'In a style that is at once intimate, well-researched and engaging, Salman Akhtar takes the reader through an exploration of patience, curiosity, privacy, intimacy, humility and dignity–matters that are rarely considered within the psychoanalytic realm. Drawing on poetry, personal reminiscences, and clinical moments that shimmer with delicate truths, Akhtar shines a light on psychic experiences that reside in the interior spaces of the mind and are integral to shaping one's core sense of being in the world. He examines benevolent and malignant forms of each trait and imparts clinical, developmental, and cultural insights with great wit, generosity and wisdom.'

Anne J. Adelman, Ph.D, Faculty Member of the Washington Baltimore Center for Psychoanalysis; *editor of Psychoanalytic Reflections on Parenting Teens and Young Adults* (2018).

'In this important book, Salman Akhtar offers an unexpected and enlivening proposal: that we should stop arguing about what makes us sick and start paying more attention to what makes us healthy, especially to the "silent virtues" of patience, curiosity, privacy, intimacy, humility, and dignity. Akhtar's generative and thought-provoking account of these virtues constitutes a profoundly moral vision of I-Thou relatedness as both the means (as strived for by the analyst) and the end (as discovered by the patient first from without and then from within) of the psychoanalytic process.'

Elio Frattaroli, MD, Faculty Member, Psychoanalytic Center of Philadelphia; author of *Healing the Soul in the Age of the Brain* (2001).

Silent Virtues

Silent Virtues addresses six areas of mental functioning, namely patience, curiosity, privacy, intimacy, humility, and dignity. Each of the areas is elucidated with the help of clinical, literary, and cultural material. The book introduces a series of novel ideas, including: (i) the distinction between patience as a component of the therapeutic attitude and the exercise of patience as a specific technical intervention; (ii) the description of the five psychopathological syndromes involving curiosity: excessive, deficient, uneven, anachronistic, instinctualized, and false curiosity; (iii) the description of four psychopathological syndromes (failed, florid, fluctuating, and false) involving intimacy; (iv) the discourse on the importance of humility in selecting patients and in deciding upon the longevity of our professional careers; and (v) the description of three forms of dignity (metaphysical, existential, and characterological) and the various ways in which they affect psychoanalytic technique.

Salman Akhtar, MD, is Professor of Psychiatry at Jefferson Medical College, and Training and Supervising Analyst at the Psychoanalytic Center of Philadelphia. He is the recipient of the prestigious Sigourney Award (2012) for Outstanding Contributions to Psychoanalysis.

Silent Virtues

Patience, Curiosity, Privacy, Intimacy, Humility, and Dignity

Salman Akhtar

Routledge
Taylor & Francis Group

LONDON AND NEW YORK

First published 2019
by Routledge
2 Park Square, Milton Park, Abingdon, Oxon OX14 4RN

and by Routledge
52 Vanderbilt Avenue, New York, NY 10017

Routledge is an imprint of the Taylor & Francis Group, an informa business

© 2019 Salman Akhtar

Chapter One was originally published in the Psychoanalytic Review 102: 93–122,
2015. Chapter Two was originally published in the *Journal of the American
Psychoanalytic Association* 65: 265–304, 2017. Chapter Five was originally published
in the *American Journal of Psychoanalysis* 78: 1–27, 2018. Chapter Six was published
in the *American Journal of Psychoanalysis* 75: 244–266, 2015. These papers are
reprinted here with the permission of pertinent author, editors, and publishers.

British Library Cataloguing-in-Publication Data
A catalogue record for this book is available from the British Library

Library of Congress Cataloging-in-Publication Data
A catalog record has been requested for this book

ISBN: 978-1-138-33215-7 (hbk)
ISBN: 978-1-138-33238-6 (pbk)
ISBN: 978-0-429-44668-9 (ebk)

Typeset in Times New Roman
by Taylor & Francis Books

To
MUGE
with love, gratitude, and devotion

Contents

Acknowledgements

Besides my patients from whom I have learned much about the human condition, I am grateful to many colleagues who have helped me in subtle and not-so-subtle ways. Prominent among these are Drs Aisha Abbasi, Ira Brenner, April Fallon, Lana and Ralph Fishkin, Rao Gogineni, Steven Gordon, Jaswant Guzder, Gurmeet Kanwal, Susan Levine, Afaf Mahfouz, Rajnish Mago, Tahir Maqsood, Henri Parens, Barry Rovner, Stephen Schwartz, Roomana Sheikh, Shahrzad Siassi, and J. Anderson Thomson, Jr. My assistant, Jan Wright, prepared the manuscript of this book with her usual diligence and good humour. Finally, I must mention Muge Alkan, whose love and support was crucial as I laboured through this project. To all these individuals, I offer my sincere thanks.

About the author

Salman Akhtar, MD, is Professor of Psychiatry at Jefferson Medical College and a Training and Supervising Analyst at the Psychoanalytic Center of Philadelphia. He has served on the editorial boards of the *International Journal of Psychoanalysis*, the *Journal of the American Psychoanalytic Association*, and the *Psychoanalytic Quarterly*. His more than 300 publications include ninety-three books, of which the following nineteen are solo-authored: *Broken Structures* (1992), *Quest for Answers* (1995), *Inner Torment* (1999), *Immigration and Identity* (1999), *New Clinical Realms* (2003), *Objects of Our Desire* (2005), *Regarding Others* (2007), *Turning Points in Dynamic Psychotherapy* (2009), *The Damaged Core* (2009), *Comprehensive Dictionary of Psychoanalysis* (2009), *Immigration and Acculturation* (2011), *Matters of Life and Death* (2011), *The Book of Emotions* (2012), *Psychoanalytic Listening* (2013), *Good Stuff* (2013), *Sources of Suffering* (2014), *No Holds Barred* (2016), *A Web of Sorrow* (2017), and *Mind, Culture, and Global Unrest* (2018). Dr. Akhtar has delivered many prestigious invited lectures including a Plenary Address at the 2nd International Congress of the International Society for the Study of Personality Disorders in Oslo, Norway (1991), an Invited Plenary Paper at the 2nd International Margaret S. Mahler Symposium in Cologne, Germany (1993), an Invited Plenary Paper at the Rencontre Franco-Americaine de Psychanalyse meeting in Paris, France (1994), a Keynote Address at the 43rd IPA Congress in Rio de Janiero, Brazil (2005), the Plenary Address at the 150th Freud Birthday Celebration sponsored by the Dutch Psychoanalytic Society and the Embassy of Austria in Leiden, Holland (2006), and the Inaugural Address at the first IPA-Asia Congress in Beijing, China (2010). Dr. Akhtar is the recipient of numerous awards including the American Psychoanalytic Association's Edith Sabshin Award (2000), Columbia University's Robert Liebert Award for Distinguished Contributions to Applied Psychoanalysis (2004), the American Psychiatric Association's Kun Po Soo Award (2004) and Irma Bland Award for being the Outstanding Teacher of Psychiatric Residents in the country (2005). He received the highly prestigious Sigourney Award (2012) for distinguished contributions to psychoanalysis. In 2013, he gave the Commencement Address at graduation ceremonies of the Smith College School of Social Work in Northampton, MA. Dr. Akhtar's books have been translated in many languages, including German, Italian, Korean, Romanian, Serbian, Spanish, and Turkish. A true Renaissance man, Dr Akhtar has served as the Film Review Editor for the *International Journal of Psychoanalysis*, and is currently serving as the Book Review Editor for the *International Journal of Applied Psychoanalytic Studies*. He has published eleven collections of poetry and serves as a Scholar-in-Residence at the Inter-Act Theatre Company in Philadelphia.

Introduction

Generally speaking, psychoanalysis has had more to say about morbid psychological states than about healthy ones. This is understandable since the discipline was born in a clinical context. Emotional suffering in the form of mental conflict, anxiety, paranoia, dread, misplaced lust, punishing conscience, and melancholic withdrawal became its customary concerns. The fact that the discipline's founder, Sigmund Freud, held a rather dismal view of human nature furthered this dark inclination. Most people, according to him, were "good for nothing in life" (1905a, p. 263) and "antisocial and anticultural" (1927a, p. 7) at their core. Any belief in human beings' inherent goodness was an "evil illusion" (1933, p. 104). Freud's followers took this to heart. Clinical scepticism got intermingled with existential cynicism. Psychoanalysts became clinicians of despair and misery was ensconced as the mother-tongue of their profession.

The stoic ethics of such 'classic vision' was challenged by analysts who subscribed to a softer, 'romantic vision' (Strenger, 1989). They replaced Freud's 'primary narcissism' and 'instinctual discharge' with 'primary love' and 'object seeking'. They held that psychopathology results not from the inherent battle between opposing instincts (or, between these instincts and the superego) but from neglect or abuse of the child by its caretakers. And, they asserted that a kind and benevolent relationship between the patient and analyst was as important for 'cure' as was insight via transference interpretation. Human goodness in the former perspective was defensive or sublimatory. Human goodness in the latter perspective was intrinsic and natural.

The book in your hands reflects the latter trend. An earlier counterpart, *Good Stuff* (Akhtar, 2013e), addressed the topics of courage, resilience, gratitude, generosity, forgiveness, and sacrifice. The current book extends my study of positive human attributes to six new and under-investigated realms: patience, curiosity, privacy, intimacy, humility, and dignity. Each topic is dealt with a nuanced approach to phenomenology, ontogenesis, cultural variations, and therapeutic relevance. The existing, if scattered, literature on each topic is critically assessed and extended. Many novel ideas are introduced. Prominent among these are the following:

- *In the chapter on Patience*: the elucidation of chronic waiting and chronic hurrying; the distinction between patience as a component of the therapeutic attitude and the exercise of patience as a specific technical intervention.
- *In the chapter on Curiosity*: the classification of the aims of curiosity into their elemental, exploratory, empathic, existential, and enactive purposes; also, the description of the five psychopathological syndromes involving curiosity. These include excessive, deficient, uneven, anachronistic, instinctualized, and false curiosity.
- *In the chapter on Privacy*: the distinction between inherent, internalized, and imposed origins of privacy as well as the finer distinctions between privacy, confidentiality, and secrecy.
- *In the chapter on Intimacy*: the description of four psychopathological syndromes involving intimacy. These include failed, florid, fluctuating, and false intimacy; also, the elucidation of some unexplored realms of intimacy, including intimacy with parts of oneself, intimacy with animals, and intimacy with God.
- *In the chapter on Humility*: the discourse on the importance of humility in selecting patients and in deciding upon the longevity of our professional careers.
- *In the chapter on Dignity*: the description of the three forms of dignity (metaphysical, existential, and characterological) and the various ways in which they affect psychoanalytic technique.

Together, these fresh proposals extend and deepen the purview of our theory and the reach of our technique. The fact that positive rather than negative emotional attitudes provide the entry points for this wide-ranging discourse is itself new and additive to the knowledge base and clinical praxis of psychoanalysis.

Part I

Sensing and searching

Patience

It takes a long time to develop from a psychically inchoate infant to a coherent adult with identity and agency. The mind has to evolve distinction between self and its objects, renounce omnipotence and magical thinking, learn to bear ambivalence, acquire self- and object-constancy, negotiate travails of the oedipal situation, enter the temporal order of life, master task orientation, learn to play, reconfigure primary internal objects and one's relationship with them, merge affection and sex together, and develop capacities for intimacy, industry, and generativity. This task-filled journey to assuming adulthood takes over two decades and demands patience from both the traveller and his or her tour guides. Neither growing-up nor child-rearing can be rushed. These processes depend upon pre-programmed epigenetic sequences that unfold from within and facilitating psychosocial inputs that come from the outer world. And, all this takes place at its own merry pace with both progressive and regressive trends competing to take control of the developing ego. No wonder enormous patience is required from both children and parents in order for this sojourn to succeed.

The same is true of psychoanalytic treatment. It is slow and time-consuming. Many years intervene between the beginning and end of this painstaking process and much forbearance is required from both the analyst and the analysand. In fact, patience constitutes a cardinal non-interpretive element of the former's technique (Stone, 1961) and an essential ingredient of the "fairly reliable character" (Freud, 1905a, p. 263) required of the latter. In light of this, it is unsettling to note that psychoanalytic literature has little to offer on patience. The puzzlement is compounded by the fact that encounter with masochistic caricatures of patience and narcissistic flurries of impatience forms an almost daily feature of the psychoanalyst's clinical life. Yet there is little to read about such phenomena. It is this lacuna that I intend to fill here. I will examine the quality of patience in its phenomenological nuance, its developmental origins, its cultural variations, and its psychopathological distortions. Then, I will elucidate the technical implications of these ideas and conclude with some synthesizing remarks.

Phenomenological aspects

The root word for 'patience' is 'patient' which, in turn, is derived from Middle English *pacient* and Greek *pēma*. This etymology results in the inclusion of the following phrases in the dictionary definition of 'patience': "1: bearing pains or trials calmly or without complaint, 2: manifesting forbearance under provocation or strain, 3: not hasty or impetuous, and, 4: steadfast despite opposition and difficulty" (Mish, 1987, p. 852). Going beyond English to other major languages like Spanish, Chinese, Arabic, and Hindi, one searches for further subtleties in delineating the phenomenon of patience. Spanish, generally a rich source of connotations, describes *paciencia* in terms that are essentially similar to English. The Chinese word for patience is *nai-sin*, which underscores the capacity for tolerance as a character trait. Arabic has two related words to cover this phenomenological terrain: *sabr* and *tahammul*. The first denotes the capacity to accept adversity with calm and the latter denotes the capacity to carry on with dignity during states of suffering. Moreover, the first Arabic word for patience is etymologically related to words that mean 'pouring' or 'emptying out', and the second Arabic word for patience to words that are linked to pregnancy. The implication of this is that patience refers to bearing less-than-full psychic states and can, in due course of time, lead to fruitful outcomes. Hindi refers to patience as *dheeraj*, a word derived from Sanskrit *dhri*, meaning steadfast, composed, calm, well-behaved, and well-bred. The linkage with 'good' behaviour and breeding has the consequence of elevating patience to a higher and desirable standard.

While mostly described as a monolithic phenomenon, upon a closer look, patience turns out to have four components. These components are (i) acceptance of external and internal reality as it exists at a given moment, (ii) absence of resentful feelings and bitterness, (iii) retention of hope that matters would change for the better and, (iv) capacity to wait for favourable times without haste and restlessness. As would be immediately obvious, each of these elements has its own developmental history and each adds its particular hue to the multifaceted phenomenon called 'patience'. The first element (i.e. acceptance of a given external or internal reality) implies the achievement of 'depressive position' (Klein, 1935), i.e. renunciation of the belief in an 'all-good' self-object discourse and deepened capacity for reality testing, mourning, gratitude, humility, and reparation. The second element (i.e. retention of hope) implies robust 'object constancy' (Hartmann, 1952; Mahler et al., 1975) whereby the overall affective valence of internalized primary object representation is not compromised by need-frustration and by intensified drive activity. The third element (i.e. absence of hostile feelings) is a corollary to the second; absence of full satisfaction is taken to be a transitory and inevitable part of life and not regarded as a deliberate, teasing withholding on the part of the love object. Finally, the fourth element (i.e. capacity to wait) reveals faith in the eventual re-emergence of the good object from the void of separation; echoes of the childhood peek-a-boo game between the mother and child are evident here (see also Kleeman, 1967).

Thus explicated, 'patience' appears to be a character trait of maturity. Pop psychology (Sherman, 1987; Ryan, 2013) and spiritually inclined literature (Dalai Lama, 1997; Armstrong, 2009; Easwaran, 2012) uphold it as a great virtue. Even without such idealization, the quality of patience is known to show its benefit and utility in a number of realms. Children's growing up and parents' efforts at guiding them through this process requires patience from both parties, as stated above. Learning new skills, regardless of whether it is during childhood (e.g. riding a bicycle, mastering arithmetic) or adult life (e.g. driving a car, learning to play golf), invariably requires patience; one fails repeatedly, lacks dexterity for a long while, and needs to stay the course in order to master the task. Patience is integral to refining and sharpening a talent; the existence of raw talent alone does not take one very far.

Patience is also required for developing genuine intimacy with others and, by implication, for love. It creates and sustains the mental space necessary for listening to others and learning about their lives. Marriage is yet another realm which demands patience, especially in its earlier phases when the two partners are adjusting to the realities of a mutual life (Akhtar and Billinkoff, 2011); they not only have to adapt to each other's idiosyncrasies but to the important external and internal objects of each other. Building and maintaining a household, raising children, and attending to aging parents also demands patience. The last-mentioned especially requires much tact, and much acceptance of human frailty that is now manifesting through the hitherto invulnerable parental figures.

All this makes sense. Many areas, however, remain unclear. For instance, can patience be focal? In other words, can one be patient in one realm and not in others? Are women more patient than men? If so, why? Can patience be taught? Is perseverance always associated with patience[1] or can the two occur in de-linked forms? Finally, is patience effortless and temperamentally inherent (Lokos, 2012) or the result of an active decision each time a situation comes looking for it (Ryan, 2013)? To answer such questions or, at least, to look for their answers, I turn to the ontogenesis of the phenomena involved here.

Developmental origins

In his paper 'Formulations on the two principles of mental functioning', Freud (1911) laid down the groundwork for understanding the childhood origins of patience, even though he did not use the word 'patience' per se. Freud declared that until the time internal needs are satisfactorily met – either by external objects or by one's own hallucinatory creation of gratification – the infant has little need to attend to reality. However, since external supplies are not always forthcoming and since hallucinatory wish-fulfilment fails to bring sustained satisfaction, the infant's psychical apparatus has to forge links with the external world in the hope of finding gratification. This necessitates moving from the 'pleasure principle' (concerned solely with pleasure and unpleasure and operating under the influence of the 'primary process' of reflexive discharge) to the 'reality principle' (based upon the ego capacities for attention, memory, reflection, and reality testing). Freud went on to state:

> Restraint upon motor discharge (upon action), which then became necessary, was provided by means of *thinking*, which was developed from the presentation of ideas. Thinking was endowed with characteristics which made it possible for the mental apparatus to tolerate an increased tension of stimulus while the process of discharge was postponed.
>
> (p. 221, italics in the original)

Freud acknowledged that the shift from 'pleasure principle' to 'reality principle' is neither complete (e.g. it leaves scope for day-dreaming) nor rapidly achieved. It occurs gradually and over a long period of time. And, it is more marked in relation to self-preservatory instincts than in relation to sexual instincts. In other words, matters of self-preservation come under the dominance of the reality principle to a greater extent than do the matters pertaining to erotic desire.

In a passage that links these ideas to the underbelly of what we are calling 'patience' here, Freud observed that:

> the substitution of the reality principle for the pleasure principle implies no deposing of the pleasure principle, but only a safeguarding of it. A momentary pleasure, uncertain in its results, is given up, but only in order to gain along the new path an assured pleasure at a later time.
>
> (p. 223)

However, for such tolerance of delay to become acceptable, the child must receive ample gratifications from his caretakers. Hearing a 'no' and bearing its frustrating consequences is only palatable if one hears a 'yes' more often. When this economics is reversed, frustration grows and tolerance of delay becomes unbearable. Abraham's (1924) tracing "impatient importunity, haste, and restlessness" (pp. 404–405) to early oral deprivation speaks to this very point. Bergler (1939), writing fifteen years later, also advocated the same dynamics to underlie characterological hurry though with a novel twist.

> All orally super-cathectic people are impelled by a peculiar haste. Apparently these persons are permanently wishing to "get something". More exact analytic inquiries show, however, that the actions of these regressed people have quite another meaning: they wish chronically to push the persons of the outer world, identified with the phallic mother of

pre-oedipal times, into the position of refusal, so that they may then be aggressive, free of a guilty conscience, and enjoy in a masochistic manner.
(p. 14)

Couching his explanations in the drive and ego psychology of his days, Fenichel (1945) noted that "among the oral traits of character are the antithetical qualities of volubility, restlessness, and haste, and the tendency towards obstinate silence" (p. 491). The oral impatience worsened if it was conflated with "urethral-erotic ambition" (p. 492) that later appeared on the developmental scene. Fenichel took the role of ego-weakness into account as well while elaborating upon the anaemia of patience and the resulting incapacity to wait. He stated that:

> There are persons whose fear of their uncontrolled id is so intense or has developed so early that they have never had the relaxation and the distance necessary for the development of ego forces to handle it. They are intolerant of tensions and unable to wait. Whenever they have to wait, they experience the waiting itself as a traumatic event. They try to protect themselves against it by any means. In any situation of excitement they look less for gratification than for an end to the intolerable excitement … Persons of this type are always in a hurry, even if there is plenty of time.
> (p. 487)

Building upon this early literature, subsequent psychoanalysts and child observational researchers contributed further to the understanding of the developmental antecedents of patience and impatience. Erikson (1950) proposed the concept of 'basic trust' which manifests, at first, in the child's willingness to let the mother out of sight with undue anxiety, anger, or restlessness. Such certitude implies "not only that one has learned to rely on the sameness and continuity of the outer providers but also that one may trust one's self and the capacity for one's own organs to cope with urges" (p. 248). Such childhood optimism grows out of frequent experiences of one's needs being met with satisfaction. Benedek's (1938) concept of 'confident expectation' constitutes an earlier formulation of a roughly similar idea. Both Benedek and Erikson describe a psychic position whereby hope is not lost quickly and faith persists in the environment's provision of libidinal supplies and in one's capacity to wait for them.

These notions regarding the early childhood roots of the capacity for patience have been refined by contemporary child observational researchers (e.g. Bowlby, 1969, 1973, 1980; Emde, 1980, 1991; Lichtenberg, 1983; Greenspan, 1989; Schore, 2001). They regard the infant and the caretaker as an evolving interactional system in which each partner is viewed as having separate competencies which affect the other's behaviour and as initiating and reinforcing the desired behaviour of the other. Internal regulation for the infant, though innately programmed within optimal thresholds of stimulation and/or deprivation, is, in the end, inseparable from the stable regularity of key exchanges with its caretaker. If the innate preparedness of each partner leads them to actively seek gratifying attachment and development-enhancing experiences, then the child becomes capable of affect regulation, stays optimally hedonic (i.e. replete with adequate pleasure), and can tolerate temporary absences of gratification. Although the word 'patience' does not appear in this literature, it is clear that the development of self-regulation (as a consequence of secure attachment) implicitly includes the ontogenesis of patience.

Linking such observationally derived notions with Freudian metapsychology, Aisenstein and Moss (2014) note that the infant first progresses from merely needing milk to desiring the breast and then from desiring the breast to waiting for the object-mother. These transitions involve psychic work and to explain the nature of such work, Aisenstein and Moss evoke Freud's (1924a) concept of 'primary erotogenic masochism'. This, as we know, refers to the deep-seated human capacity for drawing pleasure from suffering; it emanates from the inward binding of a certain quantum of death instinct by libido. Aisenstein posits this energic amalgam to be the consequence of a particular kind of mother–child interaction.[2] She declares that:

> primary masochism allows the capacity for waiting to be integrated. It is the mother's psychic work that makes this possible. A "good-enough" mother is one who is able, through her words, to help the baby wait: "Wait, my little one, I'm going to take you in my arms but not right now … you will have your feed soon, just keep calm and wait a bit". The mother envelopes the infant with words; she gives him word and thing-presentations. She thus helps him to wait, which implies confidence in the object. How is the concept of primary masochism indispensable here? Well, because if the waiting is to be tolerable, it must be "invested masochistically". The infant has to learn gradually that *there is also pleasure in this waiting due to the psychic work that it involves.* This investment of the delay is what lies at the basis of desire: I think about and imagine the pleasure to come. I am inclined to say that the *structure of desire is masochistic in essence,* for it is inconceivable without the renunciation of immediate satisfaction and the investment of waiting. Someone who is in love and is going to see the object of their desire in a week, or in a month, is able to wait because they have learned to find pleasure in psychic work and fantasy scenarios that they create of the forthcoming encounter.
>
> (p. 64, italics in the original)

While Aisenstein links the development of patience with primary masochism, her intent is to describe an essentially normative evolution. There are circumstances, however, where the masochistic element of waiting becomes more pronounced, leading to a stoic turning away from the world that sooner or later warrants clinical attention.

Psychopathology

While idiosyncratic constellations of symptoms (e.g. blissful patience in one realm associated with thorny impatience in another, patience with some individuals in one's life and not with others, contempt for others' patience) do figure in clinical practice, the two maladies analysts encounter most often are the syndromes of: (i) chronic waiting,[3] whereby a caricature of fortitude and stoicism serves all sorts of narcissistic and masochistic purposes; and (ii) chronic hurry, whereby any postponement of gratification seems unbearable and emotional contact with the 'ground' is lost in a restless pursuit of the 'figure'. I will now address these two conditions in some detail.

Chronic waiting

Some individuals appear to be very patient. They do not rush things and seem capable of remarkable peace and quiet waiting. If things do not go their way, they put matters off for a while and then resume their pursuit again. Such equanimity superficially resembles mourning but the fact is that inwardly they have not accepted defeat. The brief lull in seeking their aim is a temporary postponement, not actual acceptance, of experiencing loss. Many such individuals are highly active in chasing their dreams. Patience fuels their perseverance, though one senses that there is something excessive about such tolerance of delay. A secret plan seems to be at work here. Some goal must be achieved, no matter what price one has to pay in the process. In contrast to such overtly ambitions persons are the individuals who sit quietly and expect their mothers (or her substitutes), or their psychoanalyst, or God, or a miraculous event in reality – *Wunderglauben*[4] – to change their lives forever.

Elsewhere, I (Akhtar, 1996) have delineated the 'someday ...' fantasies that underlie this attitude. Here, it will suffice to say that the longed-for 'someday ...' refers to a time when one would be completely peaceful and conflict-free. Everything would be available or nothing would be needed. Motor activity would either be unnecessary or effortless. Even thinking would not be required. There would be no aggression from within or from outside. Needless to say, such a universe is also oblivious to the inconvenient consideration of the incest taboo and the anxieties and compromises consequent upon the oedipal situation. A complex set of psychodynamic mechanisms helps maintain the structural integrity of 'someday ...': (i) denial and negation of sectors of reality that challenge it; (ii) splitting-off of those self and object representations that mobilize conflict and aggression; (iii) a defensively moti-vated feeling on inauthenticity in those areas of personality where a healthier, more realistic, and compromise formation level of mentality and functioning has been achieved; and (iv) a temporal displacement, from past to future, of a preverbal state of blissful unity with the 'all good' mother of the symbiotic phase. The inactivity, timelessness, wordlessness, thoughtlessness, unexcited bliss, and absence of needs implicit in 'someday ...' strongly suggests that this fantasy, at its core, contains a longing for a luxurious (and retrospectively idealized) symbiotic phase.

Long before my delineation of the foregoing organization, Abraham (1924) had made reference to this dynamic when he stated that:

> Some people are dominated by the belief that there will always be some kind person – a representative of the mother, of course – to take care of them and to give them everything they need. This optimistic belief condemns them to inactivity.
>
> (p. 399)

Bergler's (1939) concept of 'pseudo-waiting' is also pertinent in this context. He declared that "the healthy strive after the current aim, the neurotic after the current defense under the disguise of the aim" (p. 13). Juxtaposing this formula to the dynamics of waiting to be rescued by the mother (Abraham, 1924) suggests that the one who is willing to wait until eternity is clinging to the defensive denial of the fact that the 'all-good' mother of infancy is lost forever and, in his case, might not have existed to begin with. Such waiting can be silent, stoic, and firmly concealed underneath schizoid indifference. Or it can accompany cheery optimism which refuses to acknowledge and psychically account for discordant sectors of external and internal reality. Many aging adults who harbour secret hopes of starting their lives all over again betray such dynamics.

Chronic hurrying

Chronic hurrying is infrequently recognized and written about though often encountered in clinical practice. One finds it in the form of impatience with tasks, restlessness with the lumbering pace of life, frequent looking at the watch, and a pressured manner of talking. The individual in a hurry constantly 'multi-tasks', takes on too much work, and tries to reach from point A to point B in the most rapid fashion possible.[5] At times, this results in cutting ethical corners and subtle compromises of morality. Such symptomatic constellation is most evident in narcissistic personalities who find 'less-than-full' states unbearable and whose ego-ideals are impossibly grand. However, oedipally fixated, competitive neurotics with mixed obsessional and hysterical personality traits can also display the tendency to hurry.

At its base, chronic hurry emanates from two complementary sources. The first is the 'push' factor of the desire to get away from being a helpless and dependent child, to bypass the developmentally mandated necessity to wait, especially as one struggles with oedipal wishes and prohibitions (Chasseguet-Smirgel, 1984), and to jettison the need to postpone instinctual gratification at the behest of the 'reality principle' (Freud, 1911). The second factor contributing to chronic hurry is the 'pull' factor of the allure of adulthood, which is imbued with omnipotence by the growing child; the frequent parental refrain, 'when you grow up, then ...' fuels the child's idealization of adulthood. Seduction by the opposite-sex parent especially results in the growing child's circumventing the need to wait; the boy becomes a man and the girl a woman, without the humbling requisite of first becoming a son or daughter, respectively. Once this structural foundation is laid down, the child finds himself/herself in a rush to 'actualize'[6] it. The child (and later, the adolescent and the adult) does not compare himself or herself with peers; instead, he or she competes with his/her elders. Wishes to get ahead quick, become someone 'big', achieve great success with minimal effort and without any waiting are other manifestations of such underlying psychic structure.

Few psychoanalysts have addressed those phenomena, with Kris (1977) being an exception in this regard. In an eloquent discussion of the state of being in a hurry, he distinguished between (i) the rush to get *away from* an experience or an object and (ii) the pressure to *move towards* a goal or an object. Kris emphasized that the former type of hurry is associated with intra-systemic conflicts whereas the latter arises from inter-systemic conflicts. He observed that:

> the appearance of being in a hurry invariably is a response to an *impending* expression of passive libidinal wishes, largely of pregenital origin, to be loved and admired and comforted as a small child is loved by his mother, but also by his father. In being in a hurry, the passive libidinal wishes on the verge of expression are repressed.
>
> (p. 96, italics in the original)

Kris added that such repression of passive aims creates an opportunity to pursue secondary goals that are mature and that represent "sublimations of *active* libidinal wishes" (p. 96, italics in the original). His observations largely pertain to well-structured neurotic patients whose hurry emanates from conflict-based issues. Hurry in individuals with 'lower level' (Kernberg, 1970) character organization is, in contrast, a manifestation of non-renunciation of infantile omnipotence and narcissistic pressures to close the gap between the ego and ego-ideal. In some of these patients, the hurried state acquires 'secondary autonomy' (Hartmann, 1939) and begins to serve as an emotionally suffused 'manic defense' (Klein, 1935) against depressive anxieties. Clearly, all this has impact upon the process and conduct of psychotherapy once such individuals enter treatment. Before taking up the nuances of this matter, however, I would like to make a brief foray into the sociocultural attitudes surrounding patience and impatience.

Sociocultural aspects

Three questions immediately present themselves in this realm: (i) are there cross-cultural differences in the prevalence of patience as a character trait; (ii) has the ability to be patient eroded with the advent of the electronic information media, especially the internet, cell phones and other transportable devices; and (iii) what is the overall attitude of civilization towards the attribute of patience? As far as the first question is concerned, stereotypes would have us believe that people from the East (especially the Far Eastern nations like China, Japan, and Korea) are more stoic, more tolerant, and more patient in facing daily adversities and deprivations than people in the industrialized nations of the West. This notion seems to be a corollary of the idealization of Eastern meditation practices (e.g. Zen Buddhism) and their mystifying, unhurried teachers. The fact that 'retreats' where such instruction is offered are frequently located in laconic settings also adds to the rosy view of their embodying fortitude. Such assumptions are strengthened by anecdotal reports and personal memoirs of having achieved greater patience and wisdom in such settings (Isherwood, 1980; Irwin, 2011). However, little scientific data exists to corroborate these assertions. The omission of Western mystical traditions of reflective solitude also makes this literature suspect. If one juxtaposes the mystical silence of the Buddhist temple in the little Japanese village of Kamakura with the spirit of prolonged isolation and self-reflection at the Carmelite retreat in Darien, Illinois, then the jury seems to be out. The non-verbal fortitude stereotypically associated with the Japanese too can readily find its counterpart in the habitual quietude of the rural folk from northern Sweden.[7] One therefore ends up wondering whether the qualities of fortitude and stoicism are differentially distributed across East or West, or do they simply reflect mystical traditions that exist across the globe?

This brings up the second question and that is whether people across the globe have become less patient with the unfolding of the twentieth and twenty-first centuries? Here the advent of the electronic information network and pathways of instantaneous communication seems to have played a role. Take the decline of letter writing, for instance. Not only has the art, with all its endearing formalities, nearly vanished, the waiting that came after one had posted a letter has become a matter of the past. Nowadays, people write electronic missives (email) that are transmitted across cities, nations, and continents in a matter of seconds and often elicit equally rapid responses. The practices of 'texting' and 'instant chatting' have caused even greater collapse of the affectively charged and realistically warranted patience (with all its delicious anguish) for obtaining a response to one's communication. Why be patient if all 'answers' are in the here and now? The past can be deleted and the future will appear on the luminescent screen in just a few minutes.

Such considerations lead us to the final question of this section and that pertains to the overall societal attitude towards patience. A striking contradiction awaits us here. *On the one hand*, human civilization puts great premium on the quality of patience; restraint of impulses, delay of desire in accordance with reality, tolerance of differences between people, and insertion of thought between emotion and action are qualities that contribute to the very basis of civilization's evolution and persistence (Freud, 1930). Patience is integral to all of them. Patience is also celebrated by all the world's religions: Judaism regards patience as a fundamental attribute of God, who is described as 'long-suffering' or 'slow to anger' (Exodus 34: 6); Jewish texts call people to emulate God's patience and state that "a person's wisdom will yield patience" (Proverbs 19: 11). Christianity reminds us that "love is patient, love is kind" (1 Corinthians 13: 4) and also, "to those who by patience in well-doing seek for glory and honour and immortality, He will give eternal life" (Romans 2: 6–7). And the Holy Quran issues the reassuring injunction: *"Inna-Allah-e-mu-al Saabreen"* ("God is with those who remain patient"). All three religious traditions speak of the prophet, Job, who suffered hardship with dignity until God rewarded him. Such legacies exalt patience to a high level of desirability and respect among human values. *On the other hand*, man has always been enthralled with fastness and speed. Originating most likely in the evolutionary fear of fast-moving animals and the advantage of quickness in avoiding dangers, then man's fascination with speed antedates the Industrial Revolution and its mechanical support of man's desire for high-velocity accomplishments. Ancient folklore, Greek epics, Roman tales, and Indo-Chinese fables are replete with exalted illustrations of the high speed with which a protagonist could run, shoot arrows, swim, and climb mountains. In the realm of athletics and sports, such idealization of speed is explicit. To this human 'speedophilia', the advent of machines, and especially electronic media, have imparted a cutting edge of procedural restlessness. Automakers proudly announce how quickly their vehicles can go from zero to sixty miles per hour and the speedometers of cars tell us that they can go as fast as 120 or 140 miles per hour, speeds at which they will never be driven. Computer manufacturers compete in how quickly the consumer can access the web ('high speed wi-fi') and the instinctualized gloating over 'instant replay', 'texting', 'instant messaging', 'Instagram', and 'FaceTime', etc., is hard to overlook.

Putting all this together, one ends up with the troubling conclusion that while society upholds patience, gradual accomplishment, step-by-step progress, and contemplation, it sells and rewards quickness and high speed. This contradiction seems to have become intensified with the profusion of electronic communication methods that have evolved over the past few decades. This has the potential of affecting the human mind but the exact nature and extent of such impact remains unclear.[8]

Technical implications

Surveying the phenomenological, developmental, and sociocultural aspects of patience prepares the ground for discussing the technical implications of these observations. Four different ways in which our understanding of patience impacts upon day-to-day clinical work are: (i) patience as a component of the therapeutic attitude; (ii) the exercise of patience as a specific intervention; (iii) patience-related phenomena as entry points for the analyst's intervention; and (iv) patience-related 'symptoms' in the countertransference and their management. I will now address these technical issues in some detail.

Patience as a component of the therapeutic attitude

Elsewhere, I (Akhtar 2009a, pp. 171–186) have delineated three components of the analyst's therapeutic attitude towards the patient, namely survival, vision, and faith. However, I acknowledged that:

> The three facets of analytic attitude (namely survival, vision, and faith) are not meant to provide an exhaustive list of all that is sustained under such an attitude. Devotion readily comes to mind but it seems to be included under "survival". Benevolence stakes its claim but seems to be included, at least the way I see things, under the category of "vision". Similarly, hopefulness appears to be a metaconstituent of "faith". This, however, does not mean that there might not be aspects of analytic attitude that lie outside the phenomenological domain of the three I have chosen to focus upon.
>
> (p. 172)

It is in the spirit of this observation that I now add 'patience' as yet another component of the analyst's therapeutic attitude, one that might underlie and/ or contribute to the other three (survival, vision, and faith) already outlined. Patience, it seems, is integral to the analyst's endeavour. He knows, from the beginning, that the work will take years to finish and that it cannot be rushed.[9] He is aware that there are beginning, middle, and ending phases to the process, each with their own twists and turns and often quite variable durations. He recognizes that the victories in overcoming resistances and deepening of insights can take a long time before being translated into actual changes in symptomatology and lived life. He accepts that interpretation – be is transference-based or genetic – is not once for all and that the tedium of 'working through' (Freud, 1914b), i.e. a piecemeal metabolism of insights, invariably awaits the two parties in the clinical dyad. He is cognizant that resistances which have been overcome keep cropping up again and again and their interpretations have to be repeated afresh. There is an inherent 'laziness' involving change and a tenacity to 'id resistance'. Both the analyst and the analysand have to revisit material that has been analysed countless numbers of times and expand, fine-tune, and deepen the insights in this process. A quick agreement and rapid behavioural change following interpretation is suspect. It is the gradual and painstaking assimilation of insights gained as a result of repeated dissolution of resistances that ultimately matters.

All this requires patience on the part of both the patient and the analyst. For the former, it might be a necessary evil that, willy-nilly, has to be transformed into a virtue. For the latter, it is a matter of ingrained attitude with which he approaches his work.

The exercise of patience as a specific therapeutic intervention

Aside from being an integral component of therapeutic attitude, exercising patience can constitute a specific therapeutic intervention. Such patience is not an absence of action; it is a purposeful choice to wait for the right time and the right reasons to intervene. Opting for this route is especially tricky at clinical moments that tug at the analyst's 'interpretive greed' (Akhtar, 2014a) and his 'compulsion to interpret' (Epstein, 1979). Sometimes it is a provocative comment or the sudden revelation of a hitherto unspoken piece of childhood history that pulls the analyst into making a premature and impulsive intervention. At other times, it is an unexplained and puzzling silence that exacts a similar effect. Resisting the temptation to offer a verbal intervention of course does not mean that the analyst is not 'doing' anything. It simply means that his patience has now moved out of the attitudinal realm and has acquired the status of an intervention.

Clinical vignette: I [10]

Marilyn McDonough, a very attractive architect in her fifties, had sought help following an emotional crisis with one of her children. Once the acute matter was settled and the treatment began to deepen, the centrality of her own mother's death when Marilyn was barely five years old came to the surface. A talented and industrious woman, Marilyn had devoted all her energies to raising her kids (after a tumultuous marriage ended in divorce) and to advancing in the profession she loved. She excelled at both these endeavours and, all along, the pain of her early maternal loss remained psychically sequestered – never repressed but not entire worked through either. Later, she got married again and had since then maintained a reasonably satisfactory marital life.

Her analysis remained focused upon the life-long effects of early loss; it coloured transference anxieties, sensitivities to separation, and fear of getting re-traumatized by losing me. Provision of ample psychic space, empathic validations, gentle uncovering of defences against the awareness of the pervasive impact of the childhood tragedy, and interpretive handling of 'survivor's guilt' (Niederland, 1968) and the resulting inhibition of healthy entitlement led to great improvement in her capacity to mourn. Energy thus freed up was then directed to deepening ties with her family and newer sublimations.

One phenomenon during this middle phase of Marilyn's analysis was outstanding. It began around the late second or early third year of her treatment and lasted off and on for a very long time, though with changing hues and increasing insight into its nature on the part of both her and myself. The phenomenon consisted of her stopping talking some five or six minutes before the end of each session and then remaining quiet until we parted for that day.

Reflexively, I wondered whether I should interrupt Marilyn's silence and explore what was going on in her mind. Something, however, told me not to do so. Then, an association occurred to me. This pertained to the diminished pressure under which gasoline gets pumped into the car just before the paid-for amount is to be reached. The gas continues to go in the car but now under less pressure. This cognitive allusion reflected a growing certainty in my inner experience that Marilyn and I were not only deeply related but still 'in analysis' during those last silent minutes of each hour. The fact that neither she nor I felt restless, dammed up, inhibited, or in need of talking confirmed the correctness of my therapeutic stance. Further reflection reminded me of the concept of a young child's 'low-keyedness' (Mahler et al., 1975), whereby his or her diminished interest in external reality, lesser motility, and sombreness of mood reflect the effort to inwardly hold on to the image of a mother who, at that particular moment, is unavailable. I surmised that, during these end of session silences, Marilyn was keeping me inside her while simultaneously separating from me. The work of mourning (her actual mother) was as evident in her silence as was the preparatory effort at separating from me (in transference). I remained 'non-interpretive' but emotionally attuned to her throughout these moments.

Confirmation of such insights came from Marilyn, who – after about a year or so after the beginning of these silences – one day said, "Do you know what I am feeling and thinking during the times we are silent towards the end of the session? I feel very peaceful and in no need to talk. I feel I have talked enough and now I can be with you without speaking. And, you know, sometimes when I am silent, I see an image of the sign infinity which is pulsating". Contrary to my usual practice of waiting for further associations and/or asking for clarification, I felt the comfort to intervene immediately. I said, "Infinity – like forever, pulsating – as fully alive. There, yes, there is the mother who's gone forever and yet fully alive within you!" Marilyn nodded in agreement.

This clinical vignette demonstrates two opposing principles of technique. On a gross and sustained level, it demonstrates the exercise of patience (vis-à-vis her silences at the session's end) as an intervention – non-verbal and 'preparatory', though it might be deemed – helped the spontaneous unfolding of the clinical process. On a sharp and momentary level, it shows that a quick intervention when the truth of the moment is staring in one's face (or what Bion (1970) has called the 'act of faith') can override the customary protocol of patience as an attitude. Such 'upward' and 'downward' titration of patience during analytic work is challenging. Limentani's (1989) quip that "psychoanalysis is an art and for this reason it needs discipline" (p. 260) is certainly pertinent in this context.

Patience-related clinical phenomena as an entry point for the analyst's intervention

Some analysands display tenacious 'someday ...' fantasies (Akhtar, 1996). At their base, such fantasies reflect clinging to the hope that the 'all-good' of infantile, symbiotic bliss shall return and that one would become conflict-free forever. The excessive, if not pathological, hope of these patients serves as character armour that keeps reality at a distance. For them, the present matters little and the longed-for future, everything. Even though such individuals can appear extraordinarily 'patient' and, for a long while seem ideal candidates for analyst who never push the analyst for quick relief, the fact is that their pathological hope is fuelled by (and, in turn, fuels) consideration narcissism and sadomasochism.

Intervention with such analysands is Janus-faced. On the one hand, the analyst must be extraordinarily patient, and permit the analysand to:

> experience for a sufficient length of time and at different levels the soundness of the therapeutic rapport, the security of being understood, the benefit of a careful and thorough working through of the transference, and a relational structure that enables him or her to contain the comprehension and the elaboration of the disruption of the transference play.
>
> (Amati-Mehler and Argentieri, 1989, p. 303)

On the other hand, the patient's pathology of excessive patience warrants confrontation. The analyst must help the patient unmask what underlies the waiting attitude. This will pave the way for the two of them to squarely face the idealization inherent in 'someday' fantasies. For instance, to a patient who, after four years of analytic work, continued to complain about the ineffectiveness of psychoanalysis vis-à-vis his short stature (a disguised but close version of his actual complaint), I once responded by saying, "You know, the pained disbelief in your voice and the intensity with which you berate me about this issue makes me wonder if you really believe that analysis could or should lead you to become taller. Do you?" The patient was taken aback, but after some hesitation, did acknowledge that all along he had believed that he might become taller as a result of our hard work.

Once such omnipotent expectations from analysis are brought to the surface, the analyst can attempt to interpret their defensive aims against aggression in transference and, behind that, towards the early objects. He might also help the patient bring forth the narcissistic and masochistic gratifications derived from these fantasies, which keep the patient's existence in a grand, suffering limbo. He might now point out to the patient the illusory nature of his 'someday' fantasy. However, even during this phase, the analyst must remain respectful of the patient's psychic 'soft spots', and be affectively and conceptually prepared to oscillate between affirmative intervention, when thwarted growth needs and ego deficits seem to dictate the transference demands, and interpretive interventions, when more traditional conflict-based transference is in the forefront (Killingmo, 1989).

In sharp contrast to such perpetually waiting patients are those who are in a chronic state of hurry. Kris (1977), whose work has been mentioned earlier in this chapter, notes that the technical stance with 'hurrying away' patients should consist of (i) drawing the patient's attention to the experience of frustration which invariably accompanies hurrying, (ii) helping unmask – and rendering bearable – the passive libidinal wishes to be loved and admired from which the analysand is trying to escape, (iii) accord equal respect to the active genital wishes and assist the patient to see that hurrying precludes their full enjoyment as well and, of course, (iv) elucidating and reconstructing the inhibiting factors that were making the analysand's passive pregenital wishes unbearable in the first place.

The clinical approach with patients who are 'hurrying towards' a life goal has received less attention from Kris. In my clinical experience, the technical stance towards this sort of impatience should consist of (i) helping the patient notice and acknowledge its existence by providing him evidence from multiple sources (e.g. intensity of ambition, bypass of the reality of time, rushing the analytic process itself), (ii) encouraging the patient to be curious about the origin and history of such haste, (iii) facilitating the patient's access to its discharge as well as defensive functions, and (iv) explicating its aims in the transference-based relatedness to the analyst. It is also my general impression that while narcissistic agendas do contribute to such hurry, its fundamental anchor is in avoidance of oedipal insecurities.

Clinical vignette: 2

Philip Robertson, a handsome forty-year-old man, was a rising star in his academic field. However, he was forever dissatisfied. Nothing was enough for him. During one session, for instance, he said, "Look, I am the sort of guy who is never satisfied with ninety-percent. I want one hundred-percent". The mere reality of his actual affluence and growing fame gave him little solace. He wanted to be bigger, have more, and in a constant hurry. Deeply enamoured by his mother as a child, he remembered always worrying about his father who had been declared mentally incompetent by Phil's mother. Indeed, father was quite boyish, which made him a good playmate when Phil was growing up but a target of scorn once Phil achieved full adulthood, graduated from a prestigious university, and got his first tenure-track job.

During the early phases of his treatment, Phil would arrive just in time, pay his bills the very next day after receiving them, and fill the session with good humour and eloquent details of his ambitions and escapades with women whom he was barely able to tolerate beyond two or three dates. It was as if he had to get some place quick, as if something or some feeling or somebody was awaiting him just around the next corner of his existence. One day, he said to me: "I am hopeless. I have no satisfaction in life. I want to be like you. You look happy. I want to have as many books under my name as you have written". I responded by a one-word intervention: "When?" Phil was taken aback. "What do you mean?" I responded by asking him what sort of time-frame he had in mind, given the obvious difference in our ages, to arrive at the number of books that I have published. At first, he tried to dispel the question by regarding it as irrelevant because it addressed reality, not his wishes, but after some contemplation, he was able to see that his warding-off that very reality constituted the source of his restlessness.

Here, my one-word intervention ("when?") unmasked the patient's inability and/or unwillingness to accept the generational difference between us. By wanting to have written as many books instantly as I had published over three decades, he was denying the importance of passage of time and accrual of experience; he wanted to advance from being a boy to becoming a man without going through the intermediate step of being a son (by accepting me as a generative father in transference). The developmental background of this patient supported such a formulation. He had been over-indulged by his mother who berated his father and reduced him to a buffoon. A seduced child, this patient grew up to be a charming man who was cocky and impatient on the one hand and guilty and hollow on the other. My interpretation was an attempt to slow him down and get him grounded. It aimed at preparing him to get in contact with the betrayal that is always implicit in such maternal seduction (Chasseguet-Smirgel, 1984; Smolen, 2013) and the deflating affects associated with it.

Patience-related 'symptoms' in the countertransference and their management

While his role as an 'ordinary devoted analyst'[11] mandates patience, there are clinical circumstances where the analyst is vulnerable to becoming restless, if not impetuous. Major changes in the patient's external circumstances and moments of emotional flooding which threaten to drown the patient's observing ego pull the analyst to act rapidly, at times to the detriment of the analytic process. Premature interventions call also be pulled forth by the emergence of a long-awaited transference manifestation.

Clinical vignette: 3

> Judith Conahan, a highly intelligent lawyer with narcissistic personality disorder, was in analysis with me. For the first year or so, all she talked about was how she felt unloved by her husband and, during her childhood, by her mother. She never made a comment about me and in effect treated me with an indifference that was quite like she had received from her mother. Then, in the eighteenth month of her analysis, I announced that I had to take a few days off at rather short notice. The patient responded to the news with immediate acceptance and the usual lack of associations. The next day, however, she began her session by telling me that one of her clients had cancelled an appointment that morning. During that hour, she went through her desk drawers and found her home insurance policy. Judith went on to tell me that she got quite upset upon reading parts of that policy. There were too many loopholes, too little coverage! Discerning unmistakable allusions to my impending absence (e.g. 'canceled appointment', 'too little coverage') in her associations, I said: "Perhaps, you find it easier to talk about an insurance policy with loopholes than an analysis with interruptions." After a long pause, she responded in a pained voice: "I can see how you arrived at what you said but it hurt my feelings because I was really worried about the policy and it seems that you are not paying attention to my concern about it."

While 'over-activity' of such sort is often brought out in clinical supervision of candidates and peer group discussion of seasoned analysts, excessive and undue patience on the analyst's part remains a largely unaddressed matter. The fact is that, at times, the analyst's hope becomes unrealistic whereby he keeps waiting for a day ('someday …') when a patient who is appearing increasingly unanalysable will suddenly become analysable. An analyst–analysand collusion around such waiting is a certain recipe for an interminable analysis. Winnicott (1971) states that in such cases

> the psychoanalysis may collude for years with the patient's need to be psychoneurotic (as opposed to mad) and to be treated as psychoneurotic.

The analysis goes well, and everyone is pleased. The only drawback is that the analysis never ends. It can be terminated, and the patient may even mobilize a psychoneurotic false self for the purpose of finishing and expressing gratitude. But, in fact, the patient knows that there has been no change in the underlying (psychotic) state and the analyst and the patient have succeeded in colluding to bring about a failure.

(p. 102)

Yet another aspect of the countertransference important in such cases is the analyst's becoming restlessly aware of the passage of time while the patient seems oblivious to the months and years that have gone by with relatively little change in his situation. The analyst's dawning awareness of time suggests approaching termination in most other analyses. In the case of patients with 'someday ...', however, the situation is just the opposite. The analyst's awareness of passing time is reflective of the fact that termination is nowhere in sight and the analysis has bogged down. Indeed, in cases where 'someday ...' fantasies are deep and subtle, this countertransference experience might be the first clue of their existence. Interestingly, such entry of "the fatal limits of real time" (Boris, 1976, p. 145) in the analyst situation might itself yield a technical intervention. The analyst might announce that much time has passed and the patient seems totally oblivious to it. This might be a catalysing intervention for the analysis and, under fortunate circumstances, might be the only comment needed to rupture the patient's illusory stance.

Concluding remarks

In this chapter, I have mapped out the phenomenological terrain of patience. I have traced its developmental origins in the growing child's acquisition of reality principle and in his capacity to tolerate temporary absence of libidinal supplies. Following this I have commented upon the two most frequently encountered psychopathological syndromes in this realm, namely chronic waiting and chronic hurry. I have then made a brief foray into sociocultural matters, including the impact of contemporary electronic media upon and the overall cultural attitudes towards patience and impatience. Finally, I have outlined the different ways in which the issues pertaining to patience impact upon the conduct of psychotherapy and psychoanalysis.

Now I wish to conclude by addressing three questions that were raised but left unanswered in the beginning section of the chapter. These include (i) are there gender differences in the extent of patience, (ii) can patience be taught, and (iii) is patience an effortless ingredient of character or an intentional praxis in a moment? The answer to the first question is that there are many indications that women are generally more patient than men. There is a widespread cultural belief to this effect that originated, most likely, in an idealized view of the beneficent mother (e.g. the Madonna) and in the motif of the patient wife that goes back to medieval literature of the West (e.g. the wives in Petrarch's *Seniles* and Chaucer's *Canterbury Tales*) and the ancient religious texts of the East (e.g. the character of Sita in the Hindu epic, *Ramayana*). Such portrayal of women is simultaneously an acknowledgement of their moral superiority and a potentially exploitative sociopolitical exhortation for women to stay calm in the face of male hegemony in the relational dynamics of the two genders. Nonetheless, the idea that women are more patient has emotional currency and, via folklore and poetry, has been transmitted from generation to generation.

Psychoanalysis too lends support to this idea. Implication of this sort is to be found in Greenson's (1960) declaration that empathy is essentially a maternal function. Winnicott's (1962) concept of the 'survival of the object', Bion's (1962a) notion of the 'container' also hint at women's greater capacity for tolerance. And, so does Altman's (1977) conclusion that women have greater capacity for commitment in love relations, which requires letting go of other options, since they have a prototype of renunciation (having shifted their love from mother to father) in their psyche that men lack. Wright's (1991) observation too is important; he notes that the maternal element of psychoanalytic technique "posits faith in the background process. Things will happen if you wait" (p. 283), it says. Couched in differing idioms, all these concepts imply a greater – perhaps inherent – capacity for tolerance and waiting in women.

Empirical research lends further credence to this notion. A survey of 3,000 British citizens, commissioned by the online parcel delivery company myhermes.co.uk showed that women tend to wait longer before getting frustrated when faced with slow service (www.sourcesive.com/about, 18 July 2011). A more methodologically sound study of 573 villagers in India (Bauer and Chytilova, 2013) revealed that women, and especially those with children, are more able to delay gratification as compared to men. These observers found that women's patience grows with the number of children they look after; they attributed this finding to the greater capacity of women for discerning their children's needs, and appreciating the benefits of investment in the future.

Moving on from the gender issue to the question of whether patience can be 'taught', one comes across the simple fact that parents, especially mothers, regularly instruct their children to take turns in playing with this or that toy; they 'teach' their children to wait. Besides such domestic didactics, there exist age-appropriate reading material for preschool kids, e.g. *It's Taking Too Long: A Book About Patience* (Wagner, 1997) and *The Pigeon Wants A Puppy* (Williams, 2008) that help nurture a child's ability to be patient. Preschool and kindergarten instructors also assure that children playing board games learn to wait for their turn to make the pieces move or throw cards. Activities such as gardening also are useful conduits for inculcation of patience. All such cognitive devices aim to consolidate the intrapsychic structures of 'confident expectation' (Benedek, 1938) and tolerance of delayed gratification that evolve from a satisfactory mother–child relationship during early childhood.

Finally, there is the question whether patience is an ingrained character trait, sustained and relatively immutable, or a mode of relating and behaviour that is deliberately chosen in a given moment. Here the answer seems to be that both these views are correct. One pertains to a capacity, the other to the exercise of that capacity. It is like *having* a book and *reading* that book. Those with well-established capacity for patience tend to act more patiently while those with weaker capacity for patience become restless and impetuous. The fact, though, is that this proposal, like almost all I have elucidated in this contribution remains tentative. My hope is that I have stirred enough interest in the phenomena at hand that others will begin to pay attention to them. This is no different from how we respond to the material our patients and even life at large offer us. We receive information, mull over it, sort out what the important questions are, and look for their answers. It is in this spirit that I end this discourse on patience with a striking passage from Rainer Maria Rilke's (1929) *Letters to a Young Poet*:

> I beg you to have patience with everything unresolved in your heart and to try to love the questions themselves as if they were locked rooms or books written in a foreign language. Don't search for answers, which could not be given to you now, because you would not be able to live them. And the point is to live everything. Live the questions now. Perhaps then, someday far in the future, you will gradually, without even noticing it, live your way into the answers.
>
> (p. 34)

Notes

1 Thomas Edison (1847–1931) and Walt Disney (1901–1966) are two outstanding examples of the link between patience and perseverance. The former conducted nearly 60,000 experiments before he was able to develop a proper incandescent light bulb and the latter survived rejections from 302 banks before obtaining funding for his Disneyland project.

2 Although taken from a co-authored paper, this particular extract is written in the voice of only one author, namely, Marilia Aisenstein.

3 This psychic position is best captured in Beckett's (1953) renowned play, *Waiting for Godot*, in which two characters wait endlessly and in vain for the arrival of someone named 'Godot'.

4 Angel (1934) first reported this phenomenon in describing five patients (three women, two men) with chronic and unrealistic hope for a magical event (*Wunderglauben*) to transform their lives. She attributed her female patients' undue optimism to their belief that one day they would obtain a penis, and her male patients' similar psychology to a wish for regressive oneness with the mother. Most likely, the latter dynamics were also applicable to her female patients but could not be entertained owing to the phallocentric restrictions of psychoanalytic theory of that era.

5 Enid Balint, in an addendum to Michael Balint's (1958) *Basic Fault*, noted that the underestimation of travel time is typical time of ocnophilic characters and results in their being always in a hurry.

6 See Akhtar (2009b, p. 4) for various definitions of the psychoanalytic term 'actualization'.

7 Ronningstam (2006) has provided an unusually candid account of her growing up in a Protestant farming village in northern Sweden and the pervasive role of silence in that community.

8 *The Electrified Mind* (Akhtar, 2011a), a collection of psychoanalytic writings on the impact of cellphones and the internet on the human mind, addresses some of the issues involved here. Abbasi's (2014) book, *The Rupture of Serenity*, dedicates considerable space to the effect of electronic intrusions in the psychoanalytic space and process.

9 This brings to mind the old quip that 'anyone who needs psychoanalysis in a hurry does not need psychoanalysis'.

10 The patients' names in all vignettes in this book are fictional.

11 This, of course, is a paraphrase of Winnicott's (1966) celebrated phrase, the 'ordinary devoted mother'.

Chapter 2

Curiosity

Allow me to begin this discourse on curiosity by recounting three personal experiences. All involve the manifestation of curiosity, though in considerably different contexts. Together these vignettes introduce us to the breadth of the terrain that needs to be covered in this discourse.

- The first incident took place nearly thirty-five years ago. I was young, enjoying a Sunday morning by staying in bed late. My daughter, barely three years old at that time, was sitting on my chest. She said, "Can I ask you something?" I said, "Yes, of course". She said, "Do boys do number two also standing up?" My daughter was curious.
- The second incident involved an important birthday of a good friend which I had to miss due to an out-of-town speaking engagement. I felt bad about it and offered to take my friend and his wife out for a nice dinner upon my return. And indeed, I did so. When dinner was over and the bill came, my friend made a gesture to split the payment but I declined, reminding him that it was my treat. I gave the waiter my credit card and within a minute or two, excused myself to go to the restroom. As I was walking back from the restroom towards our table, I noticed that the waiter had placed the bill along with my credit card in a folder on the table; my friend's wife was lifting the corner of that folder to see what amount I was to pay. My friend's wife was curious.
- In the fall of 1973, I was driving through rural Virginia and was lost in the beauty of the lush countryside. A cop stopped me. He seemed younger than me but stood tall and spoke with authority. He said that I was driving over the speed limit and he was forced to give me a ticket. While filling out the pertinent form, he looked up at me and said, "You're not black, are you?" I responded, "No". He then said, "You're not white, are you?" I said, "No". He looked puzzled and uncertain, even a bit distressed. After an awkward pause, he put forth his final question: "So, what are you?" The cop was curious.

My aim in describing these experiences here is to draw attention to the myriad forms of curiosity in daily life and to lay the groundwork for thinking further about this human attribute, especially in light of its profound importance to conceptualizations and praxis of psychoanalysis. I will first delineate the phenomenological aspects of curiosity and trace its developmental origins in the hard-wired evolutionary imperatives and the crucible of formative relational scenarios of infancy and childhood. Then, I will highlight the psychopathological syndromes involving curiosity and elucidate the role curiosity plays in the unfolding and deepening of the clinical process of psychoanalysis. I will conclude by summarizing my proposals and by addressing some areas (e.g. culture, gender) that could not be addressed in the preceding sections of this chapter.

Modalities, aims, and objects

The English word 'curiosity' is derived from the Latin *curiosus*, which simultaneously means 'inquisitive' and 'careful'. Thus an outward exploratory aim and an inward self-protective aim are both implied in the concept. The etymological linkage of 'curiosity' to the Middle French *cura* ('cure' in English) also suggests that what we regard as 'curiosity' is an attitude with self-sustaining, even self-healing, purposes. This line of thinking is strengthened by the dictionary definition of the word, curiosity, which includes phrases such as "desire to know … inquisitive interest in others' concerns … [and] … interest leading to inquiry" (Mish, 1987, p. 284).

A quick glance at other widely spoken languages either confirms or expands the definition of 'curiosity'. The Hindi, *jigyasa*, is derived from the Sanskrit *gya* (to know) and *san* (desire). It is relatively value-free and, along with the Spanish *curiosidad*, essentially reproduces what is written about the word 'curiosity' in English. The Arabic equivalent of 'curiosity', *fudoul*, however, adds an interesting dimension. Itself derived from *fadl* (giving someone something good, including attention and kindness), the Arabic *fudoul* confers a modicum of goodness to the attribute of curiosity. The Chinese expression for curiosity is the compound word, *how-chi*, which means wanting to know more about something that arouses one's interest. Though less explicitly than its Arabic counterpart, *how-chi* also assigns a positive valence to curiosity.

Putting the foregoing information together results in a nuanced portrayal of 'curiosity', one that is comprised of: (i) a mental attitude of inquisitiveness; (ii) a set of activities involving exploration; (iii) a form of kindness by showing interest in others; and (iv) a self-protective and self-enhancing function since greater knowledge of the external (and internal) reality contributes to greater mastery over it. However, curiosity is not restricted to intellectual matters. It can involve other sensory modalities. Thus, curiosity can be tactile ('I wonder if this fabric is soft, this ball squeezable, this table sturdy?'), gustatory ('What does this strange fruit taste like?'), auditory ('What are they whispering about?'), or visual ('I wonder what their house looks like'), and so on. Moreover, curiosity can be active or passive. The former is evident in raising pertinent questions, displaying genuine interest, and making forays into unfamiliar territories of knowledge and skill. Gone awry, it can lead to intrusiveness and interrogation (more about this later). The latter is evident in patiently waiting for ideas to arise from within or thought to occur from without.[1] Indeed, both these forms of curiosity, active and passive, are essential components of the working analyst's armamentarium. Before delving into that realm, however, it is important to say a few words about the aims and objects of curiosity.

While open to later modifications (by myself or others), curiosity, at this point in my thinking, seems to have five different aims: the word 'aim' is being used here for what a drive seeks to accomplish (Freud, 1915b). These are the following:

Elemental aim

This aim refers to inquisitiveness and inquiries regarding the most basic nuts and bolts of the issue at hand which, at the beginning of life, is life itself. Thus, early examples of 'elemental curiosity' might involve a growing child asking her father if boys do 'number two' standing up (see the beginning of this chapter), or wanting to know the word for penis or vagina, or questioning where do babies come from, or even how to tie shoelaces or why should one say 'sorry' and 'thank you'. The purpose of such curiosity is to gather useful information, pacify phrase-specific emotional and cognitive needs, and accrue knowledge necessary for alloplastic or autoplastic adaptation (Hartmann, 1939) to life. It should be clarified, however, that the deployment of 'elemental curiosity' is not restricted to children. A mature adult, while attempting to acquire a new skill (e.g. playing golf) or learn an unfamiliar language can (indeed, must) also display this form of curiosity.[2]

Exploratory aim

This aim of curiosity is directed towards fathoming the physical and sensate aspects of the human (e.g. mother's face, one's own hands) and non-human environment. Manifest early on in the infant's searching interest in the corporeal features of its mother, and also those of the milk bottle, toys, and the pacifier, 'exploratory curiosity' persists throughout life. It forms the basis of scientific probing, innovative feats of engineering and architecture, and, on a less exalted level, of interest in travel and geographical discoveries. Unlike 'elemental curiosity', which is aimed at building one's self, brick by experiential brick, 'exploratory curiosity' seeks to master external reality with the power of knowledge. Moreover, it can be independent of such agenda and help create the ego pleasures of recreation and play (Erikson, 1950; Winnicott, 1953, 1971).

Empathic aim

The child's curiosity is not merely 'elemental' and 'exploratory'. It also possesses an empathic aim. Dependent upon the mother for its survival and immersed in an un-thought awe of her 'transformational' (Bollas, 1979) impact upon himself, the child wants to learn more about the mother's subjective world. To be sure, his desire is to find nothing there but love for himself but with passage of time and establishment of 'object constancy' (Mahler et al., 1975), the tenor of his curiosity changes. Mother is now experienced as a 'whole object' (Klein, 1935), a separate being unto herself, and, soon in the course of development, so is the father. To know them is better for relating to them and relating to them increases the chances of knowing them. All this enhances the child's sense of safety. Gaining access to the parents' inner selves thus becomes, for the growing child, a source of self-regulation and a stepping stone for learning reciprocity and mutuality in his later relationships.

Existential aim

This designation refers to the 'cosmic' puzzlement that each thinking soul experiences in its encounter with life. Why are we on this planet? What is the purpose of life? Does God exist? Where did this universe come from? Where do all the milky-ways, all the solar systems, and all the galaxies end? What exists after that? Do human beings have a right to end their lives whenever they want? What happens after death? Does a frog know that he is a frog? Do trees think?

Thinking along these lines, the great Urdu poet, Mirza Ghalib (1797–1869), muses:

Subza-o-gul kahaaN se aaye haiN?
Abr kya cheez hai, hawa kya hai?[3]

And, Pablo Neruda (1904–1973) wonders:

Que es mas triste que un tren que paro en la lluvia.[4]

Whether raised by poets or by philosophers, such questions are endless. Our field, psychoanalysis, has traditionally skirted them,[5] but the time has come to recognize that this abdication implies an erroneous belief that matters of the sort listed above have little impact upon the inner lives of human beings.

Enactive aim

Any and all types of curiosities mentioned above can be enlisted in the service of an emotionally driven enactment. Thus, asking truly simple ('elemental') questions in the aftermath of a serious lecture can be a form of mockery.

Similarly, giving in to 'exploratory' curiosity can constitute a rationalized form of escape, intrusion, and voyeurism (more about this in the section on psychopathology, below). Just as language can serve various instinctual functions and words can stand for different bodily secretions (Sharpe, 1940), curiosity of any form and in any modality can provide avenues of instinctual discharge and for actualizing repressed relational scenarios. The fact is that curiosity can get linked with the highest and the lowest inclinations and motives in our psyche (Migdow, 2008). It can become an instrument of empathy and compassion but also of violation and sadism.

After explicating the aims of curiosity, it is imperative that the objects of curiosity be considered. These objects include (i) the self, (ii) other human beings, (iii) non-human living beings, (iv) inanimate entities, and (v) the very nature of life and death.[6] Towards each of these objects, curiosity can be superficial or deep and directed at their sensate features or at their narrative interiority. Towards each of these objects, curiosity can be independently directed or, reflecting the unlimited cathectic mobility of the system Ucs (Freud, 1915d), be a displacement from or condensation with curiosity about objects from another category. Towards each of these objects, curiosity can have single or multiple aims. And, towards each of these objects, curiosity can carry a variable admixture of genuine inquisitiveness, empathy, and projective identification.

Origins

Giving precedence to ontogenetic chronology over professional chronology, which mandates that the discussion of curiosity's origin began with Freud, I will start my comments with the evolutionary foundations of curiosity.

Evolutionary and biological basis

The trait of curiosity is hardly restricted to our species. Animals also give evidence of it. This is most evident in primates but less advanced species also seem to possess curiosity.[7] This is not surprising since curiosity serves the aims of survival and helps locate essential resources (e.g. food, shelter) and find healthy mating partners. The roots of human curiosity reside in the soil of the evolutionary concept termed 'neoteny', which refers to the retention of child-like characteristics by a species during its adult life.

> Neoteny is a short-cut taken by evolution – a route that brings about a whole bundle of changes in one go, rather than selecting for them one by one. Evolution, by making us a more juvenile species, has made us weaker than our primate cousins, but it has also given us our child's curiosity [and] our capacity to learn.
>
> (Stafford, 2012)

This internal push to learn about our environment is the basis of curiosity. The fascinating thing is that in day-to-day life, human curiosity is directed not at fulfilling survival needs but at all sorts of random aspects of life. This suggests that curiosity might not only be a way of satisfying hunger but might itself be a hunger. There is some support for this idea. In the human brain, curiosity seems to be treated as a pleasurable activity and is rewarded by a flood of pleasure-inducing neurotransmitters such as dopamine. And, it seems that the site most responsible for our sense of curiosity is the dentate gyrus of the hippocampal region of our brains (McDermott, 2009).

A counterpart to the proposal that curiosity is 'hard-wired' and phylogenetically evident is that curiosity can lead to trouble and even life-threatening occurrences. For instance, if curiosity draws one into a dark cave whose inhabitants are an angry mother bear and her cubs, the consequences can be disastrous. Seen this way, the trait of curiosity could appear counter-intuitive to evolutionary theory. However, such occurrences are infrequent and carry the potential for safeguarding us in the future and also those who learn from our mistakes. To a greater extent, the same applies to human curiosity about seemingly irrelevant and unnecessary details.[8] What appears random and a waste of time today can be stored up in our neural algorithms for good use tomorrow.

Autonomous ego functions

In contrast to the early psychoanalytic view that all ego functions were, at their root, derived from the aim-inhibition, neutralization, or sublimation of id-instincts or, at best, from a primordial id-ego matrix, Hartmann (1939) declared that certain ego functions are not "derived from the ego's relationship to instinctual drives as love objects, but are rather prerequisites for our conception of these" (p. 15). These functions include intelligence, thinking, perception, learning, motility, and speech. They have 'primary autonomy', i.e. they develop independent of sexual and aggressive instincts. However, they can get caught up into instinctual conflicts and lose their autonomy. Under such circumstances, instinctual forces (and their relational scenarios) can enhance or impede the unfolding, growth, exercise, and aims of these functions.

That curiosity belongs to the list of such 'autonomous ego functions' is stated with unparalleled conviction by Nersessian (1995, 2000). While not discarding the early view that curiosity is a displaced derivative of sexual curiosity of childhood, Nersessian emphasized that curiosity has independent roots as well. In support of his proposal, he cited the infant and child observational studies of Mahler et al. (1975), Mayes (1991), and Emde (1981, 1991), which demonstrated that curiosity is present from the earliest days of life; it is evident by the infant's explorations and the "seeking of the new and the assimilation of the new to the familiar" (Emde, 1991, p. 29). Nersessian (1995) declared that curiosity was "an attitude or attribute of the ego, which can be clearly recognized in its function and role with the emergence of language and thought" (p. 118). His conclusion echoes Stern's (1985) observation that, from birth on, infants are constantly 'evaluating', in the sense of asking, 'is this different from or the same as that?' In other words, there seems to be a central tendency in infants to form and test hypotheses about what is occurring in their world. Infant and child observational studies by Lichtenberg (1982, 1989, 2005) and Greenspan (2005) lend support to this idea.

So, is curiosity instinctual or autonomous in origin? One can take sides in this debate and go on splitting hairs. My preference is to return to Freud's (1910c, 1915a) concept of 'ego instincts' which (i) are aimed at self-preservation and self-seeking, (ii) fulfil non-sexual and non-aggressive aims, (iii) operate under the dominance of reality principle, and (iv) carry an energy of their own that is not libido but 'interest'.[9] In light of this, curiosity appears to be a function of ego-instincts, one that is deeply embedded in the self-protective and self-advancing needs of the human organism.

Infant–mother bond

Another level of curiosity's origin resides in the child's relationship with his mother. Three cardinal ideas in this realm pertain to (i) the child's curiosity about the mother's body, (ii) the use of the mother as an intermediate step in the journey of his larger curiosities and, (iii) the mother's facilitation of the child's capacity to become and stay curious. The most prominent contributor to the first of these issues is Melanie Klein. She spoke of the child's "epistemophilic instinct" (Klein, 1924, 1930, 1931) as a driving force in the child's development and the mother's body as the original 'world' it explored. However, her emphasis upon the envious and destructive fantasies embedded in such curiosity (e.g. what is inside the mother's body? Father's penis? Another baby?) led her to inadequately appreciate that the child might also regard the mother's body (including its insides) as a font of knowledge and wisdom; this aspect was to be later emphasized by Bion (1962b, 1970) and Meltzer (1986). Ready availability of pleasant contact with mother's body both soothes and excites the child's curiosity.

Early relationship with mother impacts upon the consolidation of the child's curiosity via his treating her as a trial object for his explorations. Pulling at mother's hair, necklace, and glasses informs the child not only about the distinction between her accoutrements and her true corporeal self but functions as a safe field before entering the more unpredictable world of things, plants, and little and big animals. Mother's body serves as a practice arena and also, by her holding the child's hands – literally – and directing his attention by her verbal commands ("Wow! Look at this bunny rabbit!"), becomes the guide for the child's curiosity.

In addition, by containing and processing the child's spontaneous comments and questions, maternal reverie deepens the child's capacity to think about thoughts themselves (Bion, 1963). A memory of my childhood illustrates this interactional dynamic well.

> I was about five years old. My mother was cooking something – I think it was rice, but I'm not sure – on the stove top. I was watching. And then, the lid of the aluminium pot began to rise up with the steam that was coming out from it. I asked my mother: "Ammi, why does this lid move?" She responded, "See this white thing? The one that is moving upward like a tiny little cloud?" I nodded yes. She continued, "This is called steam. It is what water turns into when heated. Being a gas, it has a tendency to move upwards. So, it pushes the lid and that's why the lid moves." Seeing me engrossed in the conversation, she added: "Now, there was a little boy in a country called Scotland and this boy's name was James Watt. He also asked the same question as you just did. And, then he thought that if we heat a lot of water, and produce a lot of steam, and pass it through a tube, and connect the end of that tube to a wheel, then that steam will push the wheel to move. And, that's how the engines for the trains we travel in came about". I was enraptured. She then added, "You are like that boy and one day, you will also do something special in this world".

As it turns out, the James Watt (1736–1819) story is apocryphal and most likely popularized by his son, James Watt, Jr; it persists because it is easy for children to understand. More important than that, however, is the love that suffuses the mother–child interaction described above. And, even more impressive, is the mother's capacity to take the child's curiosity seriously, elaborate the thoughts that the child is not yet able to have himself, and to provide him with an operative mode of thinking about thoughts. Devoid of such assistance in thinking and unsupported in his 'going-on-being' (Winnicott, 1956), the child retreats into mindlessness and indifference to subjectivity of his own and others.

Puzzlement over sexual matters

Here the work of Freud is paramount. He traced human curiosity to its sexual origins. In "Three essays on the theory of sexuality" (1905b), he declared:

> The progressive concealment of the body which goes along with civilization keeps sexual curiosity awake. This curiosity seeks to complete the sexual object by revealing its hidden parts. It can, however, be diverted ("sublimated") in the direction of art, if its interest can be shifted away from the genitals on to the shape of the body as a whole.

> (p. 156)

In later papers such as "Civilized sexuality morality and modern nervous illness" (1908b), and "On the sexual theories of children" (1908a) too, Freud linked curiosity to the child's puzzlement over genital differences, pregnancy, and childbirth. This theme was illustrated in myriad details in his case of Little Hans (Freud, 1909a) and was reiterated in his paper titled, "Some psychical consequences of anatomical differences between sexes" (1925). Clearly, Freud tended to reduce all curiosity to the child's interest in sexual matters, and so did his loyal followers of the early twentieth century (Abraham, 1907, 1913; Ferenczi, 1909, 1913).

To his credit, though, one must recognize that in his paper on Leonardo Da Vinci, Freud (1910a) regarded the protagonist's relentless instinct for investigation to have been "probably organic" (p. 77) in origin. Even more interestingly, he acknowledged that the child's sexual curiosity might itself be reflective of an "inborn need for established causes" (1908a, p. 212).[10] This later line of Freud's thinking is in close alliance with the biological, autonomous, and ego-instinct models of curiosity proposed above.

Encouragement and shaping during latency

Arising from a complex interactive matrix of evolutionary imperatives, neurobiology, infant–mother interaction, and childhood sexual inquisitiveness, curiosity finds its 'safest' and most pleasurable blossoming during the latency phase (six to twelve years or so of age). It is at this time that the child's curiosity is fully and ego-syntonically directed at features of external reality. Knowing facts, memorizing historical details, mastering problems of mathematics and science, and accumulating a pride-worthy store of landmarks in the world of sports or movies or stamp-collecting becomes the child's passion. School, which Erikson (1950) declares to be "a culture by itself" (p. 259), upholds and rewards the child's curiosity and firms up the link between intellectual robustness and the child's ego-ideal. Good teachers tend to foster curiosity in their pupils. They help students observe, think, enquire, and make connections between apparently disparate clusters of information.[11]

Psychopathology

Generally speaking, curiosity is a healthy trait but, like any other mental function, it can be drawn into psychopathology. Quantitative as well as qualitative distortions of curiosity are seen in clinical practice and in day-to-day life. In the *quantitative* realm, one encounters: (i) excessive curiosity, (ii) deficient curiosity, and (iii) uneven curiosity. In the *qualitative* realm, one comes across (iv) anachronistic curiosity, (v) instinctualized curiosity, and (vi) false curiosity. Brief comments upon these six maladies follow.

Excessive curiosity

Nunberg's (1961) detailed case report of a patient given to compulsive questioning opened the doors for the consideration that curiosity can be excessive.
Nunberg traced his patient's pathological need to know to frustrated oral
drives which had resulted in the intensification of the wish to witness and
understand the primal scene. In a sophisticated step away from id-based
reductionism, Nunberg posited that his patient's superego reacted to the
intensified drive to intrude upon parental privacy but 'biting-off' perceptual
pieces of ego, leaving it perpetually hungry for more knowledge. Afflictions of
all three psychic structures (id, ego, and superego) thus contributed to the
patient's excessive curiosity.[12]

While Nunberg's formulation is a masterpiece of the mid-twentieth-century
ego psychology, incessant questioning and the unrelenting curiosity that lies
behind it might be understood somewhat differently today or, at least, accorded some additional explanations. For instance, excessive curiosity might be
seen as a by-product of having grown up with a 'mysterious' parent and/or in
a family environment suffused with secrets. Not having received the 'usual'
amount/type of information about one's parents and other important family
members (as might happen in the case of adopted children) can leave the
child hungry for answers. Another explanation might be that faced with
insurmountable hardships of childhood, a highly resilient or 'invulnerable
child' (Anthony, 1987) can increase his vigilance and curiosity to achieve a
modicum of control over the given realities.

Bion (1957) offers a third explanation. He describes the triad of arrogance,
curiosity, and stupidity in which the excessively inquisitive person smugly fails
to recognize that his questioning might result in serious trouble. In order to
make clear the relationship between the elements of this triad, Bion considers
the Oedipus myth from the perspective where the Prince's sexual transgression
is deemed secondary. Greater emphasis is laid upon his hubris in "vowing to
lay bare the truth no matter what cost" (p. 86). To be sure, the same can be
extrapolated to Adam and Eve's serpent-like curiosity which led them to be
cast out from the Garden of Eden.

Finally, by putting the question as to what is 'excessive' about excessive
curiosity on its head, one can end up with the conclusion that it is a depressed,
physically ill, and uninvolved parent (and, later on, an unduly abstinent analyst)
who has mislabelled a normal amount of curiosity as 'excessive'.

Deficient curiosity

The individual with this malady never asks questions, remains indifferent to
people and events in his surround, and comes across as either bland or smug.
These qualities play havoc with his or her interpersonal relationships; the
outcomes of such incuriosity[13] range from awkward and ludicrous to cold

and hurtful. Richard Nixon, for instance, is reported to have been surprised when, after five years of living in the White House, he invited his best friend (and Chief of Staff) Robert Haldeman for dinner in the private living quarters and the latter showed up with his wife. Nixon did not know that his best friend of decades was a married man (Woodward and Bernstein, 1974). Unlike the traffic cop who asked me, "what are you?" (mentioned at the very beginning of this chapter) out of provincial ignorance, Nixon's incuriosity was most likely grounded in narcissism. Being self-absorbed forecloses the ability and desire to know others.

Pallor of knowledge about others and the infirm curiosity that lies behind it also accompanies racial and religious prejudice. Elsewhere (Akhtar, 2007), I have noted that prejudice arises not due to unavailability of facts but by the active jettisoning of facts that *are* available. To be sure, there is some postmodern slippage in the very concept of 'facts', but lack of knowledge still seems to play a lesser role than an agenda-driven repudiation of information in the sustenance of prejudice and, at times, for unleashing violence. The 'realities' (e.g. Saddam Hussein's possessing weapons of mass destruction) invoked to justify the US invasion of Iraq constitute one such example. It is well-known that a vast majority of nations regarded the American 'facts' to be untrue and President Bush had been told as such by Ambassador Joseph Wilson (Clarke, 2004; Woodward, 2004) but this information was put aside to carry on the *a-priori* decision to wage war. Indeed, Jean Edward Smith, biographer of Presidents Franklin D. Roosevelt, Ulysses S. Grant, Dwight D. Eisenhower, and George W. Bush, concludes that the dominant theme of Bush's presidency was "a toxic blend of arrogance and incuriosity" (cited in Jablow, 2016, p. H-10). Such self-perpetuated lack of knowledge is also evident among the current Islam-bashers, most of whom know few facts about the religion and the demography and culture of its 1.4 billion followers.

On closer, more personal levels, too, lack of curiosity has deleterious impact upon self and its relationships. It does not permit deepening of self-knowledge and keeps relationships superficial. One becomes alienated from oneself and others. But if the result of incuriosity is not good, what gives rise to it and what sustains it? Three etiologies present themselves, though their hybrid forms might also exist.[14] First, lack of curiosity can result from lack of 'mentalization' (Fonagy and Target, 1998) in general or of this-and-that particular content. The mislabelling, or even non-naming, of a female child's genitals (Lerner, 1976) carries the potential of obliterating the pertinent anatomical curiosity, for instance.[15] Generally speaking, when a child's curiosity cannot be contained by maternal reverie, the child is reduced to defensive self-reliance and has to abandon curiosity (Bion, 1957). Culturally transmitted taboos on verbalization can also lead to all sorts of areas of the mind becoming 'silenced' (Fivush, 2010) and devoid of curiosity.

A second source of deficient curiosity is the opposition that exists between curiosity and narcissism. Poland (2009) states it most eloquently: "Narcissism speaks of emotional investments aimed inward, while curiosity refers to those aimed outward" (p. 259). While Poland warns against an overly fastidious distinction between the two, it remains likely that excessive self-absorption diminishes interest in others. Freud's (1914a) wry observation that nothing robs one of the capacity for love more than a toothache sums up this equation well. The miscarriage of empathy that characterizes the marriage and sexuality of narcissistic individuals (Akhtar, 2009a, pp. 99–110) is a frequently encountered clinical counterpart of it.

The third etiology of deficient curiosity is seen in association with a 'higher level of character organization' (Kernberg, 1970), namely those with neurotic formations around unresolved oedipal conflicts. Here, the pioneering work of Freud (1908b, 1909a, 1924b), and his early pupils (Abraham, 1907; Ferenczi, 1909, 1913) is pertinent. Elucidated in the section on the developmental origins of curiosity, this line of thinking views childhood curiosity as arising from interest in anatomical differences between the sexes, primal scene, pregnancy, and childbirth. The anaemia of curiosity in adult life is thus attributed to the superego-driven inhibition of sexual curiosity. Actually, such ego-blockage represents many agendas and seeks to accomplish diverse aims. Fenichel (1945) explicated the underlying compromise formations most clearly.

> A repression of sexual curiosity may block the normal interest in know-ing and thinking. Often the inhibited sexual curiosity corresponds to an intense unconscious scoptophilia or stands in intimate relationship to sadistic impulses; the consequent "stupidity" may represent simulta-neously an obedience to and a rebellion against the parents from who the patient had suffered frustrations of his curiosity ... The "stupidity" that manifestly explores the inhibition of curiosity may unconsciously be used in various ways to satisfy this very curiosity by gaining access to scenes that would be kept secret from a "less stupid" child.
>
> (p. 181)[16]

Nearly five decades later, Sarphatie (1993), a Dutch child analyst, noted two different ways by which such inhibitions can come about. When the child's parents do not understand his or her "instinctual curiosity" (p. 197), the child condemns his inquisitiveness and the resulting suppression of this ego capacity can spread to non-sexual realms. The same can happen if the parents react in an over-stimulating manner; the child becomes anxious and defensively wards off his epistemic pursuits.

Uneven curiosity

Excessive and deficient curiosities can co-exist. Someone can be very curious about a particular area and surprisingly indifferent towards another. Freud's insatiable curiosity about psychology, literature, history, mythology, and antiquities was accompanied by a peculiar disinterest in music (Cheshire, 1996; Barale and Minazzi, 2008), for instance. Mohammad Ali Jinnah (1876–1948), the Muslim separatist leader of mid-twentieth century India and founder of Pakistan, showed no interest in reading the Quran or in learning Urdu, the national language of the country he founded (Akhtar and Kumar, 2008). Many more examples of such sort can be given. Cezanne's not attending his mother's funeral and Rilke's not sparing time from his poetry to attend his daughter's wedding must be multiply determined but a certain lack of curiosity also seems at work here.

Less illustrious individuals in daily life and during clinical work can also display unevenness of curiosity. The 'energic' distribution of inquisitiveness in them is tilted towards one particular matter at the cost of others. Knowledgeable in their field of work or study, they might turn out to be shockingly ignorant about matters unrelated to it. They are simply not interested in learning other things. For some, such deliberate restriction of focus works well and productively. For others (e.g. the so-called computer-phobics), it depletes ego resources and makes life devoid of adventure.

The dynamic substrate of uneven curiosity is wide-ranging and includes cultural biases of what is important to know and what is not, inhibitions of specific ego sectors arising out of epigenetically unfolding instinctual conflicts, and 'mirror complementarity of the self' (Bach, 1977), whereby a curious part of the self exists side by side with an incurious part; the two could arise from contradictory identifications with parents of markedly different ego organizations. Similar contradictions can be found in individuals with the syndrome of identity diffusion (Kernberg, 1975; Akhtar, 1984).

Anachronistic curiosity

The first among the three qualitative forms of pathological curiosities, 'anachronistic curiosity' refers to an individual's preoccupation with questions that are not customary for someone his age. A forty-year-old man wondering if the clouds or moon run along with him when he breaks into a sprint is an illustration of anachronistic curiosity. Drawing from the earlier phenomenological section of this chapter, anachronistic curiosity can be seen as the persistence of curiosity's 'elemental aims' long after their thirst ought to have been quenched. Take another example. A thirty-year-old woman who wants to know if pregnancy results from sexual intercourse is displaying anachronistic curiosity. This is an adult asking child-like questions. Conversely, a child asking 'adult' questions also shows anachronistic curiosity. A five-year-old boy asking his mother whether it is time for them to pay their electricity bill, and a ten-year-old girl asking her parents what sort of funeral she should have are also displaying anachronistic curiosity.[17]

A host of etiological factors (e.g. parental discouragement of the child's assertive questioning, familial and cultural taboos, delayed ego maturation) can underlie anachronistic curiosity. Of greater significance are the ways in which the afflicted individual manages such predicament. One common manoeuvre is to withdraw, remain quiet, and sit tightly over one's questions; this is because of the great shame associated with elemental ignorance. Many so-called schizoid individuals 'prefer' to appear disinterested in others over revealing their deep puzzlement over extremely basic matters (e.g. 'do you also defecate?', 'did you fuck your husband and is that how you got pregnant?', 'how often do you shower and how did you come up with that frequency?', and so on).

Instinctualized curiosity

While "the truth drive is the operative agent of curiosity" (Grotstein, 2007, p. 146), an onslaught of wayward instinctual drives can readily pervert the nature of curiosity. Prominent among such scenarios are those involving voyeurism and sadism. In the former case, looking and looking intently become emotionally charged vehicles of curiosity. Such drive to 'see' tends to arise from multiple sources. It might compensate for a traumatizing state of premature separateness from the mother with vision taking on the life-sustaining function of "distance contact" (Mahler et al., 1975, p. 67) with her.[18] Klein's (1925) early observation that sexual curiosities of children are aimed not only at gaining knowledge but also at exerting control over parents is pertinent in this context.

Voyeurism that rises up to the status of a sexual perversion is invariably tinged with sadism. The rage at premature separation from the mother spills into phallic-phase curiosities and oedipal competitiveness, leading to violent intrusions in parental privacy. The associated castration fear is defended by counterphobia, denial of sexual difference, and regression to anal themes (Freud, 1905b; Chasseguet-Smirgel, 1984). Curiosity, under such circumstances, becomes an eroticized defilement of others (who stand for a nourishment-withholding mother and/or the parents in intercourse). To the extent that such perverse defiance of superego is never absolute, guilt lingers in the corners of the psyche and adds a masochistic tinge to the acting out; the more one intrudes by watching, the more one feels excluded and impotent.[19] This further fuels rage and the quest for omnipotence.

In addiction to pornography too, the major agenda is one of eroticized misogyny, omnipotence, and erasure of separateness. The preconscious awareness that the pervert and the pornography addict have of their psychic hollowness and lack of generative sexual prowess necessitates a measure of idealization. The eye, unable to locate the nourishing mother and intolerant of sexual difference, constantly searches for beauty as a reassurance against its depressive and paranoid anxieties.[20]

Milder symptoms, especially obsessive questioning of obscure facts, also serve instinctual aims since they simultaneously express a need to understand corporeal matters while also denying them (Fenichel, 1945). Kramer's (1983) description of 'object-coercive doubting' is also a case in point here. The result of sexual overstimulation of children by their mothers, this condition is characterized by the child engaging the mother in endless arguments in which she is 'forced' to take the opposite side of what the child feels is true at a given moment. Their struggle "often ends in an orgasm-like fury for both, thus re-enacting the earlier sexual play them" (p. 345).

All in all, 'instinctualized curiosity' can lead to voyeuristic perversions tinged with sadomasochism, obsessive questioning, object-coercive doubting, and also to certain character traits such as voracious reading and also the tendency to teasingly induce curiosity in others. Displaced forms of 'instinctualized curiosity' are evident in minor acts of prying (e.g. my friend's wife checking the amount of the restaurant bill, as mentioned previously) and its sublimated versions are found in certain professions, prominent among them being photography, archaeology, and historical research. Grinberg (1962) has, however, proposed that interest in becoming a physician can also derive from childhood curiosity regarding the insides of the mother's body.

False curiosity

Subscribing to the 'classic' view that inquisitiveness of any kind is displaced sexual curiosity, one might regard any non-sexual curiosity as inherently false. But that is not what 'false curiosity' is intended to denote here. The designation is used for inquiries that have little or nothing to do with their purported concern. In this realm, there are two kinds of false curiosity: benign and malignant.

Benign false curiosity is evident in the socially accepted (and expected) 'corridor chatter' or 'water fountain' queries such as "how are you doing?" and "how was your weekend?" These utterances act as 'politeness-grease' necessary for congeniality between office-mates and neighbours. Such curiosity is preconsciously recognized as a mere formality by the two parties in dialogue. It serves a useful purpose.

Malignant false curiosity is maliciously intended to seduce, mislead, or discombobulate others. The fraudulent psychopath, armed with exquisite 'state-related empathy' (Gediman, 1985) often engages his unwitting victim by a seemingly innocuous display of interest in him while actually he is planning to rob or exploit him. The narcissist with little actual concern for others' subjectivity might fake interest and display curiosity while his mind is on sexually seducing or monetarily manipulating the other.

Between the extremes of 'benign' and 'malignant' false curiosity reside professional activities where asking misleading questions is an important part of one's daily repertoire. The work of a detective, lawyer, spy, and undercover agent often includes such 'false curiosity'.

Implications for clinical work

Freud's (1915d) paper, "The unconscious", is the single most important paper in the corpus of psychoanalytic literature. It lays bare the characteristics of unconscious mental functioning, delineates the distinction between such psychic activity and conscious mentation, and indicates the avenues for discerning the unconscious (e.g. dreams, parapraxes, negation, and derivatives). The varied and nuanced proposals contained in this masterpiece (see Akhtar and O'Neil, 2012, for details) undergird all the following conceptualizations, be they about the curiosity of the analyst or of the patient.

The analyst's curiosity

One clinical 'gift' that has come wrapped in Freud's 1915 paper on the unconscious is that of sceptical listening; the analyst is topographically attuned, looks for what is hidden, what is implied, what is being warded off and why. In the spirit of Freud's 'archaeological metaphor', the analyst wants to dig deeper, find out more. He listens to what is being said but keeps his 'third ear' (Reik, 1948) open for omissions, undue emphases, negations, and unsolicited denials. In simple words, the analyst is curious. His curiosity differs from that of the neurotic or the pervert.

> Through personal analysis, sexual curiosity is purged of its infantile characteristics, it is no longer of the "peeping Tom" variety. Curiosity becomes adult and benevolent, because the psychoanalyst is not engaged upon a surreptitious gratification of his own immature sexuality.
>
> (Sharpe, 1947, p. 121)

Curiosity is central to the analyst's therapeutic armamentarium and keeps him alert. At the same time, the analyst is told to "not direct one's notice to anything in particular" (Freud, 1912, p. 111) while listening to his or her patients. The requirement of such 'evenly suspended attention' tends to blunt the sharp edges of the analyst's curiosity. A tension thus arises.

On the side of maintaining free-floating attention is the valuable fact that such attitude prevents the analyst from selecting this or that bit of material and foreclosing the possibility of surprise and discovery. It also allows the analyst's "unconscious memory" (Freud, 1912, p. 112) to effortlessly capture important links between the seemingly disparate and even 'irrelevant' aspects of the patient's associations. The clinical posture accompanying this listening attitude is one of quiet receptivity and passive curiosity.

On the side of the analyst yielding to momentary increases in his curiosity is that it leads him to ask questions. These, in turn, "destabilize existing compromise formations ... [and] ... further the development of self-observation, which is such an important concomitant cause and consequence of structural change"

(Boesky, 1989, p. 579). Well aware that analysts' questions might emanate from impatience, Boesky (1989), in his remarkable paper on this matter, notes that more often than not such inquiries are in the service of learning more and avoiding a quick conclusion. Indeed, a question can be "the emblem of the analyst's benevolent curiosity" (p. 591).[21] A decade after Boesky's proposals, Brenner (2000) emphasized that "in listening to a patient, one pays attention now to defence, now to what is defended against, depending upon what is apparent in the patient's communications" (p. 548). The clinical posture accompanying such listening attitude is one of direct questioning and active curiosity.

In the first mode described above, "curiosity is the silent partner of attention" (Nersessian, 1995, p. 121). In the second mode, curiosity is a vocal player on the stage. Most practising analysts attempt to strike a balance between these two clinical postures and their attendant passive and active modes of curiosity. Shifts between them are mostly smooth and barely noticeable. Finding himself biased in favour of one or the other of these postures, the analyst needs to examine his countertransference resistance to staying passively receptive or to become actively inquisitive; it might help to remember that boredom is a frequent defence against passive curiosity (Goldberg, 2002a) and undue abstinence a commonly used shield to ward off active curiosity.

The tension between passive and active curiosity is more marked in the very early phases of treatment during which the analyst wishes to uphold the 'fundamental rule' (Freud, 1900) by interfering less in the patient's associations and yet his lack of familiarity with the patient's inner workings propels him to be actively curious. Nersessian (1995) notes that on the other temporal end of the clinical work, i.e. during the termination phase, there also develops the risk of "constriction of curiosity" (p. 125) on the analyst's part. The analyst often ceases to be curious about the past and thus misses an opportunity for additional reconstructions.

Yet another matter to consider here is that spikes in the analyst's 'active' curiosity can also be caused by the patient's way of presenting (or not presenting) the material. Mumbling[22] and talking inaudibly can pull the analyst to ask the patient to repeat what he or she said. A pause, especially one that follows a proposition (e.g. 'and', 'but') can transform the analyst's curiosity from being passive to active. 'You want to move to New York and ... and what?', the analyst might say. An extra-analytic encounter that is blithely omitted by the patient in the next session contributes yet another clinical moment of such co-created active curiosity of the analyst. Major omission in an otherwise detailed and emotionally significant narrative can also have a similar impact upon the analyst's attention. I, for one, was made a bit irritably curious when my last patient of 9/12 (i.e. the day after the 9/11 attack) would not mention the national tragedy; I wondered if I should question the patient about this omission but, to my relief, the topic appeared in her association towards the end of the session. The fact, though, is that the patient's silence about 9/11 until the end of the session left me a little shaken up and, inevitably, curious about my reaction itself.[23]

Clearly, no fixed guideline can be established for the analyst's shifting from passive to active curiosity. The decision to move this or that way is at times spontaneous and at other times deliberate. Under ideal circumstances, the analyst maintains curiosity about his technical choices, regardless of their form, and the impact of his action (or inaction) upon the analyst process.

The patient's curiosity

The most obvious manner in which the patients' curiosity enters the clinical dialogue is via the questions they ask their analysts. The scope of such questions is large and ranges from the procedural aspects of treatment (e.g. frequency, fees, recumbent posture) through minor aspects of their shared reality (e.g. 'you know the intersection between Lancaster Avenue and 34th Street?', or referring to the renowned NFL team, 'you know the Cowboys, right?') to personal aspects of the analyst's life (e.g. 'do you have children?', 'are your parents alive?'). Given the great variability in the nature, intensity, purpose, and extent of instinctual agendas implicit in such questions, no uniform policy for answering or not answering them can be evolved (Greenson, 1967; Schlesinger, 2003). Each instance has to be taken up individually. However, some 'soft' guidelines for responding to patients' questions do exist.

First of all, questions raised by the patient at the end of the initial evaluation, especially if they pertain to the therapeutic frame (e.g. frequency of session, use of couch), should be answered in a factual manner. The analyst should not derail or mystify the patient by 'interpreting' the reasons behind such questions. For instance, if a patient asks, 'what is the advantage of lying of on the couch', the analyst should respond in a simple and straightforward way, keeping the exploration of fantasies and anxieties that might be hidden here for later. The patient is not only a patient; he or she is a consumer, too, and this fact should not be overlooked.

Second, a similar straightforwardness should be maintained towards questions that reflect pathic communication and are merely intended to assure a background of common reality. Thus, if a patient says, 'you know Jack Nicholson, right?', the analyst might simply respond, 'yes, the actor', and let the flow of the patient's association continue. To act 'like a shrink' and remain quiet or respond with 'why do you ask?' at such junctures has the potential of disrupting the patient's 'going-on-being' (Winnicott, 1956) and iatrogenically derailing the conversation.

Third, as Schlesinger (2003) eloquently puts it, "it is useful to distinguish between answering a patient's question and responding to the patient's act of questioning" (p. 173). By asking a question, the patient is imploring the analyst to do something and, at least for that moment, ceasing to be curious about his own self. At such junctures:

The governing principle is the logic of the interpretive process. Our first concern is for the *function* of the question: what is it doing here now? We could adopt as a new analytic aphorism, "A quick answer can ruin a good question." It captures the point precisely: there is much more to understand about a question than its content, and a quick answer might preclude further inquiry. But that would be the case only if the analyst (as well as the patient) were satisfied that the quick answer had eliminated all further interest either in the question or why it had been asked just then. There is no reason, in principle, why an inquiry into the act of questioning, and into the circumstances in the stream of associations that forced the interruption and substituted the question, could not continue after the analyst offered some information by way of an answer.

(p. 175, italics in the original)

Reed (1997) also warns against "misplaced valorization of anonymity" (p. 529), noting that the unconscious is not permanently altered by external information and the patient will continue to perceive the analyst's action to disclose (or not disclose) a piece of personal information according to the transference fantasies active at the moment.

Fourth, some questions of the patient might be better left unanswered (e.g. 'were you sexually abused as a child?') since factually answering them can reverse the ameliorative gradient in treatment setting, with the patient needing to become the healer of the analyst. Further, at times, firm limit-setting seems to be a prerequisite for deeper exploration of the patient's curiosity.

Clinical vignette: 4

Rebecca Cohen, a young clinical psychology intern, whose father was a survivor of the Holocaust, called me seeking psychoanalysis. She was well-informed about analysis and had been given my name by an elderly analyst. While setting an appointment on the phone, she asked me: "Are you an Arab?" I responded by saying that while I was interested in her question and what lay behind it, I could not answer it on a factual basis. I added that if we were going to undertake any kind of in-depth work together, my reality was less important than what she made of it in her mind. The patient, however, persisted, saying, "Look, I am a devout Jew and an ardent Zionist. I know that if you are an Arab, your sympathies in the Israelis-Palestine conflict will be with the Palestinians. And I am not about to give my money to someone who will support terrorism against my own people." I was taken aback by the sadomasochistic proclivity I sensed under a thin patina of ethnic rationalization. I responded by repeating what I had said and adding that if she found herself willing to tolerate ambiguity and investigate what had already begun to take place, then perhaps we could meet. Otherwise, she might have to go elsewhere. She came for her appointment and did enter analysis with me.

Her presenting symptom was inability to be romantically intimate with Jewish men. Perhaps this had propelled the referring analyst, who was Jewish, to give her my name (and, as it turned out, a Christian analyst's name, too). Rebecca underwent a rather stormy analysis over the following six years. Provocative limit testing and recall through enactments pervaded the early phase. Three things then took centre stage: (i) the Holocaust and her contradictory identifications with her father's 'survivor's guilt' (Niederland, 1968), and his persecutors' sadism, (ii) the 'separation guilt' (Modell, 1984), involving a depressed mother, and (iii) a negative oedipal defence against guilt-ridden positive oedipal strivings. These shifts, interestingly, were associated with her changing perceptions of my ethnicity: first, an Arab (equated with a Nazi), then an Indian Muslim (a minority individual, hence equated with a Jew), and, finally, a reasonably assimilated immigrant American.

Such shifting transferences and their corresponding ethnic embodiments are not the points of concern here. What is important to register is that an early 'blockage' of the patient's curiosity about the analyst led, over time, to deepening curiosity about herself.

Fifth, enhancement of the patients' curiosity about themselves is of course a crucial task during the early phases of analysis. Comments such as "I wonder what you make of this reaction of yours", "Let us see where this line of thinking leads us", or simply, "let us be curious about this" are commonplace measures for this purpose. Another point of intervention is when a patient himself asks, "why did I get so tense while watching that movie?"; the analyst faced with such a question must resist offering an explanation and instead invite the patient to deepen his curiosity about his affective life. Yet another opportunity for such enrichment is provided by the first few enactments in the course of analysis. By maintaining equanimity and composure, the analyst can help the patient transform the frustration of his action-oriented desire into an empowered observing ego.

Clinical vignette: 5

At the end of a session in the second month of her analysis, Melanie Wright, an otherwise psychologically minded young woman, got up from the couch and offered me a bag full of apples. She said that she had gone apple-picking over the weekend and wanted me to have some. I was taken aback. Neither her characteristic way of being nor the material in the session had prepared me for this. I responded, "I appreciate your bringing me this gift but I cannot accept it. See, our task here is to understand, enlighten ourselves to your mental functioning and, thus, come to grips with your difficulties. We cannot, therefore, move into actions, especially ones whose meanings are unknown to us. Now, I regret if my stance hurts your feelings, but I do not apologize because my intent is not to hurt you". She listened carefully and nodded in agreement. I then spontaneously added, "For instance, apples. What comes to mind about apples?" She answered, "Adam's apple! ... Adam and Eve ... forbidden fruit." She smiled, blushed, and left shaking her head, saying "I understand, I understand".

Sixth, in the middle and late-middle phases of analysis, the patient might become able to carry the ball of self-directed curiosity by herself, raising questions and then going on to associate to them. At such occasions, the analyst's function is largely that of 'witnessing' and "respecting the patient's essential aloneness" (Poland, 2000, p. 21). Such stance has a dialectical relationship with interpreting; interpretation enhances self-object differentiation and thus allows for more witnessing which, in turn, yields material for further interpretation. Take a look at the following material.

Clinical vignette: 6

Marilyn McDonough, an attractive architect in her fifties, had sought help following an emotional crisis with one of her children. Once the acute matter was settled and the treatment began to deepen, the centrality of her own mother's death when Marilyn was barely five years old came to the surface. A talented and industrious woman, Marilyn had devoted all her energies to raising her kids (after a tumultuous marriage ended in divorce) and to advancing in the profession she loved. She excelled at both these endeavours and, all along, the pain of her early maternal loss remained psychically sequestered – never repressed but not entirely worked through either. Later, she got married again and had since then maintained a reasonably satisfactory marital life.

Her analysis, for a long time, remained focused upon the pervasive effects of her early loss; it coloured transference anxieties, sensitivities to separation, and fear of getting retraumatized by losing me. Provision of ample psychic space, empathic validation, gentle uncovering of defences against the awareness of the deep impact of the childhood tragedy, and interpretive handling of 'survivor guilt' (Niederland, 1968) and the resulting inhibition of healthy entitlement, led to great improvement in her capacity to mourn. Energy thus freed up was then directed to deepening ties with her family and newer sublimations. Such progress did not preclude the repeated return to mourning the loss of her mother at a very young age. The resurgence of this material during later phases of analysis was often accompanied by new recollections and new questions.

One day in the fourth year of her analysis, Marilyn came for her session right after visiting her stepmother, Meg, in the nursing home where she had resided for the past few months. Marilyn began the session by talking about how frail Meg had become and how readily she got fatigued. Soon, the thoughts of Meg's death surfaced. Marilyn sobbed. And, she began wondering about Meg's funeral. This led to the memory of the day Marilyn's biological mother, Mary, had died. A question that had never occurred to her now emerged. Marilyn said, "I think I was told by my father that mom would not be coming back from the hospital and that she had gone to heaven or something like that – I am not sure – around three or four p.m. that afternoon. Since I was four-and-a-half, I suppose my bed time then must have been something like eight p.m. The question is what did I do between four and eight p.m.?" Marilyn went on to say, "I really want to know that. I don't know but I want to, in fact, I need to know that. What did I do? I know I used to write on the walls with crayons and carve something on the coffee table but all that came much later, not that afternoon. Maybe I was just wandering around the house, I don't know. But I want to know, though I am not sure why I want to know". As she was speaking, I found my mind wandering. I recalled that long ago, I had seen Wilhelm Stekel's (1924) monograph on wandering in a psychoanalytic library but had not actually read it. I felt a sense of loss and an aching desire to undo that loss. Taking a cue from this 'concordant countertransference' (Racker, 1968) and from this bit of free association of my own, I said, "Of course, you would like to link up with that missing fragment of your life. It's natural for all of us to try to fill in the gaps in our memory to help us experience a sense of continuity. It's like if you lose one ear-ring and are holding on to the other of the pair; you would search for the lost one". Marilyn responded, "But why can't I remember?" I said, "I do not really know but think there are many possibilities. One, that you were in a state that is best called 'forlorn' and being only four-and-a-half years old, could not think properly about what had happened. Two, perhaps all the grown-ups in the house were themselves preoccupied. So, left to your own meagre resources, you could not feel or think clearly. And, since you were not able to clearly register what was going on during those hours, you cannot recall it now. It is all a fog". Marilyn nodded in agreement and cried. Composing herself, she said, "It is like there is a piece of a puzzle … something absent, something not to be found". I responded, "Something and someone! For the very person who could have helped you 'think' about your mother's death – to the extent you could – was your mother and she was gone, not to be found, so to speak". Marilyn listened peacefully. The quiet of the office encased our mutuality. Then I added, "And, of course, we also have to consider if the search for the memory of those missing four hours is a version of a search for her and if the reference includes our four 'hours' and the wish that I would be with you all those hours so that you never feel forlorn now".

Reconstructive and interpretative work, both in the transference and extra-transference realms, was a response to this patient's self-directed curiosity. It helped fill the throbbing and un-mentalized gap in the narrative of her trauma and linked it up with her experience in the here-and-now of the analysis.

Seventh, a point of technique also arises when the analyst notices a remarkable absence of curiosity in the patient. Faced with this situation, the analyst might benefit by trying to establish a differential diagnosis of this 'symptom' by raising – privately, of course – the following questions. Does the patient appear incurious because he or she has already satisfied their curiosity by Googling me? And, if this a genuine absence of curiosity, does it reflect an ego defect or a defensive manoeuvre? If it is of the former variety, what has foreclosed the mental space for engagement with the other? Narcissism? State-related preoccupation? If it is of the latter variety, what is being pushed aside by seeming aloofness? Dread of dependence? Shame at the nature of one's questions? Fear of making the analyst uncomfortable? Besides such 'silent inquiries', the analyst also has to consider if he or she has somehow contributed – unwittingly, one hopes – to the patient's lack of curiosity. Did the analyst show discomfort at the earliest manifestations of the patient's curiosity and that discomfort has taken hold of the latter's psyche in a powerful way and now eliminates all analyst-related curiosities from his mind? And, similar questions need to be raised about the patient's lack of curiosity about themselves. Is it defect-based, a sort of alexithymic situation? Is it defensive? Or, has the patient's curiosity become externalized *in toto* and is manifesting as excessive curiosity about the analyst? In such a case, the analysis runs the risk of turning into a constant verbal acting-out by the patient which needs to be interrupted either by confrontation or by refusing to respond to the patient's inquiries and maintaining silence (Maldonado, 2005).

The manner of handling striking absence of curiosity in the patient therefore varies greatly. Most practising analysts strike a balance between patience and intervening; the former is an attitudinal requisite for the analyst but can be actively exercised as specific intervention[24] and the latter can include gentle encouragement, asking questions (Boesky, 1989), or defence interpretation. Each instance has to be tackled in an individual manner guided by the analyst's empathy and the dominant idiom of the dyad.

Concluding remarks

I began my discourse by delineating the phenomenological characteristics of curiosity and by noting that it can involve many sensory modalities and serve multiple aims. I posited five main aims of curiosity, namely (i) elemental, (ii) exploratory, (iii) empathic, (iv) existential, and (v) enactive. Following this, I traced the origins of curiosity to hard-wired and evolutionary necessities as well as to the formative influences of early object relations. I then outlined the psychopathological derailments and defilements of curiosity, both of quantitative and qualitative varieties. The former include (i) excessive, (ii) deficient, and (iii) uneven curiosity and the latter included (i) anachronistic, (ii) instinctualized, and (iii) false curiosity. Moving on to the clinical realm, I highlighted the role of curiosity in the analytic process and dealt with the patient's curiosity, analyst's curiosity, and co-constructed curiosities of the dyad.

A few matters, however, remain unaddressed. One of these pertains to gender. The question whether men are more curious than women or vice versa has not be satisfactorily answered, to the best of my knowledge. Child development observation provides contradictory answers. The fact that female toddlers possess a "lesser degree of motor-mindedness" (Mahler et al., 1975, p. 214) and do not venture as far from their mothers as do male toddlers would have us believe that they lack exploratory curiosity. Cultural valorization of boys' adventuresomeness, horseplay, and even counterphobic forays into the external world might also support this idea. However, the interiority of female genital sensations as well as the early 'necessity' to imagine organs that are not visible (e.g. the womb) might intensify curiosity in girls. Early psychoanalysts (Freud, 1925; Fenichel, 1945) held that the curiosity in girls and boys was qualitatively different. In the girl, peeping might form a substitute for sadistically castrating; often this tendency is displaced externally. "Curiosity in women sometimes is more or less openly aimed at witnessing catastrophes, accidents, war scenes, operations, hospital scenes, and the like; such curiosity represents active sadistic castration tendencies reduced from action to observation" (Fenichel, 1945, p. 348). In the boy, visual curiosity specifically is aimed at reassuring him against the dread of castration.[25] Perhaps, that's why men's curiosity is directed to any and all features of external reality but the female genital itself. In this context, a tongue-in-cheek observation by the Argentinian analyst, Ariel Arango (1989) is germane:

> As a matter of fact, if we conducted a random survey among men, asking them for an accurate description of the vulva – its shape, size, and color – we would have a puzzling result: they are not able to do so ... only then would they notice with surprise that they hardly look at it when making love. They hardly every stop to observe the details of the "secret entrance" even those who enjoy *lambendo lingua genitalia* (licking the genitals) would realize that they do not study it thoroughly. A man who has no difficulty in recalling the smallest feature of a drawing, or the slightest line of a statue, or the most delicate typographies of a book, will not be able, however, to describe the vulva accurately! It would be difficult to find a territory so ignored by men as the geography of the cunt.
>
> (p. 99, italics in the original)

Arango's (1989) 'random survey' leads us to the consideration of the impact of culture-at-large upon curiosity. Cultures where religion is a major organizing force tend to discourage questioning whereas cultures which have accorded science a greater hermeneutic premium tolerate inquisitiveness to a larger extent. Of course, such categorization is spurious since all cultures embody both religious and scientific proclivities; it is a matter of predominance and strict categorization. Modal child-rearing practices, too, impact upon the flowering or suppression of curiosity. Generally speaking, societies with punitive child-rearing, sexual segregation, exaltation of authority and tradition, and limited access to sources of fresh information tend to suppress curiosity whereas societies that reflect opposite values and opportunities support curiosity in their members. Preferred modes of pedagogy also play an important role.[26] Students, regardless of whether they are elementary school children or at a postgraduate level, are encouraged to question their teachers in some but not in other societies. The resulting ambiance, in turn, has powerful impact upon guilt-free exercise of inquisitiveness and curiosity. Finally, the rapidity with which a given society produces and adapts to new accoutrements of life (e.g. changing information technology, fresh electronic gadgets) or welcomes unfamiliar additions to its population (e.g. culturally diverse immigrants) can affect the necessity and rewards of sustained curiosity in its members. Stability and predictability of the environment, while soothing, can lull people into cognitive somnambulism.

This also applies to the microcosm of psychoanalytic culture. The discipline upholds curiosity as premium yet psychoanalysts, beginning from Freud, have often sought to suppress curiosity about themselves and about alternate perspectives on psychological matters (see Rudnytsky, 2011, in this regard). Even today, one encounters psychoanalysts who refuse to consider perspectives that are out of their orbit of comfort. Tenacious commitment to this or that theoretical model of technique can lead to diminished curiosity and impede collegial dialogue (Wolstein, 1977; Zusman et al., 2007; Poland, 2009; Stern, 2009). Take a look at the following anecdote:

- Some years ago, I presented an invited paper at a prestigious psychoanalytic institute in this country. In that paper, I proposed that while the origins of the death instinct concept in Freud's personal life (e.g. the death of his daughter, Sophie; his own struggle with cancer) are well known, the intellectual sources of this idea remain inoptimally explored. I then went to demonstrate how Freud's contact with the German physicist, Gustav Fechner (who coined the term 'constancy principle' and was an avowed Buddhist), French biographer of many Indian mystics, Romain Rolland (of 'oceanic feeling' fame), and the British scholar, Barbara Low (who coined the term, 'Nirvana principle' and was a well-known expert in Sanskrit), had influenced his thinking in this regard. Since all these individuals were deeply involved with India and were immersed in Hindu mysticism, it seemed reasonable to surmise that Freud's 'death instinct' concept had a fundamentally Eastern touch. During the brief break after my presentation, I overheard two senior analysts talking about my proposal. One said, "What do you think about this Hindu stuff and all?" The other responded: "Humbug!"

Leaving personal experiences aside, I do wonder about our profession's lack of curiosity about a whole range of clinically and academically important matters. The following questions especially come to mind.

- Why do African Americans, who constitute 13 per cent of the US population, amount to a mere 0.007 per cent of the membership of the American Psychoanalytic Association?
- Why does the IPA have only three 'regions' (Europe, North America, and South America) while all major Asian nations (e.g. China, India, Israel, Japan, South Korea, and Turkey) as well as Australia, have well-functioning psychoanalytic societies and institutes?
- What are the reasons behind our current enthusiasm for propagating psychoanalysis in China, while we show little interest in India, which is largely English-speaking and has had a functioning psychoanalytic society since 1921?
- Will the major psychoanalytic journals ever require that papers submitted for publication be 'vetted' through PEP Web so that a proper anchoring in the existing literature is assured?
- How do we really feel about the fact that the time a patient spends undergoing psychoanalysis has gone from 300 minutes per week (six sessions of fifty minutes each) to 180, or even 135, minutes per week (four or three sessions of forty-five minutes each)? Does this reflect a healthy loss of weight or an alarming step towards therapeutic marasmus?

Such ruminations pale, however, as we – all of us –come face to face with the ultimate curiosity of our existence. What is this life about? What will happen to us after death?[27] And, why should we die at all? After some eight or nine decades of grooming ourselves, striving hard to achieve this or that goal, and trying our best to be useful to this world, is death the final trophy we get? What logic is inherent in this? Like others of my age group, I wonder about such questions. And, more. Does dying mean that I will never get to see my children again? Never? How would my patients be affected? What will happen to my carefully collected artwork and rugs? What about all the books I have? Will I never drive a car again? Will I never spend any more time with my friends? Never visit India? No wine? No ice cream? Ever? Such dark musings mostly return empty-handed. At times, they yield some professional writing on the topic of death, such as my papers on childhood parental loss (Akhtar, 2001, 2011b), comparison of Freud's *Todesangst* and Ghalib's

Ishrat-e-Qatra (2010),[28] mortality (Akhtar, 2011c), graves (Akhtar, 2011d), bereavement (2017), and so on. At other times, they prompt late-night scribblings that crystalize into a poem or two, poems whose ironic surrealism seeks to defy the ultimate sadness of it all. And it is with one such poem that I end this meandering meditation on the topic of curiosity. The poem is titled *Questions* (Akhtar, 2014b, p. 63):

Does a parrot know that he is not a dove?
When would Walmart start selling love?
Where do all the highways actually end?
Why do mystics like a river's bend?

At what point does the coward finally turn bold?
What is sadder than a dog in a bitter household?
How many selves do I have, how many faces?
Why can't Mexico and Scotland change places?

Notes

1 The origin of sudden and unexpected appearance of solutions to quandaries one has been mulling over is traditionally traced to the problem-solving function of the system Ucs (Freud, 1915d; Kris, 1952; Rangell, 1969; Weiss and Sampson, 1986). Bion (1963), however, suggests that such thoughts 'pre-exist' and can only be found by emptying the mind and remaining receptive to their appearance.
2 Some psychoanalytic candidates falter because they fail to ask extremely basic questions at the outset of their training.
3 Literally translated, this couplet means: "where have all this greenery and all these flowers come from?/what actually is a cloud and, pray tell, what is air?"
4 Literally translated, this means: "What is sadder than a train stopped in the rain?"
5 Allen Wheelis (1915–2007) was an exception as a psychoanalyst in this regard. He continually sought to explicate such issues in his writings (Wheelis, 1966, 1973, 1975). Outside of organized psychoanalysis, Rollo May (1953, 1969), Victor Frankel (1959), and Irvin Yalom (1980) have been important contributors to the matters of existential curiosity.
6 Psychoanalysis has generally held that interest in animals, things, and nature at large constitutes a displacement from this or that curiosity about human bodies and human object relations (Freud, 1927b; Volkan, 1981; Winnicott, 1953). Only a few analysts (e.g. Searles, 1960; Denford, 1981; Bollas, 1992; Akhtar, 2003, 2005) have allowed the possibility of psychic relations with the inanimate world being independent and not always symbolic of human to human relatedness.
7 A team of researchers from the Max Planck Institute in Munich have discovered a 'curiosity gene' in the great tit songbird (2007). This gene, Drd4, is responsible for enhancing the brain's dopamine reception and birds showing a particular variation on this gene have a greater propensity to visit new areas and explore unfamiliar objects placed in their cages.
8 Anyone who has enjoyed the game of Trivial Pursuit will testify to this. And, of course, the love of trivia extends far beyond the confines of this particular board game. We psychoanalysts have our own private collections of such juicy tidbits of

gossip and history: 'In which year did Mrs Benvensite give the "original" couch as a gift to Freud?' 'Who said that Ferenczi can analyze a horse?' 'What are the names of Michael Balint's three wives?' 'Which President of the American Psychoanalytic Association declared the following: "I am an id-ego-superego-internal-external-psychoanalyst-psychosynthesist"?' And so on.

9 I have elsewhere (Akhtar, 1994, 1999a) elucidated the theoretical controversies that seem to have resulted from the eclipse of this important early concept of Freud.

10 Nunberg (1931) also spoke about the 'need for causality' and I included it among the six basic human needs in my paper on the distinction between needs and wishes (Akhtar, 1999a).

11 See the research output of Harvard's Project Zero program (2010) as well as the important explications of such pedagogy by Ritchhart and Perkins (2005, 2008) and Salmon (2010).

12 Children with intense preoccupation with primal scene can also show excessive, though displaced, curiosity. Their psychodynamics is, however, simpler. Ferenczi's (1909) description of the case of Little Chanticleer is an illustration par excellence of this.

13 Even though not particularly elegant or popular, 'incuriosity' is a recognized and proper English word (Mish, 1987, p. 590).

14 One must rule out organic causes (e.g. autistic-spectrum disorders) before considering the psychogenic etiologies proposed here.

15 In this context, see my case of an adult Indian woman who asked me what her genital was called in our shared mother-tongue (Akhtar, 2011e, pp. 228–229), and also, see my concept of 'unmentalized silence' (Akhtar, 2013a) of the mind.

16 Three years before the publication of Fenichel's (1945) encyclopaedic text, Mahler (1942) had described childhood 'pseudo-imbecility', which worked as "a means of restoring or maintaining a secret libidinous rapport with the family" (p. 4).

17 Anachronistic curiosity can manifest in a 'negative' form as well. Thus, a seventy-eight-year-old man showing no curiosity about his mortality (and its impact upon his family) is anachronistically 'incurious'.

18 Greenacre (1953) specifically noted that the "uncanny reaching out with the eyes" (p. 90) of children not sufficiently held and cuddled by their mother.

19 An outstanding depiction of the condensation of curiosity and sadomasochism is evident in Michael Powell's (1960) disturbingly-graphic movie, *Peeping Tom*.

20 In less pathological states too, curiosity can serve instinctual aims more than ego aims. Voracious reading, for instance, might be undertaken more for its 'filling' and narcissistic yield than for actual accretion of knowledge.

21 Writing from a relational perspective, Viola (1992) termed analytic curiosity as "an activating instrument" (p. 376). The fact is that analysts fear sexualizing their curiosity and therefore repeatedly add prefixes to it. We thus end up with phrases like 'legitimate curiosity' (Low, 1935), 'benevolent curiosity' (Jones, cited in Sharpe, 1930; Herold, 1942; Boesky, 1989), 'neutral curiosity' (Cecchin, 1987), and 'educated curiosity' (Nersessian and Silvan, 2007).

22 Devereux (1966) noted that inhibition of infantile auditory curiosity regarding the primal scene can result in compromised hearing in adult life as well as in habitual mumbling. Thus, one produces incomprehensible sounds that simultaneously blur obscene words and imitate ill-understood primal scene noises.

23 Upon checking with two analytic colleagues (Drs Jennifer Bonovitz of Philadelphia and Axel Hoffer of Boston), I found that both had seen one patient each who did not bring up the 9/11 disaster in their sessions on 9/12.

24 For the explication and clinical illustration of using patience as an active intervention, see Akhtar (2015a).

25 Such distinctions between male and female curiosity would now be regarded as representing the phallocentricism of early psychoanalysis. Contemporary analysts would most likely believe that girls' and women's curiosity might have more interior references (both corporeally and relationally speaking) and boys' and men's curiosity more externally oriented focus. It seems the jury is still out on this matter.

26 A sweet example of such informal 'pedagogy' comes from the way my grandmother told bedtime stories. She would regale us with statements such as, "Upon getting this news, the king first cried and then laughed". We children were expected to then ask, "Why did the king cry?" She would gladly answer. Then, we were expected to ask, "Why did the king laugh?" This would give her immense satisfaction as she provided the answer to our questions.

27 It turns out that death and curiosity have very close links. To be curious, sooner or later leads to encounter limits, including the limits of our lives. Curiosity thus reveals the open secret of our mortality. To not be curious on the other hand suffocates intellect and passion leading gradually to a psychic death of sorts (Goldberg, 2002b).

28 The German and Urdu expressions mean 'fear of death' and 'the ecstasy of the raindrop that has fallen on the river', respectively.

Part II

Restraining and relating

Chapter 3

Privacy

Fall of 1978. I am in the library of a prestigious North American psycho-analytic institute. Not to borrow a book or to skim through the pages of a journal. I am there to be assessed if I am suitable for psychoanalytic training. The room has a benevolently stern air to it. Bookshelves made of dark mahogany cling obediently to all its walls. They contain wisdom, promise to yield secrets of human emotional life to the devoted seeker. The long table in the centre of the room with twelve high-back leather chairs around it has witnessed psychoanalytic history. It is weighted with experience. I am sitting at one head-end of the table, my mouth dry, my heart beating fast. Leaving one or two chairs empty on both my right and left sides, seven training analysts sit, who are to simultaneously interview me in a strictly measured one hour time. They are all old white men in the vestimentary homogeneity that is the product of scepticism towards authentic strivings of any sort. They are seasoned analysts, some quite well known. There is no woman in the room there so that it is not possible to breathe one whiff of maternal tender-ness, real or imaginary as it might be. I feel very brown, very small, and very alone. The interview begins and its perfunctory nature is over with lightning speed. Then, as one bespectacled, bearded, and balding man in a grey flannel suit is asking me something about my childhood, another man interrupts him and says that he has made an observation about me over the last ten minutes or so and that he wants to check if I agree with him. This is a famous analyst, known for his sharp intuition, sudden bursts of deep interpretive comments, and a scathing sense of humour. He confronts me with something about my behaviour and, disregarding my intimidated and mumbling response, con-fronts me again with his point. I am devastated. The trauma of this particular moment remains with me for years afterwards. It appears again and again in my training analysis in a different institute,[1] a few hundred miles away. It turns out that what the 'astute' interviewer had pointed out was not wrong but that he pointed it out was. He addressed a part of myself that was not prepared to be brought into conversation.

In Freud's (1895a) terms, the inner storm caused by this interviewer's comment ruptured my 'protective shield'. In Kundera's (1991) terms, it transgressed "a certain border that must not be crossed" (p. 23). And, yes, there does exist an intrapsychic barrier that separates the public and the private while permitting us to live in both worlds, sometimes in an overlapping and intermingled manner and other times in categorically separate ways. This inner border between the public and private selves might be thick or thin, and might vary from individual to individual and culture to culture and era to era.[2] But it does exist and its safeguarding a private sphere of mental life is what forms the topic of my contribution here.

I will open my discourse with an attempt to define privacy and differentiate it from secrecy. Following this, I will elucidate the intricate linkages between form and origin in this realm, highlighting three different pathways to the inception and sustenance of a private mental life. I will then describe the psychopathology of privacy and discuss the role of privacy in the conduct of psychotherapy and psychoanalysis, making comments upon the patient's privacy, the analyst's privacy, and the mutual dialectics between them. I will conclude by summarizing the ideas presented in this chapter and by making some brief comments about the impact of gender and aging upon one's need for privacy.

A nosological conundrum

The dictionary definition of 'privacy' includes such phrases as "the quality or state of being apart from company or observation ... [and] ... freedom from unauthorized intrusion" (Mish, 1987, p. 927). At first glance, this seems perfectly serviceable. However, careful scrutiny leads to misgivings. There seems to be an over-emphasis here upon solitude which may or may not be a component of privacy; one can maintain privacy while mingling with people in a cocktail party, for instance. The dictionary also overlooks that the absence of 'unauthorized intrusion' might, at least in the case of children and adolescents, translate into neglect; being ignored and being private are certainly not akin. Surely, there has to be a better definition of privacy.

What is privacy?

Leaving lexicon behind, we encounter the widely influential explication of privacy by the pre-eminent legal scholar, Alan Westin (1967): "The claim of individuals, groups, or institutions to determine for themselves when, how, and to what extent information about them is to be communicated to others" (p. 47). Satisfaction with this definition also evaporates very soon. Two problems exist. One, according to this definition, the consent-less release of *any* information is an invasion of privacy; all information about a person or group could then be deemed private, overextending the concept of privacy to an absurd extreme. Two, the definition equates the individual's or group's control over information with privacy and thus leaves open the possibility that if an individual or a group is not permitted to exercise such control (e.g. via a prohibition to release their information), that too becomes an invasion of privacy. And if a person/group willingly reveals its deepest secrets, it is not losing privacy since it is exercising control over the flow of information.

What all this leads one to deduce is that a satisfactory definition of 'privacy' is hard to find. Psychoanalytic literature turns out to be of little help in this regard. There is no entry for the word 'privacy' in the indexes of the collected works of Freud, Abraham, Ferenczi, Fenichel, Klein, and Winnicott. The word appears just one time in the entire corpus of Freud's work (Guttman et al., 1980, p. 998) and even there without a working definition of it.[3] PEP Web, the electronic compendium of over a century's psychoanalytic writings, yields a total of eleven full-length papers with 'privacy' in their titles (Melzak, 1992; Meares, 1994; Weatherill, 1995; Reed, 1997; Alfonso, 2002; Covington, 2003; O'Neil, 2007; Novick and Novick, 2008; Cooper, 2008; Kantrowitz, 2009; Gabbard, 2015). While containing important ideas about privacy (to which I shall refer in pertinent parts of this chapter), none of these provide a coherent definition of what the word stands for.

Frustrated, one returns to 'non-analytic' literature and encounters three useful monographs. The first of these is by Wacks (2010), the second by Keizer (2012), and the third by Francis and Francis (2017). All three survey well-known legal and sociological tracts in this realm and cover roughly similar territory. However, independently, each monograph offers useful nuggets about the nature of privacy. Wacks (2010) recommends that one should settle for describing the characteristics of privacy and hope that such illumination of the periphery might shed light on the centre as well. In other words, by describing the components of privacy, we might stumble upon its essential nature. Wacks proposes that privacy consists of a triad of (i) *secrecy* (information that is tightly guarded), (ii) *anonymity* (attitude that wards off attention), and (iii) *solitude* (lifestyle that restricts access to the subject). While the three components seem to capture the essence of privacy, they are disparate and insufficiently weighted; a person might lead a hermit-like existence but pour out his innermost thoughts and feelings on an internet blog, for instance. Or, a person might be a social butterfly and the life of the party but carry on a totally hidden secret life. Wacks' triad is alluring but does not yield a solid definition of privacy.

Keizer (2012) takes up matter as diverse and wide-ranging as the birth of American privacy movement, the feminist critique of privacy, the cult of sanctimonious exposure, and technology and privacy. Of significance to our nosological concerns here, are the following statements by Keizer: (i) privacy "exists only by choice" (p. 14), (ii) many languages do not contain a word equivalent to the English 'privacy', (iii) protection of one's privacy can be a gesture of respect to others' sensibilities, and (iv) privacy is essentially grounded in a "creaturely resistance to being used against one's will" (p. 20). Keizer declares privacy to be a prerogative of the powerful, and secrecy to be a defense of the weak. He concludes his struggle to come up with a fool-proof definition of privacy by a statement of dignified resignation: "What preserves mystery might also be mysterious" (p. 22).

Francis and Francis (2017) start their discourse with the now well-established 'right to be let alone' (Warren and Brandeis, 1890) doctrine. Not surprisingly, they give pride of place to the protection of one's body against unwanted access and safeguarding of a location against uninvited entry. Such 'spatial privacy' might involve "a home, a bedroom, a workplace, a purse, a locked suitcase, or a car trunk" (p. 6). Intrusion into such private spaces might be physical or visual (e.g. by a Peeping Tom); technologically advanced eavesdropping devices raise increasingly complex challenges to 'spatial privacy'. Francis and Francis also note that privacy is often needed to protect people against discrimination. "The inability to control sensitive information such as medical conditions, sexual orientation or disability, may subject people to loss of insurance, employment, or housing" (2017, p. 20). Like Wacks (2010) and Keizer (2012), Francis and Francis distinguish privacy from secrecy. Unlike them, they link privacy with self-respect, dignity, and, to certain extent, with altruism. Keeping somethings to oneself precludes burdening others.

The insights in these monographs are important. Any attempt to define privacy can hardly overlook them.[4] My preference, however, is to focus upon the functions of privacy (especially as these pertain to an individual subject) and then, turning full-circle back, postulate that 'privacy' is that psychic structure which carries out these functions. I have the following four functions in mind:

- Privacy allows the separation of the exposed and covert sectors of personality.
- Privacy acts as a reservoir of thoughts, feelings, fantasies that one avoids revealing to others and actions that one is loath to undertake publicly. The latter include "minor physical self-involvements such as humming, whistling, belching, and flatulence" (Goffman, 1959, p. 128).
- Privacy regulates the choice of how, when, and to what extent one shares intimate thoughts and feelings with others. By sharing tightly held information with a spouse, individual privacy can morph into a couple's privacy.
- Privacy enhances "a certain inner reserve [thus] enabling the capacity to sublimate" (Weatherill, 1995, p. 151). It also allows for the ongoing "dialogue with one's own self" (Sandler and Sandler, 1998, p. 97) to get refuelling and affirmation, through the perception of cues, that one's self is one's familiar self.

Putting these functional dynamics together yields some useful hints about the nature of privacy: it is that psychic space that allows subjectivity to remain self-enclosed (or to be shared voluntarily with select others) so that thinking can become layered, self-reflection ongoing, and sublimation possible. While it makes sense to agree that privacy refers to the capacity to maintain certain information about oneself away from others' scrutiny, what renders some pieces of information 'private' remains unclear.

What makes some personal information private?

On the surface, it would seem that one's name, postal address, and profession would be less 'private' than, say, one's medical records or sexual preferences. In the same vein, one's fantasies might seem more 'private' than one's day-to-day actions. The following observation made by Freud (1908c) in connection with the link between children's play and creative writers' day-dreaming underscores the deeply private nature of one's fantasy life.

> People's phantasies are less easy to observe than the play of children. The child, it is true, plays by himself or forms a closed psychical system with other children for the purposes of a game; but even though he may not play his game in front of the grown-ups, he does not, on the other hand, conceal it from them. The adult, on the contrary, is ashamed of his phantasies and hides them from other people. He cherishes his phantasies as his most intimate possessions, and as a rule, he would rather confess his misdeed than tell anyone his phantasies.
>
> (p. 145)

However, such distinctions between what one readily exposes and what one guards as private are not invariably true. And, at this juncture, we return to the monograph by Wacks (2010) which 'proves' this assertion by evoking the following five variables.

- *Context*: what is deemed 'private' by an individual depends upon the context in which the concealment or disclosure of the information takes place. Take, for instance, one's home address. It appears the sort of data about oneself that does not appear 'private'. But what if one were a terrorist hunted by the FBI? Now where one resides suddenly becomes a very private matter. Take one's erotic fantasies involving a family member. These are generally kept tightly hidden but sooner or later become a topic of discussion in a psychotherapist's office. More examples can be given but the point, I think, has been made. What is and is not private is not a static entity. It changes with changing context.
- *Culture*: some cultures permit conversation about money but treat sex as taboo. Others are just the opposite. Self-praise is acceptable in some cultures but not in others. Cultures also vary in the degrees to which they uphold altruism, sacrifice, and reverence for elders. Such differences drive some aspects of mental content towards concealment and others towards public

expression. Thus what is considered 'private' in once culture (e.g. one's income) might not be regarded as such in another. Individuals who migrate from a considerably different cultural topography to another might thus reveal too much or too little about themselves and ask questions that others might find invasive and puncturing of their privacy (Akhtar, 1999b, 2011e).

- *Time*: curiously, time can play a role in according some personal information the status of privacy. For instance, the front page coverage of a government official's lurid affair, which certainly is as public as things can get, unearthed some twenty-five years later by a zealous journalist can seem an invasion of privacy to the protagonist. Public past can turn into private present. The converse can also happen. A wealthy man loves to talk about the days of his poverty and how he slept on pavements and had no money to buy food. What was a shameful secret from others then is now paraded out as a trophy of resilience. Private past has become public present.

- *Volition*: each person decides for himself what about his life is to remain private. Depending upon his culture and his characterological make-up, he also selects the people to whom he reveals this 'private' sector of his mind. As he exerts control over the flow of such traffic, he can 'declassify' information and no longer hold as 'private' something he has decided to make known to others. Thus what was one moment private, the next moment is not. Of course when such disclosure happens without his awareness and consent, then the shift from 'private' to 'public' is not only traumatic but retrospectively confers an even greater degree of privacy to the exposed material.

- *Implication*: this too is important. What is guarded strenuously and considered most private is what, if revealed, is expected to cause most damage. Conversely, what does not cause damage even in 'technically' intimate is generally not considered private information. Illustrations of the former might include both negative (e.g. plan to embezzle money from one's employer) and positive (e.g. secret crush on a teacher) types of information, the revelation of which would result in embarrassment, distress, and even punishment. Illustrations of the latter include intimate tidbits of quotidian vanity (e.g. which toothpaste one uses) and personal details of little significance to others (e.g. that one does not ever eat ice cream before 6 p.m.). Privacy involves matters of greater 'weight' and consequence.

The foregoing points establish the fact that it is not easy to define 'privacy' and 'private' mental content. As if this were not enough, we are also faced with the not-so-easy task of distinguishing 'privacy' from 'secrecy'.

How does privacy differ from secrecy?

As defined by *Webster's Dictionary*, secrecy represents "the habit or practice of keeping secrets ... [and] ... the condition of being hidden or concealed" (Mish, 1987, p. 1061). However, there is more to secrecy than this; it is often mobilized by shame and can also have sadistic and corrupt aims. Secrecy stops ego-growth by keeping a psychic sector frozen in time. It also exerts a deleterious impact upon interpersonal relationships by robbing them of fullness and honesty. Prominent among psychoanalytic authors who have written about secrets and secrecy are Gross (1951), Sulzberger (1953), Margolis (1966, 1974), Hoyt (1978), Jacobs (1980), Khan (1983a, 1983b), Kulish (2002), and Balsam (2015), though this list is by no means exhaustive.

Gross (1951) defined 'secret' as that which is known by one person and not by others around him. He noted that a 'secret' is invariably associated with powerful impulses to retain it as such and to reveal it as well. While anal phase derivatives are evident here, Gross emphasized that secret-keeping (and trying to pry open parental secrets) reaches its developmental zenith during the oedipal phase. Sulzberger (1953) underscored the phallic-exhibitionistic qualities of secret-keeping and observed that women are more likely to reveal others' secrets and men their own. Even more far-reaching papers on 'secrets' and 'secrecy' were written by Margolis (1966, 1974). Comprehensively reviewing the literature and encompassing the developmental (psychosexual and identity-related), literary, and technical realms, Margolis concluded that

> whatever is eventually rendered unconscious involves aspects of life that are first kept secret from parents or others and that therefore the formation of neurosis proceeds from conscious secret keeping by the child to keeping things secret from its own superego and ego.
>
> (p. 292)

Margolis pointed out that exactly the reverse occurs in psychoanalytic treatment. "The patient is encouraged to reveal all of his conscious secrets to the non-condemning analyst and, after he is able to do so, to no longer hide unconscious secrets from his own ego and superego" (p. 292).

Hoyt (1978) focused upon deliberate secret-keeping which can be accompanied by open declarations ('I have a secret and I will not tell it') or by complete silence about its existence. He noted that secrets serve many purposes on intrapsychic and interpersonal levels. Hoyt makes the important observation that a secret is inherently social and can be used for shutting people out as well as for drawing them closer. Jacobs (1980) added that existence of family secrets often necessitate overt or covert pacts between involved family members to preserve the secret. He also noted that the content of family secrets, regardless of their being based on facts or fantasies, can have a significant impact upon the child growing up in that family.

Khan (1983) put greater emphasis upon the *act* of keeping something secret and the *existence* of a secret than upon *what* it is that's being kept secret. He made the point that, at times, having a secret helps the child protect an emotionally significant part of himself from being impinged upon. This is necessary since the growing ego cannot tolerate such impingements. The secret also protects the caretakers from the affects and behaviours that would surface were a part of the self was not cloistered. Like the repressed material which Freud (1915c) said "exercises a continuous pressure in the direction of the conscious" (p. 151), the secret aspires to be known. And, when a secret is shared, secrecy is transformed into mutual privacy. I agree with Khan's formulations but question his neglect of the secret's content and the non-defensive, 'discharge' (e.g. sadomasochistic) functions of secret-keeping. A clandestine addiction to pornography, a tucked-away bank account, and a tightly guarded sexual affair, all might have ego-protective functions and serve as defences against expected attacks from external (interpersonal) or internal (superego) agencies but one can hardly overlook the narcissistic and sadistic aims of such sequestering of one's psychosocial existence. Keeping an eye on both the 'defensive' and 'discharge' functions, I think, is important in the course of clinical work with patients who keep important secrets from their family and friends.

Kulish (2002) emphasized that secrets are integral features of female sexuality and Balsam (2015) extended this line of thinking by referring to "complex secrets of the body, sex, and gender" (p. 33). I will refer to these two authors' views in greater detail while discussing the links between gender, child development, and privacy. At this point, however, I wish to return to secrecy's relationship to privacy.

Putting all the findings in the literature cited above, it seems that differences between 'privacy' and 'secrecy' consist of the following: (i) privacy is consistent with mental health, secrecy may or may not be; (ii) privacy is ego-syntonic, secrecy only partly so; (iii) privacy is about form, secrecy about content; (iv) privacy is not emotionally charged, secrecy almost always is; (v) privacy facilitates reverie while secrecy is an "intrapsychic cul-de-sac" (Akhtar, 1985, p. 82) which mobilizes defensive processes; (vi) privacy adds to dignity[5] and secrecy diminishes it; and (vii) privacy is content with itself while secrecy has an ambivalent agenda: it wants to bury itself deeper and yet longs to come out and breathe fresh air of consensually shared knowledge. Even if this helps delineate the concept of privacy, it remains unclear whether privacy is a monolithic concept as far as its origins are concerned or are there different 'royal roads' to this sanctuary of the mind?

Origins of privacy

Considered one way, the three pathways to the creation of private mental space pertain to the realm of 'origins' or, to employ a medical term, etiology. Considered another way, they also refer to different forms of privacy since the extent to which the 'private' material accrued under these scenarios can be consciously experienced varies. Even their 'preferred' modes of expression might not be alike. Given this complexity, we are forced to talk of origin, form, and function in a blended way and not in neatly separated categories.

Inherent origins

Since the prefix 'inherent' denotes an attribute "involved in the constitution or intrinsic character of something" (Mish, 1987, p. 601), it might be worthwhile to ask whether the human need for privacy has an animal substrate to it; in other words, do animals demonstrate a need for privacy? And, the answer to this question is a resounding 'yes'. Studies of territoriality and social organization have clearly demonstrated that virtually all animals seek periods of aloneness or small group intimacy (Westin, 1967). Frans de Waal (2016) notes, for instance, that chimpanzees have sufficient control over their sexual impulses "either to refrain from them or to arrange privacy first" (p. 224). So do human beings. In this and many other ways, man's quest for privacy seems to be rooted in the evolutionary need for self-protection and self-replenishment.[6]

Within psychoanalysis, the notion of inherent privacy is implicit in the psychic space under 'primal repression' (Freud, 1895b). This represents the rudimentary affective and cognitive material accrued during the non-verbal period of infancy. In Frank's (1969) phraseology, this is "the un-rememberable and the unforgettable" (p. 48) substrate of the human psyche. The elements it contains cannot be verbally and sequentially recalled but only somatically re-lived or metaphorically expressed.

Winnicott's (1960a) concept of 'true self' which denotes the unthought psychosomatic continuity of existence and whose essence is "incommunicado" (Winnicott, 1963, p. 187) also exemplifies 'inherent privacy'. Winnicott assumed the existence of a core self from the very beginning of life which blooms if it is protected and not impinged upon. Indeed, he declared that "it seems necessary to allow for the concept of the isolation of this central self as a characteristic of health" (1960b, p. 46). Elaborating upon the isolated and deeply private aspect of the true self, Winnicott stated that he was "putting forward and stressing the importance of the permanent isolation of the individual and claiming that at the core of the individual there is no communication with the not-me world" (1963, p. 190).

Another illustration of 'inherent privacy' of the mind pertains to what Balint (1968) called 'the area of creation'. In this realm of psychic experience, there is no external or internal object present. "The subject is on his own and his main concern is to produce something out of himself; this something to be produced may be an object but not necessarily so" (p. 24). Besides artistic creativity, mathematics, and philosophy, this private sector of mind includes "understanding something or somebody, and last but not least, two highly important phenomena: the early phases of becoming – bodily or mentally – 'ill' and spontaneous recovery from that 'illness'" (p. 24). The subject, during these moments, is perhaps engaged with 'pre-objects' (dim fragments of non-self representations) that congeal into recognizable objects (including poems and paintings) only after much preconscious work. In Seamus Heaney's (1995) words, this is a move from "delight to wisdom" (p. 5).

Internalized origins

Freud's (1900) topographic theory laid down the groundwork for the conceptualization of psychic privacy. It differentiated mental contents that were readily accessible, perception-based, and logically oriented from mental contents that were deeply buried, wish-based, and operated according to the illogical primary process. Moreover, there existed censorship barriers between the systems Cs and Pcs as well as between systems Pcs and Ucs, with the latter barrier being less permeable. Freud (1915d) emphasized that the repressed did not constitute the entire content of the system Ucs; instinctual representations, 'primal phantasies' (Freud, 1915e), and material accrued due to primal repression (see above) also resided there. It is the repressed material, however, that forms the core of 'internalized privacy' since whatever wish, fantasy, thought, or impulse is repressed, it has met that fate due to a perceived sense of danger in its expression; this danger was originally perceived to be coming from the parents though it might later come from ego's own counter-cathectic interests and from the superego's autarchic dictates. Upon hearing the child say something and seeing the child do something, parents threaten him with withdrawal of love and even with physical punishment. Such admonitions were later internalized as ego interests and superego commands; they drove fresh activations of prohibited wishes into a state of repressed privacy.

Bick (1968) and Khan (1963, 1972) approached the childhood origins of privacy from a different perspective. Bick stated that during early infancy, parts of personality have no intrinsic binding force and must therefore be held together by the maternal holding function. "Later, identification with this function of the [maternal] object supersedes the unintegrated state and gives rise to the fantasy of internal and external spaces" (1968, p. 484).[7] Khan (1963) extended Freud's (1895a) concept of 'protective shield' or a threshold of stimulation by the *external* world to include the regulation of *internal* stimuli also. More importantly, he traced the origins of such stimulus barrier to early mother–infant interactions which regulate the extent of the child's stimulation from both within and outside, assuring that the child is neither over-stimulated nor under-stimulated. A safe, inner space was thus created. Khan (1972) also asserted that ample and satisfying experiences of "shared trust" (p. 294) in early childhood strengthen the child's sense of selfhood and permit the elaboration of psychic privacy.

These developmental observations are, of course, undergirded by the fact that being civilized condemns human beings to live in a divided state (Freud, 1930). The elemental and the instinctual is forced to hide behind the fig leaf of the socially acceptable. This large-scale development is replicated at a microscopic level during child-rearing. By direct or indirect affective or motor signals, parents convey to the child what thoughts and feelings can be publicly expressed and what must be kept private. The child is told to keep the 'private parts' of his anatomy covered and, with further growth, learns that parents guard certain aspects of their privacy too quite tightly. Still later, he learns that family matters of this or that sort are not to be told to others; they are to be kept within the family.

In contrast to such shared privacies or at least agreed-upon limits to openness within the family is the child's finding the private domain of his or her own mind. The first successful lie spoken by the child breaks the spell of parental omniscience. The child begins to feel that he has a mind of his own, the contents of which are not always known to his parents. Tausk (1933), who first made this observation, places such development in the period of toilet training, say, around two years of age. The child learns that he has a will, he can hold back, he can mislead the person doing the training, and that he can keep something to himself. Such anal transformation of inherent and early infantile privacy (Khan, 1963, 1972; Bick, 1968) into secrecy acquires further colouration from the oedipal phase developments where curiosities about sexual intercourse, pregnancy, and childbirth play an important role. Adolescence, with its prime agenda of identity consolidation and individuation (Erikson, 1950; Blos, 1967) further deploys privacy as a psychic retreat and a space for reverie essential for growth. When families avoid the tensions that inevitably result from the adolescent's need for privacy and when an evasive 'niceness' is employed to skirt difficult confrontations, there develops a failure to conceive an outer reality that is different from personal reality (Sullivan, 1956). The internal space for privacy suffers a collapse and the lack of "personal boundedness" (Meares, 1994, p. 98) can lead to omnipotence of thoughts.

Dealing more specifically with female development, Kulish (2002) noted the importance of secrets for girls and women. Here are some excerpts from her eloquent advocacy of this idea.

> The configuration and functions of the female body conveys powerful, secret-bearing meanings ... a woman's body contains sexual openings and unseen powers that lie within its cavities ... Women's sexual arousal can be kept hidden and secret within the body ... Little girls can masturbate secretly and indirectly, sometimes not registering the secret to themselves ... The hiddenness and secretness of their sexual feelings may give girls a sense of power in the ability to keep a secret and to choose to share it or not ... [During the oedipal phase] Because the mother is typically the major caregiver in most families and societies, sexually competitive feelings are perceived as a threat to continued safety and nurturing care. The girl feels, therefore, that she must hide her sexual feelings from her mother. Sexuality, which is seen as belonging to the mother, must be inhibited and driven underground.
>
> (pp. 155, 158)

Balsam (2015) acknowledged "the importance of the mother in the girl's development and the implicit oedipal challenge that entails" (p. 55). However, she challenged the received theory that when it comes to knowledge of body and sexuality, boys/men are clear-minded and girls/women are confused. She emphasized that

> the "secrets" nowadays – which we all know but which *still* can be hard to acknowledge in a sustained way – are that each sexed body, formed as male or female in the womb, is lived out as equal over its years, when weighed in balance with its own characteristic pains and characteristic pleasures. I believe that we must resist the developmentally regressive temptation to keep *comparing* males and females, if we want to build a neutral developmental theory.
>
> (pp. 41–42, italics in the original)

This does not rule out the external, sociocultural variables that are at work here. Kulish (2002) reminds us:

> that in a very real sense, it has been necessary throughout the ages and across cultures for women to keep their sexual urges secret. When a woman is seen as the property of father and husband, whose honor depends on her chastity, it was, and still is, too often a matter of life and death for her that her sexuality be bound, veiled, hidden … In this sense, I will admit that women's pleasure in secrecy may be making a virtue out of a necessity.
>
> (pp. 155–156)

And, here the difference between 'introjection' (Ferenczi, 1909), i.e. willingly bringing the whole or part of an object inside oneself, and 'interjection' (Bollas, 1999), i.e. the forcible and traumatizing insertion of unacceptable external realities into someone's self, becomes paramount. Internalized origins have given way to imposed origins of privacy.

Imposed origins

In contrast to the 'inherent' and internalized origins of privacy are those sources which, by external force, drive mental contents into hiding. Children and adolescents raised by tyrannical and torturing parents, women brutally beaten by hateful men, spouses gas-lighted by paranoid partners, and ethnic groups terrorized by totalitarian dictators are all subject to such 'imposed privacy'. Melzak (1992), who has poignantly described the vicissitudes of privacy, secrecy, and survival under repressive regimes, states:

> The mistrust between people leads to the conscious keeping of secrets, the unconscious internalization of divisiveness and secrecy, and limitations

on the ability to assess reality. People may be organized and traumatized by overwhelming fear. People may pretend not to acknowledge the acts of repression they observe. They may also unconsciously fail to notice such manifestations.

(p. 215)

Underneath such ego surrender often lie fantasies of rebellion and revenge, and hopes for breaking the chains of their psychosocial imprisonment. In Fivush's (2010) terminology, these are instances not of 'being silent' but of 'being silenced'.

Less malignant versions of 'imposed privacy' are found in compliance with widely accepted societal taboos on topics of conversation. Variable from culture to culture, such restrictions result in pockets of unspoken and even unmentalized psychic material. Repudiated thoughts and feelings of this sort can range widely and involve matters as diverse as personal income, worries of children, political leanings, bowel habits, ownership of property, sexual life, and belief in life after death. The longing to express such thoughts and feelings might find a fortunate outlet if one migrates to a cultural terrain more accepting of such ideas, makes friends with someone with similar persuasion, or finds oneself a truly non-judgemental therapist. Otherwise, the taboo mental content is condemned to remain veiled and the distance between privacy and secrecy gets blurred.

Psychopathology

While hybrid and oscillating forms might exist, more often the two types of psychopathology of privacy are relatively rigid: too much privacy or too little privacy. Brief comments on these maladies follow.

Excessive privacy

Some individuals seem to need too much privacy. They lead a solitary existence, have few friends, despise 'small talk', do not intermingle with neighbours, and eschew interaction with peers at their workplace. While it is tempting and often not inaccurate to label them schizoid or paranoid, it is far better to attempt comprehending the forces behind such retreat.

A prominent dynamic in such people is their dread of loving. They have felt chronically deprived of affection during childhood and this has made them very hungry for love. This hunger stirs up a horrible fear that one's love has become so devouring and incorporative that it has become destructive (Fairbairn, 1940). Unlike depressives who fear destroying their love objects by hate, schizoids fear destroying their desired objects by love. The 'pre-history' of this loving–destroying link goes back to their childhood when their robust affectionate gestures were regarded by their parents as grievous assaults.

Retreat into indifference became the subsequent defence against the love which felt too dangerous to express.

A related dynamic is that the projection of one's suppressed love-hunger results in love objects beginning to take on cannibalistic qualities. Guntrip (1969) eloquently summed up the resulting turmoil.

> So the schizoid not only fears devouring and losing the love object, but also that the other person will devour him. Then he becomes claustrophobic, and expresses this in such familiar ways as feeling restricted, tied, imprisoned, trapped, smothered, and must break away to be free and recover and safeguard his independence; so, he retreats from object-relations. With people, he feels either bursting (if he is getting them into himself) or smothered (if he feels he is being absorbed and losing his personality in them).
>
> (p. 35)

Yet another mechanism causing retreat into privacy is narcissism. The narcissist's love objects are all within him, often in an idealized form (Kernberg, 1975). No wonder he confuses self-love with loving in general (Freud, 1914a). He evolves a pattern of intense idealization and coercive control of the other with no deepening of actual knowledge of that person over time (Akhtar, 2009a, pp. 99–111). Or, a periodically selfish 'affair' with the love object is carried on alongside a blithe indifference towards it in reality.

Clinical vignette: 7

> Sofia Anderson, a college professor married to a renowned poet, told me the following story. Once she had gone to visit her parents who lived a few hundred miles away from her marital home. A few days later, she took a flight back to her city, a flight that arrived quite late at night. She asked her husband to pick her up from the airport and he said that he would. However, when she landed, he was nowhere to be found. To her further dismay, he wouldn't even return her phone calls. Finally, she took a cab and went home. When she reached there, she found her husband sitting in the living room, absorbed in his thoughts. He would not even talk to her for another half hour or so. Sofia was truly distraught and also deeply puzzled since he would not offer any explanation for his not showing up at the airport and his near mutism at home. Finally, he broke his silence, appeared in their bedroom where she lay crying on the bed, and revealed that all this time, he was writing a poem about how much he loved her. He felt quite happy with himself and wanted her to hear him read the poem right then, assuming that this declaration of love was far superior than his coming to meet her at the airport.

This vignette clearly illustrates how private discourse with internal objects can replace relationships with actual objects. The former can be omnipotently manipulated while the latter require reciprocity. The former are parts of one's own psychic apparatus while the latter have an autonomous and separate existence. The former can be retained in a 'pure' and idealized form, while the latter, being human, are inherently less than perfect.

All three dynamic patterns (fear of loving, fear of being loved, and loving only internal objects) contribute to a defensive need for excessive privacy. Lack of 'basic trust' (Erikson, 1950) and sociopathic tendencies can further complicate the clinical picture, often resulting in formidable resistances to engagement with the analyst. The patient wants, needs, and clings to privacy/ secrecy while the analyst encourages openness and self-revelation.

Deficient privacy

An opposite condition is seen in individuals who seem utterly unable to keep things confidential. In contrast to tight-lipped secret-keepers, such persons blurt everything out. Upon being asked a formal, 'How are you?', they begin to rattle off all their problems of the day. They cannot keep confidences and are relentlessly inclined to gossip. Ferenczi (1915) long ago noted that many patients talk a lot but say nothing of value and Fenichel (1945) observed that "compulsive loquacity originates in a need to gain the approval of other persons for something inwardly felt as prohibited" (p. 166).

At times, such "counter-secrecy" (Hoyt, 1980, p. 407) is intended to aggressively shock others, test sympathy, or avoid a serious discussion of private matters by 'getting them over with' with a quick admission. On the other hand, undue transparency about oneself might relate to a profound lack of entitlement that extends to one's mental contents. It is as if one was not permitted the ownership of one's thoughts and emotions (for a parallel failure of ownership of one's body, see Laufer, 1968). Clearly, issues of separateness are involved here; by not keeping anything to oneself, one achieves (or, at least, strives to achieve) a seamless merger with (m)other(s). Yet another way of looking at this malady is to regard it as internalization of a leaky 'container' (Bion, 1962). Perhaps, boundaries between individuals, especially between the mother and the child, were blurred in these families. Inability to retain any modicum of privacy – at times rationalized as candour – is a repetition of such adhesiveness. Remaining quiet and keeping one's thoughts private becomes tantamount to separation at a deep psychosomatic level and stirs up annihilation anxieties.

Diagnostically, many such individuals have a hypomanic character. They desperately avoid solitude and do not wish to encounter their inner selves. Deutsch (1933), who wrote the first psychoanalytic paper on chronic hypomania, stated that despite excessive socialization, such individuals remain empty and devoid of substance.

If we look more closely, we note the hollowness of their success in comparison with the energy expended, how the love relationships lack warmth, in spite of their apparent passion, how sterile the performance is in spite of continuous productivity. This results from the monopolization of psychic energy in service of the goal we have described: the silencing of the narcissistic wound, of aggression, and of guilt reactions.

(p. 215)

This is a 'defence' hypothesis of characterological hypomania; deficient privacy is viewed here as a shield against early loss that gave rise to rage and guilt. This perspective stands in contrast with the hypothesis offered above which deploys a 'defect' model: the lack of capacity to maintain privacy is based either upon the identification with an excessively porous mother or upon a fundamental lack of entitlement which renders keeping mental contents to oneself difficult.

Just as excessive privacy results from many sources (e.g. mistrust, fear of love, narcissism), deficient privacy can arise from many sources (e.g. defence against guilt, counterphobia, merger hunger). And both conditions can reveal themselves to be based upon etiologies that are hybrids of defects and defences. Keeping this in mind is of paramount importance in clinical work with patients whose conflicts revolve around issues of privacy.

Technical implications

Throughout the course of psychoanalytic treatment, attention to privacy is needed. This mostly involves the concern for protecting the patient's privacy but the analyst's privacy also needs to be safeguarded. The following six measures aim to achieve this:[8] (i) establishing a privacy-assuring therapeutic frame; (ii) protecting the patient's privacy when clinical information needs to be shared with others; (iii) preserving the patient's privacy in extra-analytic contacts; (iv) respecting the patient's need for privacy during the analysis sessions themselves; (v) safeguarding the patient's privacy in case of the analyst's falling sick, retiring, or dying, and (vi) managing to sustain a modicum of privacy for the analyst, both during and outside of clinical hours. Brief comments on each now follow.

Establishing a privacy-assuring therapeutic frame

Privacy is integral to the psychoanalytic setting in both its external (Carpelan, 1981; Akhtar, 2009a) and internal (Parsons, 2007) representations. Clinical work is done in an enclosed space, with doors closed and little intrusion from the outside world. However, such space need not be sterile. It must embody a certain pleasant ordinariness, a point well-captured by Winnicott (1954) in the following passage:

This work was to be done in a room, not a passage, a room that was quiet and not liable to sudden unpredictable sounds. Yet not dead quiet and not free from ordinary house noises. This room would be lit properly, not by a light staring in the face and not by a variable light. The room would certainly not be dark and it would be comfortably warm ... and probably a rug and some water would be available.

(p. 285)

Winnicott's description contains a home-like soothing stability. And, most likely, it pertains to an office at the home of an analyst. Elsewhere (Akhtar, 2009a) I have discussed in detail the differential impact of the analyst's office being located at home or in a professional building upon the patient's and the analyst's psychology. Here I will suffice to say that the home office creates a risk to analyst's anonymity by increasing the chances that the patient might encounter the analyst's relatives, draw conclusions about the analyst's financial status, and learn about the analyst's talent (or lack thereof) for the maintenance of the exterior of the house (e.g. driveway, garden). All this will of course be 'translated' backwards into the patient's private idiom and transference-based inferences. The point to consider is the analyst's privacy is at greater risk and "the analyst needs to have clearer internal boundaries since external boundaries are permeable in such a situation" (p. 115). A counterpoint that needs to be taken into account is that generally speaking, a home office provides the patient somewhat greater privacy than an office in a professional building with increased people traffic and thus more chances of him or her being seen by acquaintances and friends.

Such 'external' concerns for assuring privacy, however, must not make us overlook that the therapeutic frame on an 'internal' basis also ought to assure privacy and confidentiality. Verbal assurances are hardly the panacea here. It is the attitude of the analyst that counts.

Clinical vignette: 8

Michelle Park, a twenty-four-year-old graduate student, sought a consultation with me for panic attacks and increasing social phobia. She arrived in time for her appointment and the initial assessment proceeded smoothly. However, as we were about ten to fifteen minutes into the session, she abruptly stopped, looked at me, and said, "I am pretty sure that you know my father but just want to confirm. Do you?" This had not occurred to me as I set up the time to meet with her and even as I welcomed her into my office. But now that she asked, and looking at her face, I could see the resemblance with a physician I knew. He was on the staff of the medical school with which I am affiliated; he was not in psychiatry and my contact with him was restricted to an occasional, formal greeting in the school's corridors. Going over all this in my mind, I responded to Michelle's inquiry by saying: "Yes, in fact I do. I had not thought of it when we talked on the phone but now upon seeing you and especially upon your asking, I realize whose daughter you are. So yes, I do know him but from a distance only. We are not friends or anything like that. But I think a bigger question than whether I know him or not is whether despite knowing him, can I listen to you peacefully *and* also maintain whatever little contact I have with him without any alteration." She nodded in agreement. I continued, "Now, I know that you might need a reassurance to that effect but I doubt that words are the right vehicles to convey that I will protect your privacy. Only time and actions can prove that for you. So, if you are comfortable, we can proceed further with our conversation. What do you say?" Michelle seemed quite relieved by my response and the interview soon continued along the lines that were already beginning to unfold. Soon, the fact that she had sought me out knowing that I might be acquainted with her father itself became a topic for investigation.

Such moment-to-moment stability of the analytic position in the face of temptations to act out this or that scenario (e.g. in the above-mentioned case, becoming a quickly reassuring parent) is what transmits the confidentiality and respect for privacy in the clinical ambience to the patient. The analyst's 'holding' and 'containing' functions facilitate the patient's ego-relaxation and emergence of deeper intrapsychic material. Sitting behind the couch, maintaining 'abstinence' (Freud, 1915a), and remaining un-hurried permits the analyst to have the private space necessary for reverie, conjecture, and formulation of interventions.

Protecting the patient's privacy while sharing information with others

While confidentiality of the patient's communications is an essential condition for psychoanalytic treatment, situations do arise where the analyst needs to consult a colleague. Common examples of such situations include (i) when the clinical process becomes continuously confusing or seriously disturbing to either the psychoanalyst or the patient, or both; (ii) when there is a grave threat of physical harm to the patient or the analyst or a minor who is dependent upon the patient (see Hoffer, 2015, in this context); (iii) when the analyst recognizes a powerful countertransference pull to commit a boundary violation; (iv) when the analyst makes or is considering making an intervention that seems highly unusual (Akhtar, 2011f); (v) when the analyst is diagnosed with a terminal illness or decides to retire or relocate to a distant city; and (vi) when a patient is threatening to bring a lawsuit against the analyst. To be sure, more illustrations can be given but the point, I think, is made. The analyst needs peer consultation from time to time. Protection of a patient's confidentiality does not entirely preclude this need. However, certain guidelines must be followed. APsA's code of professional ethics is a good source to consult here. It states:

> A psychoanalyst must take all measures necessary to not reveal present or former patient confidences without permission, nor discuss the particularities observed or inferred about patients outside consultative, educational or scientific contexts. If a psychoanalyst uses case material in exchanges with colleagues for consultative, educational or scientific purposes, the identity of the patient must be sufficiently disguised to prevent identification of the individual, or the patient's authorization must be obtained after frank discussion of the purpose(s) of the presentation, other options, the probably risks and benefits to the patient, and the patient's right to refuse or withdraw consent.

Such restrictions have to be reconciled with the need of written case reports for the advancement of clinical education. The implicit tension between 'privacy-protection' and 'need for reporting' has served as the impetus for considerable literature over the past three decades (e.g. Klumpner and Frank, 1991; Renik, 1994; Tuckett, 2000; Gabbard and Williams, 2001; Alfonso, 2002; O'Neil, 2007; Kantrowitz, 2009). This wide-ranging corpus can hardly be summarized here though it must be registered that Gabbard and Williams (2001), in their capacity, at that time, of co-editors of the *International Journal of Psychoanalysis*, provided succinct guidelines and options for psychoanalysts seeking to achieve a balance between protecting their patient's privacy and keeping their published reports honest and useful.

> Authors may choose to disguise superficial details of the patient's external life so that the patient is essentially unrecognisable to a reader. Some analysts may ask for written consent from the patient in addition to disguise. If one is writing about a clinical syndrome involving a group of patients, it may be possible to use case material that is a composite of several patients. When an analyst wishes to make a point about psychoanalytic process, theory or technique, the "process approach" may be useful, in which dialogue between analyst and patient is presented in play script fashion without biographical features of the patient. Finally, some analysts have conveyed clinical experience through a colleague as author, who often may be a consultant or supervisor for the case described, thus masking both the identity of the analyst and that of the patient. One variation of this last strategy is to publish clinical material from an ongoing study group composed of several colleagues, where specific authorship is unclear.
>
> (p. 1067)

Which of these five methods the analyst chooses as he undertakes writing a case report should be based upon specific clinical considerations; it would therefore vary from case to case[9] and would benefit from consultation with a colleague.

Preserving the patient's privacy during extra-analytic encounters

The analyst is responsible for protecting the patient's privacy if an accidental encounter between them occurs outside of clinical hours. For instance, if he becomes aware that his patient is going to be present at a small intimate gathering to which he too is invited, he should decline to be there (Glover, 1955). And, if the analyst enters a restaurant and sees his patient seated there with family members or friends, it is best for him to acknowledge the patient with a minimal gesture, if at all. To visibly smile at the patient or wave or nod can appear well-mannered but carries the risk of those sitting around the patient becoming curious about who the person gesturing at the patient is and force the patient either to lie or to reveal that he is seeing an analyst; an inadvertent breach of patient's confidentiality might thus ensue. Needless to add that all reactions of the patient to an accidental extra-analytic encounter should later be explored in an analytic manner (Tarnower, 1966; Strean, 1981).

The situation is different if the patient is alone when the analyst runs into him. Thoma and Kachele (1994) emphasize that under such circumstances, the analyst should maintain an attitude of informed naturalness and might even enter into a bit of small talk. They wryly comment that "it would be inappropriate for the patient to let himself freely associate in public, and the analyst would behave conspicuously if he refused to talk about the weather or vacation plans and instead remain silent or interpreted the conversation" (p. 298). Acting naturally protects the patient from the potentially traumatizing effects of a stereotypically silent analytic attitude. The special importance of such matters to training analyses is self-evident. According to Thoma and Kachele:

> it is essential that in their training, candidates develop an uncomplicated relationship to the various roles they will play in and outside their professional lives. The degree of natural behaviour by their analysts that candidates experience both in and outside psychoanalysis is an instructive measure for such tolerance towards the diversity of roles.
>
> (p. 299)

While respecting the patient's privacy and avoiding deliberate self-exposure, the analyst must be vigilant towards the transferential fantasies aroused by extra-analytic encounters and be prepared to handle them in the customary analytic fashion. He must also keep the possibility open that the patient's witnessing his "fallibility and humanity" (Zuckerman and Horlick, 2006, p. 351) can exert a growth-promoting influence upon his patient.

Respecting the patient's need for privacy during sessions

On the one hand, the analytic patient is expected to abide by the 'fundamental rule' (Freud, 1900) and renounce conscious censorship and verbalize all that enters his mind. On the other hand, the appreciation of the place of solitude and privacy in mental life (Winnicott, 1958; Khan, 1983) allows the patient to take his time and use his discretion in revealing his thoughts, feelings, and fantasies. Since the former pole of this 'free association–respect for privacy' spectrum is better known, I will focus upon the latter pole. In this context, it is to be noted that Ogden (1996) has gone to the extreme of telling a patient, at the onset of analysis, that each of the two participants needs to maintain a place for their privacy. Cooper (2008) astutely unmasks the risks inherent in such a directive.

> I have concerns that telling a patient that "we must both have a place for privacy" may run the risk of unnecessarily conveying something about my own wishes for distance or of emphasizing my attunement to the patient's need for distance. In my experience, patients are quite adept at maintaining privacy and editing their thoughts, despite my invitations to tell one what is one their mind. Moreover, I am concerned that I might be construed as issuing a kind of non-impingement promise – that is, that I am saying that I will try not to invade the patient's privacy. While I think that respect for the patient's privacy is paramount to analytic work and even a precondition for analytic exploration, I can not *promise* not to impinge on or invade the patient's privacy.
>
> (p. 1049, italics added)

Cooper's stance is congenial to my own way of thinking. I believe that concern for the patient's need for privacy *during* the session is better conveyed by the analyst's respectful attitude than by verbal assurances. This is most evident in handling certain kinds of patient's silences. Long before the *au courant* relational analysts, Loewenstein (1961) and Arlow (1961) in the United States, and Khan (1983c) in England, noted that silence is, at times, a necessary mode of relating during the clinical hour and such silences must not be punctured by interpretations. During these moments, the patient is expressing the need to be alone, contemplate, establish control over his feelings, and/or re-generate inner resources before proceeding further. In other words, the patient is asking for privacy and the analyst must respect that desire. I have discussed divergent ways of handling such silences elsewhere (Akhtar, 2013a, pp. 25–56) and now want to consider another expression of the patient's need for privacy.

Clinical vignette: 9

Matt Smolen was in his mid-forties when he sought psychotherapeutic help. His 'problem' centered upon the chronic and intense anger he felt towards his father. It consumed him, leaving little mental space for relaxation except via drinking wine – excessively and each night. He had a loving wife and this did bring him a modicum of peace but his inner life remained turbulent.

Born with a visible congenital deformity, Matt felt like an object of contempt and ridicule by his father. This abuse, unstopped by his weak and submissive mother, continued throughout his childhood. Matt became reclusive and kept his mental life and, later, his social activities secret from his parents. Matt hated them and also hated his five-year younger sister, Ann, who was their father's darling.

During a session early on in his work with me (face-to-face, twice weekly), Matt said that he wanted to tell me two things but was finding it hard since he was very ashamed of them. I remained quiet and waited. Then Matt asked me if he could turn his chair away a bit so that he wouldn't be facing me while he revealed those things. I told him it was fine with me if that would help him talk. He turned his chair to face away from me, remained quiet for a while, and then revealed that as an eleven-to-twelve-year-old, he would frequently touch his sister's genitals as she slept at night. He paused and added that the 'second thing' was harder to tell and he needed to postpone its disclosure to the next session. I accepted that 'request', letting him keep the 'second thing' to himself for the time being. Matt shifted his chair back to its usual position. Feeling 'un-shamed' by me, he relaxed. We talked about his touching his sister's genitals, the shame around it, and what might have motivated him to do so in the first place.

In the next session, Matt again expressed the desire to face away from me and upon my silent agreement, did so. With great difficulty, he told me that for a long time, he had been picking his nose and eating his snot. Both of us were quiet for a while. Then, I said that while I cannot be sure but I had a feeling that those two secrets had something to do with each other. Matt turned around and the session went on in a halting but mostly customary way for us.

There is a lot that can be unpacked here. However, the point I wish to emphasize is that my letting him have some 'spatial privacy' (Francis and Francis, 2017) by shifting his chair to face away from me *and* my going along with his need to tell one secret at a time and thus respecting his 'decisional privacy' (Wacks, 2010) were the measures that strengthened the therapeutic alliance between us and led to the deepening of our work.

Keeping one's 'analytic greed' (Akhtar, 2017) firmly in check is the key here. Interpretive over-enthusiasm must not be permitted to crudely knock on the doors of the patient's privacy.

Safeguarding the patient's privacy if the analyst falls sick, retires, or dies

An infrequently discussed aspect of protecting the patient's confidentiality (hence privacy) pertains to the analyst's retirement or sudden inability to practice due to severe illness or death. The first of these situations might require referral to a colleague. This, in turn, necessitates obtaining the patient's consent as well as a balanced, matter-of-fact discussion of how much and what kind of information the analyst intends to impart to the colleague to whom he is referring the patient. No more and no less than what is mutually agreed upon in such an exchange ought to be revealed. The second and third of the situations mentioned above (namely, severe illness and death) might shift the traffic in the opposite direction. A professional colleague of the analyst might have to contact the patient and inform him of the analyst's inability to continue working or of his or her death.

O'Neil (2007), in a singularly important research study of analytic confidentiality and privacy, comments upon this matter. She notes that:

> Only 15% of respondents were aware of guidelines for handling confidential material when closing a practice. The "professional will" model suggested by APsA is not widely used. Neither the British nor the Canadian societies have such forms. The BPaS, however, requires that all analysts provide the office with the name of a colleague or a list of their patients: upon the analyst's incapacity or death, that colleague or a member of the Society takes the responsibility of closing the analyst's practice. The procedure is now mandatory for the right to practice analysis as a BPaS member.
>
> (p. 697)

Often the antecedents of such instances are the analyst's aging and slowly increasing infirmity. The dangerous consequences of denial of this issue, either by the patient or by the analyst, have to be squarely faced. Frank and factual discussions about reality aspects are necessary. These could involve compromises of analyst's privacy and the risk of over-stimulating or under-informing the patient. Ethical dilemmas posed by these situations must not be handled only according to the rules and regulations of a given analytic society. Matters of transference and countertransference must also be considered. Consultation with a colleague or, at times, more than one colleague, provided they are able to bear and state the truth, is often quite helpful.[10]

Managing to sustain and utilize analyst's privacy

The 'blank screen' model of the analyst's participation in clinical work has now been cast aside and it is agreed upon that the analyst's character, subjectivity, and even countertransference experience (e.g. Racker, 1968; Searles, 1979; Hoffman, 1983; Renik, 1995) are inevitable components of the clinical process. At the same time, a certain asymmetry has to be maintained in order to preserve boundaries, let transferences flourish, and achieve an ego stance from which to make interpretations. For this asymmetry to be achieved, the analyst must retain relative anonymity and refrain from undue self-revelations. Any belief in the total opacity of the analyst is naive since patients draw all sorts of conclusions from our names, our skin colour, our office locations, our academic degrees, our office décor, and, nowadays, from internet sites, like Google, etc.; this can become a bit of a problem for analysts who are well-known. Nonetheless, the protection of the analyst's privacy is vital to the analytic process in many ways.

In responding to the patient's questions about his personal life, the analyst has to make a choice between (i) answering minor, reality-based conversation-facilitating questions right away (Greenson, 1967); (ii) viewing the patient's question as an answer to a deeper question that has arisen in his mind and therefore bringing the patient's attention to *that* question (Schlesinger, 2003); (iii) answering the question when a thorough exploration does not reveal the potential of any further difficulty; and (iv) at times, telling the patient who is insistent upon knowing the factual answer that it is inadvisable for the analyst to do so for this or that reason. The following bullet points illustrate these four responses.

- Patient (in the middle of a lively, smoothly progressing talk): "You know Jack Nicholson, right?" Analyst: "Yes, the movie star", and the conversation proceeds.
- Patient: "Do you have a daughter?" Analyst: "Something you are thinking or feeling or noticing has given rise to that question, it seems to me. Can we be curious about what *that* something might be?"
- Patient: "Where are you going for these two weeks?" The analyst might choose to answer it factually after some exploration and in the case of ego-fragile patients who cannot maintain psychic connection with such information, the analyst might answer it immediately.
- Patient: "Were you sexually abused as a child?" Once again, the analyst might explore the reasons behind the patient's curiosity but if the patient is absolutely insistent, the analyst might have to declare that he would not answer this question because any factually answer, positive or negative, could have a deleterious effect upon the gradient and direction of care between them. It risks the patient becoming the therapist.

But questions from the patient are not the only arena where the therapeutic importance of the analyst's privacy is tested. Writing about countertransference and sharing one's clinical experiences with supervisors and peers are other arenas where "exposure of personal limitations and conflicts means a sacrifice of privacy" (Kantrowitz, 2009, p. 795) on the analyst's part. However, the advantages of seeking consultation, preferably on an ongoing basis, outweighs the shame and anxiety over letting go of a tight grip on one's privacy.

> One solution is an ongoing, mutual sharing with a trusted colleague; this both eases the tension that develops internally in clinical work and keeps one aware of blind spots. With a compatible partner, our openness to, and our revelation of, deeper levels of ourselves increase. As in analysis itself, the listener's perspective on the presenting analyst's characterological tendencies, conflicts, and blind spots can help the other recognize and work through how they influence the treatment. Communicating details of analytic process increases both insight and the capacity to contain intense affect.
>
> (p. 800)

Finally, there is the privacy afforded by the analyst's sitting behind the couch and by his commitment to an un-hurried stance. This facilitates thinking, provides a space for reverie, lets the analyst sort out his emotional responses, allows the analyst 'working ego' to consult his 'working self' (Bolognini, 2008),[11] and permits time to put together the initially disconnected mnemic and perceptual stirrings within the analyst's mind to form a composite understanding of the clinical moment.

Concluding remarks

In this chapter, I have attempted to deconstruct the concept of privacy. Pooling together the scattered observations in psychoanalytic, philosophical, clinical, and literary traditions, I have portrayed as the mental space that keeps intimate thought and emotions apart from public aspects of the self. It permits reverie, facilitates elaboration of fantasy, and enhances contact with the deepest layers of oneself and others. I have also outlined the distinction between privacy and secrecy. Following this, I have delineated the inherent, internalized, and imposed origins of privacy and demonstrated that complex biopsychosocial variables help create and sustain private mentation. I have also discussed some psychopathological syndromes in this realm and highlighted the role of privacy (both the patient's and the analyst's) in the course of intensive psychotherapy and psychoanalysis.

Before concluding, however, I wish to make brief comments upon an area that has remained unaddressed so far. This pertains to how the psychic significance of privacy varies with age. Generally speaking, the privacy literature focuses upon the mid-part of the human life span. And, perhaps, this is rightly so. Infants and little children have no sense of privacy and the elderly might have less need of it. The former phenomenon has been addressed by child development theorists (see above). The latter has received little attention. Psychoanalytic literature on aging is sparse and the few references it contains to the intensification of merger-longings (Cath, 1989) and the emergence of a second symbiotic phase (Maddow, 1997) during old age do not specifically mention a diminution in the need for privacy. However, reading between the lines, something like this can indeed be discerned. Cath notes that "life-long repressed yearnings for an ideal father's or mother's love become intensified" (p. 101) during old age and Maddow sees the elderly "traversing in reverse the infant's growing independence as it moves forward from symbiosis" (p. 164). Both imply a weakening of self–object boundaries and thus reduced privacy. Powerful desires for merger are also mobilized by the anxiety about the approaching final and complete separation from this world. The time for secret-keeping is other. Further motivation for diminution of privacy is provided by the guilty need for confessing one's 'crimes'. Desperate holding on to life by loudly recounting one's most alive moments and clutching to whatever connections can be found can also break the boundary between one's public and private selves. Keizer (2012) describes such terminal erosion of privacy in the following tongue-in-cheek passage:

> With the increasing loneliness of aging and sole survivorship, coupled with my generation's emphasis on "relating", I anticipate a level of intrusiveness and self-exposure that my octogenarian parents would find obscene. I am occasionally tainted by a vision of waiting for my medicine in a nursing home as some fellow inmate shanghais the nurse on duty to hear about his dreams, his lovers, his concerts (the ones he remembers), his experiments in spirituality, and the zodiac signs of all nineteen of his grandchildren – or of trying to navigate my walker down the hall toward a quickly cooling bowl of soup only to be waylaid every ten feet and told I look like I could "use a hug". Physician-assisted suicide may not be a legal option even then, and with global warming well under way, my chances of being adopted by an Arctic Circle tribe and set adrift on an ice floe are depressingly slight.
>
> (pp. 11–12).

And, this brings me to the end of my discourse. I do so with the evocative and provocative quip by the celebrated novelist, Gabriel Garcia Marquez, who declared that "each individual lives three lives: public, private, and secret" (cited in Martin, 2008, p. 69). I find this assertion congenial to my way of thinking. It does provide a coherent answer to the mysteries of our existence. At the same time, it raises further questions: How are the public, private, and secret lives related to each other? When is such separation adaptive and when maladaptive? What governs the proportion of mental life that gets assigned to these three sectors? And, finally: does one of these sectors more clearly reflect the truth about the person than the other two? Or, should we treat Marquez's aphorism as a Zen *kōan* and regard such questions, especially the last mentioned, as something too private to ask?

Notes

1 I was accepted for training in the institute where this group interview took place but decided to go elsewhere.

2 The evolution of the concept of privacy over the last 800 years has been painstakingly traced by Vincent (2016).

3 The one place Freud (1926) used the word was in his address to the B'nai B'rith where he attributed his attraction to "Jewry and Jews" (p. 274) partly to "the safe privacy of a common mental construction" (p. 274).

4 Here, I am talking about only the nosological parameters of the privacy concept in these three monographs. I will return to other aspects of these volumes in later parts of the chapter.

5 I have elsewhere (Akhtar, 2015b; reproduced in this book as Chapter 6) elaborated on the metapsychology and clinical relevance of the concept of dignity.

6 Such self-replenishment provided by privacy is compellingly contained in Khan's (1983b) concept of 'lying fallow'. This is a state of alert quietitude with three characteristics: (i) slowed mentation, (ii) reduced relatedness, and (iii) peaceful self-acceptance. Together these three replicate the infantile calm after a good feed. Working in unison, they exert a replenishing effect upon the ego.

7 See also Anzieu's (1990) metapsychological correlations of the body ego and the topographical model of the mind, in this context.

8 My comments are restricted to the treatment of adult patients. For a consideration of privacy-related concerns in the treatment of children and adolescents, see Novick and Novick (2008) and Smolen (2018).

9 See also (Cliff, 1986) for some useful pointers for disguising patients' identities for publication purposes.

10 For thorough discussions of the impact of an analyst's illness and death upon the analytic process and, ultimately, upon the patient, see Abend (1982), Dewald (1982), Freedman (1990), Firestein (1990), Schwartz and Silver (1990), and Wolman (1990).

11 Bolognini refers to the analyst's conscious and preconscious data collecting apparatus as his 'working ego', and the knowledge of theory and technique stored in his unconscious as his 'working self'.

Chapter 4

Intimacy

In keeping with the topic of this chapter, I will begin with the intimate act of telling you a few things about my late father, Jan Nisar Akhtar. He was a renowned poet of the Urdu language and a well-known Bollywood song-writer. His literary output was large and his dexterity and speed in writing astonishing. He was a shy man who could be charmingly eloquent in the presence of younger poets who frequently gathered in his living room. Appearing a bit sleepy and inwardly absorbed during the day, my father would turn charismatic in late evening recitals of poetry. He wrote many poems about intimacy but here I quote only two *shers* (couplets). Here is the first one:

> *Tu is qadar mujhe apne qareeb lagta hai*
> *Tujhe alag se jo sochooN, ajeeb lagta hai.*

And here is the second:

> *MaiN teri zaat meiN gum ho saka na tu mujh meiN*
> *Bahut qareeb huye, phir bhi faasla to raha.*

Literally translated, the first couplet means: "I experience you so very close to me/ that it feels very strange to think of you as a separate being", and the second one: "I could not lose myself into your being, nor could you/ We did grow very close but some distance still remained".[1] The two couplets (J.N. Akhtar, 1975, pp. 65, 84) capture the tension between intimacy and privacy, describe the illusory nature of emotional union, and shed light upon the limits of interpersonal closeness. Putting reality-based chronological quibbles aside, the psychological sophistication of such poetry brings to mind Freud's humble admission that "everywhere I go, I find a poet has been there before me" (cited in Nin, 1966, p. 14). The poet knows that intimacy and privacy are Siamese twins of subjectivity: separate and connected at the same time.

But let me not get ahead of myself. Permit me to take a few steps back and start by defining the concept of intimacy. Once that is accomplished, I will delve into the developmental substrate of intimacy, its psychopathological derailments, and its socioculturally based variations. After this, I will discuss some unexplored realms of intimacy and then conclude with the technical implications of the concept of intimacy.

Definition and description

The English word 'intimacy' has roots in three eras of Latin language (Mish, 1987, p. 613). In Old Latin, its progenitor is *interus*, which means 'inward'. In Middle Latin, its origin can be traced to *intimus* or 'innermost'. And, in Late Latin, its ancestry goes back to *intimatus*, which means 'to put in'. Combined, the three etymological roots refer to psychic interiority, softening of personal boundaries, and closeness with another being. Of note is the fact that the Late Latin *intimatus* also means 'to declare'. Thus intimacy comes to acquire a sense not only of letting something deeply private of the other being put into oneself but also of putting something deeply private of oneself into someone else. It involves a seamless blending of the psychic convexities and concavities of two individuals. Doing so requires mutual trust and lack of shame between the partners. Balint's (1968) phrase "harmonious interpenetrating mix-up" (p. 66), while clumsy and used specifically in a clinical context, captures the essence of what intimacy is all about.

In the three other most widely spoken languages of the world, namely, Spanish, Chinese, and Hindi, the situation is roughly the same. The Spanish '*intimidad*' is akin to the English 'intimacy' but is infrequently used in spoken communication. In Chinese, the phrase that approximates the English 'intimacy' is *chin-mi kwan-si*. It refers to romantic closeness; there is no comparable expression for friendly intimacy in Chinese. In Hindi, the counterpart of intimacy is *aatmiyeta*, which means 'belonging to oneself' or 'one's own'; it implies that a certain degree of self-other merger is the core feature of intimacy.

In psychoanalytic literature, references to intimacy are largely made in two contexts: romantic relationships and clinical work. I will address the latter in the technical section of this chapter and focus here on intimacy in love. Freud's scattered remarks on how the ego surrenders itself to an idealized object while in love (1917a), puts such object in the place of ego-ideal (1921), and itself becomes utterly defenceless (1930), long anticipate Paris' (1985) declaration that "when we fall in love, there is a loss of ego boundaries, at times verging on ecstatic delight. We look into the beloved's eyes and believe that nothing separates us" (p. 505). However, Paris is wise enough to add "that this is illusory, that many sectors of our self are inviolate" (p. 505).

Nonetheless the "pleasures of self disclosure, confidence sharing, and the state of jointly possessing a secret" (Brody, 1978, p. 527) form central elements of intimacy. Indeed, Rubin (1989) emphasizes the 'positive' side of this intimacy–privacy tension. He declares that intimacy involves "trust, tenderness, caring, the exchange of feelings, cooperation, joy in each other's self-realization, and satisfaction" (p. 1). Cooperative relating and "benevolent closeness" (p. 2) are central to the experience of intimacy, according to Rubin.

Mention of 'closeness' brings up Burch's (2004) interesting viewpoint which holds closeness and intimacy to lie on a continuum. He sees closeness as being in the conscious realm and intimacy as arising from the unconscious. Closeness does not preclude intimacy but does not necessarily include it. Physical proximity and frequency of contact can lead to 'closeness' but not necessarily to 'intimacy'.[2] Moreover, intense engagement with another person can exist without closeness, for instance, during states of anger (Schimel, 1987). Shared situations of fear (e.g. disasters) and excitement (e.g. football games) can lead to closeness with others without actual intimacy. Perhaps closeness refers to sharing focal areas of experience whereas intimacy involves much greater trust and a more diffuse and far-reaching psychological nakedness on the part of the two parties involved.

Putting such speculation aside, I return to Burch and note that he gives premium to the experience of 'tenderness' in the context of intimacy. He cites Thorne (1991) who declared that "when tenderness is present in a relationship, I believe there is the possibility of finding wholeness and of recognizing the liberating paradox" (p. 77); giving oneself over to someone leaves nothing to be desired anymore and taking someone in fully allows them to be truly themselves.[3] Though neither Thorne nor Burch mention it, the work of pre-eminent Finnish psychoanalyst, the late Veikko Tähkä (1993) is outstanding in this context. Tähkä described tenderness as an affect arising from

> empathic sharing of the object's pleasure and subsequent leaving of the pleasure for him. In a loving relationship, this letting the object keep the pleasure for himself is followed by a second re-pleasure in the subject for the loved person's feeling and for the knowledge of having contributed to that oneself.
>
> (p. 244)

The maternal quality of this experience brings up the issue of gender-transcendence during intimacy. Brody (1978) emphasizes that "true intimacy may require the abandonment of some conventional aspects of gender identity" (p. 521), giving credence to Binstock's (1973) earlier statement that "the state of being in love completes the lover's identity as part of a male-female duality" (p. 104). And, it is true that identification with the partner's excitement during sex makes it possible to derive pleasure from his or her erotic desire. Kernberg (1995) notes that under such circumstances, there is a sense of

> temporarily overcoming the ordinarily unbreachable barrier separating the genders, and a sense of completion and enjoyment of the penetrating and encompassing, penetrated and enclosed aspect of sexual invasion. In this connection the symbolic displacement of all "penetrating" parts of the anatomy and of all "penetrable" openings signals the condensation

of eroticism from all zones ... and the consequent confluence, in sexual activity or contact, of fantasies and experiences reflecting the entire body surface of both participants ... Unconsciously identifying with both genders eliminates the need to envy the other gender, and, in remaining oneself while becoming the other as well, one has a sense of having achieved intersubjective transcendence.

(p. 23)

While marked during the actual sexual encounter, a loosening of roles customarily held proper for one or the other gender occurs in most states of intimacy within a romantic couple. This is more 'visible' among heterosexual couples but no less true for homosexual dyads, even though their intrapsychic traffic across genders is more layered and nuanced.

All in all, the experience of romantic intimacy involves the following eight characteristics: (i) physical and emotional closeness, (ii) trust in the essential goodness of the partner, (iii) relaxation of personal boundaries, (iv) overcoming of shame about one's actual or imaginary blemishes and gently overcoming the partner's proclivity to shame, (v) sharing of private thoughts, fantasies, emotions, and expectations, (vi) empathic immersion in the subjectivity of the other, (vii) tenderness, i.e. joy in the other's self-realization and in facilitating that to occur, and (viii) oscillating and partial transcendence of gender boundaries. Intimacy in non-romantic contexts, such as friendship, follows the same pattern though the erotic element is not integral to it (or is 'aim-inhibited')[4] and there is lesser requirement for gender transcendence. While sex dissolves gender boundaries, friendships solidify them. This is true of both same gender and cross-gender friendships.

Developmental substrate

While Erikson's (1968) declaration that it is "only when identity formation is well on its way that true intimacy – which is really a counterpointing as well as fusing of identities – is possible" (p. 135) seems true, it is also true that the foundations of the capacity for intimacy are laid down in the earliest stages of infancy and childhood. The components of intimacy, especially those subsumed under the "affectionate current" (Freud, 1910b) of love, include trust, concern, porousness of self-boundaries, mutuality, absence of shame, sharing of experiences, and tenderness. All of them have their origins in the early mother–child relationship and to this we must turn at this point.

With differing metaphors and theoretical lexicon, all important theoreticians of early development emphasize that a comfortable fit between the infant and its mother is the basis of psychic stability, safety, and confidence. Concepts such as 'absolute dependence' (Fairbairn, 1952), 'primary attachment bond' (Bowlby, 1969), the state of 'illusion' (Winnicott, 1960b), and 'dual-unity' (Mahler et al., 1975) all indicate that the availability of reliable maternal care leads the child to develop trust in its own abilities and to evolve a benevolent view of the world at large. Benedek's (1938) and Erikson's (1950) notions of 'confident expectation' and 'basic trust', respectively, speak to this very point.

With such self-assurance and a charitable worldview, the growing child becomes capable of forays in external reality; continued access to the primary object for "emotional refuelling" (Furer, cited in Mahler et al., 1975, p. 69) helps sustain the necessary 'we-ness' (Bergman, 1980, 1999) during such assertions of 'me-hood'. By the time the child acquires self- and object-constancy, he can defer gratification, indulge in fantasy enactments, and enjoy role-playing. Fusion of good and bad object representations enhances his capacity to cope with simultaneous love and anger towards self and others (Kernberg, 1975). By age three or so, the average child can attend nursery school, showing that he is capable to accept a mother substitute. His dialogue with his internalized mother makes it possible for him to feel a modicum of intimacy with his kindergarten teacher (Kramer, 1996). Still later, during the oedipal period, sexual curiosities arise and the nature of parental intimacy becomes a matter of great concern for the child. He tries to understand sexual matters and succeeds to a certain extent but many things still remain mysterious. Repression then sets in, leading to compartmentalization of the mind, layering of the self, and aim-inhibition of erotic desires typical of this developmental period (Freud, 1924b).

During the subsequent phase of latency (from six to twelve years or so), relationship with school teachers and same-sex peers broadens the child's emotional arena. Friendships in latency and, later on, during adolescence allow sharing secret ambitions and sexual curiosities. Much intimacy characterizes such relationships as they are replete with exclusivity, mutuality, and tenderness. The onset of adolescence especially pushes the young individual towards seeking intimacy, this time with a romantic and sexual partner. Love and sex, hitherto existing as separate, now come to be fused. Counterphobic disidentification with parents (Blos, 1967; Tyson and Tyson, 1999) and 'hyper-intimacy' with peers in the service of identity consolidation gradually settles and a return to conventionality becomes evident. This marks the beginning of young adulthood. Parents are still loved and so are friends, but deeper confidences are now shared only with one's romantic partner (homosexual or heterosexual, with or without marriage). Becoming a parent oneself and raising children opens up new avenues for intimacy with one's partner. Still later, the accrual of shared memories offers the intimacy of mutual nostalgia. At the terminal end of life, accommodations to changes in biological functioning propel the couple to seek novel ways of sustaining romantic intimacy (Kaplan, 1990). Clearly, throughout the lifespan, psychological health

> includes the idea of tingling life and the magic of intimacy. All these
> things go together and add up to a sense of feeling real and of being,

and of the experiences feeding back into the personal psychic reality, enriching it, and giving it scope. The consequence is that the healthy person's inner world is related to the outer or actual world and yet is personal and capable of an aliveness of its own ... each person has a polite or socialized self, and also a personal private self that is not available except in intimacy.

(Winnicott, 1984, pp. 31, 66)

To this relatively 'conservative' survey of developmental literature, one must add some significant newer contributions. The following six certainly merit inclusion here though much more literature than I can cover exists in this realm. I summarize them in chronological order of their appearance.

Levenson (1984) proposed that the mother's differing attitudes towards her male and female offspring contribute to the differences between their varying patterns of closeness and distance from her: "while the boy can differentiate via gender, the girl must struggle to differentiate via generation" (p. 531). Boundaries remain more porous for the latter as she grows further. As a result "at the point of marriage – the adult intimate dyad – a man's basic issue is how to be intimate and *stay* autonomous; a woman's is still how to be intimate and *become* autonomous" (p. 533, italics in the original).

Horner (1986) devoted a monograph to the tension between the search for intimacy and the desire to preserve independence and authenticity. She traced the healthy capacity to strike a balance between these polarities back to the amalgamation of the mother's supportive-holding activities on the one hand and individuation-promoting functions on the other.

Stern (1985), in his well-received book, *The Interpersonal World of the Infant*, highlighted the interactional synchrony between the mother and her baby *and* the mother's joy in the child's pleasure in his efficacy as the founding units of mutuality and intimacy in the child. Stern described four stages of developing self: emergent, core, subjective, and verbal. It is only at the third stage (beginning around eight months of age) that actual intersubjective exchange with mother becomes possible. Capacity for intimacy is born at this point. Revisiting his book thirteen years later, Stern (1998) added the concept of 'narrative self' which followed the 'verbal self'. This constellation gives rise to the first true and false stories one develops about oneself; these can include facts and fictions about one's capacity or incapacity for intimacy with others.

Ehrlich (1998) delineated two experiential modalities, those of 'being' and 'doing'. Both must be present for consolidation of identity and healthy functioning of the self. Ehrlich went on to say that:

A resolution of intimacy based exclusively on the modality of *Doing* will at best be a portrait of drive domination and will never extend far beyond the erotic question of who is doing what to whom. On the other hand, intimacy that is resolved exclusively in the *Being* modality will be of the kind encountered in deep spiritual unions, like those met in intensive religious and mystical experiences. Exclusively, unalloyed to at least a modicum of what can be provided by the *Doing* modality, it cannot provide an alternative to the necessary encounter between members of opposite genders, whose mental, spiritual, physical, and instinctual union leads to cross-fertilization, offspring, and family formation.

(p. 157, italics in the original)

Alperin (2001) emphasized that the need for intimacy is inborn and finds strength from empathic attunement between the infant and its mother. The adult desire for intimacy reflects a wish to return to this early stage and "undo the primordial separation from the mother" (p. 140). Alperin included the following among obstacles to intimacy in adulthood: the 'alienating individualism' (Rotenberg, 1977) of capitalist societies, fear of psychic dissolution during closeness, paranoid hostility, and incestuous anxieties.

Orbach (2007) focused upon this last issue and explored it in the context of romantic couples. She noted that in such a setting, three different attachment schemas are at work: that of each individual and that of the entity itself. This last one is what matters in the end. Helping to elevate it above individual attachment patterns and safeguarding the space it provides in the form of 'separated attachment' and 'connected autonomy' makes it possible for the couple to recover and/or sustain sexual intimacy between them.

Finally, I wish to add a developmental notion of my own. This pertains to there being some difference between the sort of intimacy a child has with its mother and with its father. 'Maternal intimacy' is overarching, not necessarily verbal, and provides psychic nourishment and sustenance. 'Paternal intimacy' is focal, didactic, and geared towards external reality.[5] Superimposed on top of these are the different types of intimacies with the same-sex and the opposite-sex parent. In the girl's case, the 'maternal intimacy' and the 'same-sex parent intimacy' are harmonious; this deepens the capacity for intimacy in her but also increases the fear of autonomy. In the boy's case, the 'maternal intimacy' and the 'same-sex parent intimacy' involve two different figures; this weakens the capacity for intimacy but increases the regressive fear of merger. I will return to how these two forms of relatedness act in unison in the technical section of this chapter. Before discussing such technical issues, however, it is necessary to consider scenarios where things have gone wrong and where the possibility of intimacy is grossly compromised.

Psychopathology

Like all character traits, capacity for intimacy is subject to derailments of personality development, psychic trauma, and unfortunate vicissitudes of adult life. Morbid forms of intimacy thus emerge. These include: (i) failed intimacy, (ii) florid intimacy, (iii) fluctuating intimacy, and (iv) false intimacy. Brief comments on each follow.

Failed intimacy

Not all people are capable of developing and sustaining intimate relationships with others. Their efforts to achieve intimacy fail due to various deficit and defence-based impediments from within. Four levels of psychopathology are generally evident under such circumstances. The *first level* pertains to schizoid anxieties regarding emotional closeness with another person. As a child, the schizoid has felt chronically unloved and unseen in his psychic veracity by his parents (Ferenczi, 1929; Fairbairn, 1952). His overtures of playfulness and love were treated as intrusions by them. As an adult, he dreads expressing his affectionate and needy feelings to others lest these be rejected all over again. He relates to them via intellect and reason, becoming didactic or preachy in the process. Others do not understand him, cannot relate to his aloofness, and, at times, feel intimidated by him. Consequently, the schizoid individual finds himself devoid of friendships. There is little or no genuine intimacy in his life since he dreads (and, using rationalization, derides) the ordinary messiness and unpredictability of human relationships.

The *second level* of failed intimacy is caused by paranoid fears. After all, emotional closeness with others requires that one trusts the other person and finds it safe to be with him or her in a relaxed, self-disclosing way. This is difficult for individuals whose lives are structured around viewing themselves as the object of others' hostility, interference, and oppression. They are suspicious and feel unjustly treated by others. As a result, they erect defensive walls of humourless rigidity and vigilance. As a character trait, mistrust becomes a formidable barrier to intimacy in both social and romantic spheres of life (see Akhtar, 2016, for details).

The *third level* of deficient empathy involves narcissistic character traits. Freud's (1914a) 'U-tube theory' of the relationship between self-love and object-love still holds water: the more one loves oneself, the less one can love others. However, more nuances have come to be recognized in this context (Kohut, 1971, 1977; Kernberg, 1975, 1984; Akhtar, 1992a, 2009a; Bach, 1977). It has been noted that the narcissistic individual is forever busy burnishing the image he presents to others and this preoccupation siphons off the psychic energy needed to listen to others. He cannot grasp the psychic depth of others. And, if he presents himself as shining, perfect, and above any criticism, then others cannot reach his inner self. Either way, the door to intimacy gets closed. Moreover, letting others know oneself requires acceptance of one's total self and not of one's strengths only. In other words, deep and genuine interaction with others requires humility[6] and the narcissist is incapable of self-effacement. To complicate matters further, knowing others fully has the dual risk of encountering their blemishes as well as their strengths. The former warrants restraint of criticism and the latter requires tolerance of envy. Both tasks are difficult for the narcissist and therefore he avoids intimacy with others. Yet another difficulty arises from the narcissist's profound internal attachment to "an ideal object with whom one would never have to feel aggression and from whom no aggressive actions would have to be tolerated" (Richards and Spira, 2003, p. 357). This condemns him to a never-ending search or life-long wait for this perfect object. Meanwhile, the capacity for meaningfully relating to imperfect and 'ordinary' objects is seriously compromised.

Finally, the *fourth level* of difficulty in achieving intimacy exists in the context of a neurotic or 'higher level of character organization' (Kernberg, 1970). Problems of this sort are generally milder in intensity, often ego-dystonic, and limited in their relational scope. They mostly involve the sexual realm and manifest as inhibitions of pre-genital sexuality, especially during foreplay. Capable of trusting, deep, and sustained bonds on a selective basis, individuals with neurotic restrictions of intimacy can end up with restricted sexuality and an unexciting social life suffused with 'unmentalized xenophobia' (Akhtar, 2007).

Regardless of the levels of psychopathology outlined above, a common defence against intimacy is to 'elevate' its lack into a proud insistence upon freedom.

> One experiences not the threat of intimacy, but that one needs space, can't stand coercion, loves freedom, isn't ready yet, and so forth. In its easiest formulation, the quest is for freedom and the avoidance of anything that compromises it. Commitment, even the idea of commitment, threatens that quest. To maintain freedom, affects and associations arising in opposition are censored within, through psychic defences. Hence, freedom-seeking persons, in extreme instances, need to avoid wishing for anything or caring about anyone. Intimacy with another and caring for another mobilize anxiety that is attenuated through denial, detachment, contempt, rationalization, and the sabotage of trust.
>
> (Ingram, 1986, p. 77)

In contrast to this spectrum of psychopathology leading to deficient or failed intimacy are situations and characters which facilitate the development of 'hyper-intimacy'.

Florid intimacy

Using the designation 'florid' in its sense of being extravagant and declamatory, I wish to describe characters and situations where a certain kind of ready-made bonhomie prevails and where intimacy develops quite rapidly between strangers or near-strangers. Five scenarios come to mind.

- Someone older, affluent and resourceful but deeply traumatized encounters a younger and financially compromised person with a similar traumatic background. The former has an uncanny empathy for the latter; he wants to 'rescue' the less fortunate of the duo. They develop a quick and tight bond of intimacy.
- A lonely immigrant poet living in a land where hardly anyone understands his language finds out that another poet of his language is visiting town. They meet. A long and intimate discourse ensues. In what Kretschmer (1925) called an "enlarged autism along people of similar persuasion" (p. 162), the two become deep friends and continue to communicate with each other long after the visiting poet returns to his land.
- In the living room of a Bollywood movie star, young aspirants spill their guts and on the slightest cue from the matinee idol reveal their deepest secrets. The star is not moved towards reciprocal disclosure but a fellow 'minor artist' present there (an 'extra' in old terminology of the film industry) becomes enamoured and shares his or her private thoughts with fervent desire for closeness.
- A sexually perverse man and woman with mutual consent and with precisely matching depth of regression decide to eat each other's faeces. They regard this ego-polluting ecstasy as evidence of their profound intimacy with each other.
- In contrast to this grotesque illustration is the following elegant passage describing the instantaneous development of intimacy between two sadomasochistic strangers. "The large wide-open eyes contain a hint of reproach. The gaze sinks deeply into me. She plays a fallen woman, the victim of a need for love that leads her repeatedly to villainous men who will use her and forsake her. She is stuck with her vulnerability, her hidden masochism, and I am stuck with my secret sadism. Across that gulf our glances meet, we recognize each other. We are a pair" (Wheelis, 1994, p. 86).

What all these illustrations have in common is the triad of (i) extraordinary porousness of self-boundaries, (ii) uncanny mutuality of 'tongues' between the parties involved, and (iii) rapidity with which emotional engagement takes place between them. Situational (e.g. immigration, Bollywood drama), aesthetic (e.g. poetry, other common interests), and characterological variables (e.g. perversion, hypomanic tendencies) all contribute to the development of 'florid intimacy'. Let me hasten to add that rapid development of intimacy must not be reflexively devalued. To be sure, not all such instances have happy endings[7] and many evaporate with the speed with which they developed. However, some of them can give rise to long-term friendships. I fondly myself recall my first ever conversation with the London-based South African psychoanalyst, Julian Stern, which lasted for eleven hours and has resulted in a deep and mutually gratifying and ongoing friendship of twenty-five years.

Fluctuating intimacy

Seemingly a co-existence of 'failed' and 'florid' intimacies, the syndrome of 'fluctuating intimacy' usually arises from an equipotent mixture of object hunger and merger anxieties (Guntrip, 1969; Mahler et al., 1975). Object hunger propels closeness and giving 'hundred percent' of oneself to others in the hope of becoming indispensable to them. Merger anxieties stir up fear of losing all autonomy and becoming enslaved. One's own object hunger is projected upon the object leading to phantasies of being cannibalized. As a result, such individuals (often termed 'borderline') withdraw from closeness. But this exposes them to the pain of stark aloneness and lack of belonging. Wanting to avoid this latter dread, they return to the object only to get anxious all over again. Like Schopenhauer's (1851) porcupines, partners caught in such a relational matrix fluctuate between intimacy and distance, trust and mistrust, betrayal and confession, and separateness and merger. They cannot live peacefully together nor can they do without each other. For such individuals, emotional involvement stirs up a characteristic 'need-fear dilemma' (Burnham et al., 1969): to be intimate is to court engulfment and to be apart is to court aloneness. Not surprisingly, they keep going back and forth and remain inconsolable at either end of the intimacy–separateness spectrum (Gunderson, 1985; Melges and Swartz, 1989; Akhtar, 1990). That such oscillations of 'optimal distance' (Akhtar, 1992b) disrupt their relationships is beyond question. What remains dubious is whether their closeness with loved ones can be accorded the status of genuine intimacy. Their inability to accept others fully, metabolize aggression, and master merger fears attendant upon close contact impede their grasp of others' subjectivity. Their 'intimacy' is not only transitory but superficial as well.

False intimacy

Since intimacy, by definition, means psychological integrity, interactional transparency, emotional truthfulness, and mutual trust, any departure from these components contaminates the experience. Individuals who have not achieved self- and object-constancy (Mahler et al., 1975) and who lack the capacity for relating to 'whole objects' (Klein, 1935) can only muster pale facsimiles of intimacy; they relate from parts of their selves to parts of others.

Such developmentally determined failure is, however, not the main origin of false intimacy. Mandatory insertion of a part object or a lubricated accoutrement of desire into romantic intimacy is what renders it false. Freud's (1927b) description of fetishism whereby an interposition of an inanimate object (e.g. shoe, earrings, stocking) or some part of the body (e.g. foot, lock of hair) becomes a requirement for a man's achieving sexual union with a woman is the prototype of false intimacy. Khan (1979) extended this theme and declared that "the pervert puts an *impersonal object* between his desire and his accomplice; this object can be a stereotyped fantasy, a gadget, or a pornographic image. All three alienate the pervert from himself, as, alas, from the object of his desire" (p. 9, italics in the original). Going into further details of the pervert's "technique of intimacy" (p. 20), Khan noted that such a person is incapable of relating to a truly separate object. For him, the object occupies an intermediary position: not entirely subjective and yet treated as subjectively created. Through such manoeuvre of intimacy, he "tries to *make known* to himself and *announce and press into* another something pertaining to his innermost nature as well as to discharge instinctual tension in a compulsive and exigent way" (p. 22, italics in the original). The relational consequences and the paradoxical pallor of such turgid closeness elicits the following eloquent passage from Khan.

> The capacity to create the emotional climate in which another person volunteers to participate is one of the few real talents of the pervert. This invitation to surrender to the pervert's logic of body-intimacies demands of the object a suspension of discrimination and resistance at all levels of guilt, shame, and separateness. A make-believe situation is offered in which two individuals temporarily renounce their separate identities and boundaries and attempt to create a heightened maximal body-intimacy of orgastic nature. There is always, however, one proviso. The pervert himself cannot surrender to the experience and retains a split-off, dissociated manipulative ego-control of the situation. This is both his achievement and failure in the *intimate* situation.
>
> (p. 22, italics in the original)

A more recent rendering of such pseudo-intimacy can be found in Celenza's (2015) clarification that in both male and female sexual perversions, the prevailing dynamics involve objectification of the woman's body. Pleasurable and orgastic though the interaction might be, it can hardly claim the status of being intimate since both partners have colluded in eliminating the subjectivity of the female partner, replacing it with complicity and dehumanizing compliance.

Outside of the sexual scenario, postures of false intimacy can also be discerned in the social lives of narcissistic and sociopathic characters (Kernberg, 1984, 1992; Akhtar, 1989, 1992a, 2007). Elsewhere, I have commented upon the former's inability in the following manner.

> He or she does not wish to renounce total autonomy while also not permitting a separate mental life to the other. Under the pressure of instinctual drives, the narcissistic individual comes too close to the other person and defending against the aggression, inevitably mobilized by intimacy, he withdraws and becomes cold and aloof. In contrast to the mature relatedness in love which gradually deepens, narcissistic

relatedness is characterized by cycles of need-based intimacy and defensive withdrawals. Or, there develops a pattern of intense idealization and coercive control of the other with no deepening of actual knowledge of that person over time.

(Akhtar, 2009a, pp. 102–103)

In the sociopathic character, corrosion of superego functions and deterioration of ethical foundations of human relatedness leads either to the total incapacity of intimacy or to a peculiar kind of transitory and false intimacy arising mostly out of "glibness and charm" (Abraham, 1925, p. 299) which pulls the other person close, and 'state-related empathy' (Gediman, 1985) which permits a sharp though transitory attunement to the other person's needs. The sociopath, like a skilful puppeteer, is able to seduce the other person to take steps towards intimacy while waiting to make his exploitative move.

Sociocultural aspects

Since intimacy, by definition, involves the relationship between two or more individuals, it is likely to be affected by a given society's provision of prototypes of such experience during childhood, facilitation of close interpersonal relationships during adult life, and the endemic sustenance of belief in the value of human relatedness and mutuality. To be sure, all societies offer such avenues to its members. However, to the extent they do so differs. And, this difference can account for cross-cultural variations in the degree of intimacy and the value accorded to the experience.

In the age of the 'Protean Man' (Lifton, 1971) and the 'culture of narcissism' (Lasch, 1979), great emphasis is placed upon appearances, acquisitions, ambitions, and self-benefitting 'adjustments' to circumstances. Family life suffers when parents are consumed by demands of work and pressure to make money. Childhood is aborted.[8] Children have fewer siblings and limited contact with their cousins, who often do not live in the same city. Miller (2013) eloquently describes the toll all this takes upon the emotional lives of children and I quote him at some length.

> The lot of children seems to have deteriorated in a number of ways. First and foremost, the combination of accelerating family breakdown and economic pressures requiring two incomes has meant that children have less and less personal relationship with their parents and virtually no experience of normal family life. Second, the dangers of road traffic and fear of paedophiles and other predators make it extremely rare for children to be able to play with their neighbors and friends unsupervised, and close to their home. The result is something of a siege mentality. Inside the "safe houses" (home, nursery school, school, after-school clubs, etc.) life is barren, two-dimensional, and stressful. During leisure

hours, three-dimensional, practical experience of building, inventing, and constructing is a thing of the past. Computer graphics replace reality and the television screen and the headphone enforce passivity. School hours are dominated by the pressure of tests, attainment levels, examinations, inspections, and the coercive nature of league tables. The joy of learning the importance of living co-operatively are replaced by the pressure to succeed and the preoccupation with competition.

(pp. 200–201)

On an earlier, developmental level too, the contemporary scenario in the West (especially in the United States) seems grim. Capitalism thrives on the induction of 'false needs' (Akhtar, 2011e) which makes people conclude that they have to make more money to purchase more things; this partly contributes to the unquestioned norm of the two-income family. Since paid maternity leave is short (e.g. six weeks in the United States), babies are put in 'day care', and then into 'preschool' centres. Mother–child bonding suffers and what is lost due to the lack of comfortable leaning upon the mother for care and assurance is 'compensated' by the familial and societal exaltation of autonomy. Expressions such as 'take care of yourself' and 'do it yourself' go unquestioned and 'assisted living', which is actually an existential requirement of all human beings, becomes a subtly derided accommodation for the elderly and terminally ill. The pallor of 'we-ness' produces a 'me-generation' that is replete with ambition, hesitant about dependency, and compromised in the capacity for intimacy. Work-mates, especially in white-collar settings, do not socialize with each other. Friends know little about each other's personal problems and have to make appointments to share a meal often weeks and months in advance.

Matters are different in most Latin American, Mediterranean, and Asian cultures. Though the juggernaut of American-style consumerism is beginning to impact these societies, their distinction from the North American norms is still noticeable. In many such places, women do not work outside the home, quit their jobs upon having babies, or are afforded fully paid long maternity leave. Joint or extended families still exist and the child is not left with paid strangers from six weeks onwards (as is frequently the case in the United States). Often a group of women (mother, grandmother, aunts, older female siblings and cousins) are available to care for the child (Roland, 1988; Kurtz, 1992) and assure a certain continuity of skin-to-skin contact and emotional dependence. Children have more siblings and greater access to their maternal and paternal cousins. They play with each other and thus engage in the emotional lives of their peers on a regular basis. Neighbours constitute an important part of a relationship network. Ordinary human competitiveness is sacrificed at the altar of mutual respect and social cohesion. Workplace offers opportunities for life-long bonds. Friendships are deep and involve great sharing of information, personal feelings, and even secrets. Intimacy abounds and loneliness is exceptional.

Lest these contrasting portrayals be deemed caricatures, some 'softening' of their hard edges is needed. *First*, profiles of modal character do not rule out individual variability within a given society. Thus warm and friendly people with capacity for deep intimacy do exist in the West and cold, aloof, and mistrustful ones in the East. Group tendencies painted with the broad brush of generalization must not be permitted to gloss over the finer nuances of individual psychodynamics. *Second*, both within the East and West, there might exist sub-cultural, regional, and ethnic differences in the extent of interpersonal intimacy. For instance, the personal reserve deemed prototypical of White Anglo-Saxon Protestants ('WASPS') is not valid for African Americans or Italian Americans in the United States. And, in India, people of the states of Punjab and Tamil Nadu differ greatly in the extent of talkativeness, need for privacy, and ease with which they make new friends. *Third*, economic class also plays a role here. Generally speaking, families of lower socioeconomic classes live in close proximity with each other. This necessitates greater interaction with relatives and with neighbours and other community members. Overcrowding within living quarters can lead to 'thinness' of personal boundaries and greater tolerance of intimacy. Even a cursory look at upper middle class, predominantly White, North American suburbs reveals the isolationism and crusty self-reliance of their inhabitants. Contact with neighbours is perfunctory and one sees fewer children playing outside the house. To paraphrase Freud's "anatomy is destiny" (1924b, p. 178), observations such as these make one conclude that 'economy is destiny'. *Fourth*, a related variable pertains to rural versus urban societies. The former provide great necessity and opportunity for close human relationships. The latter facilitate cloistered existence. Thus in rising world nations like China, Brazil, and India, where rural to urban migration is occurring at an astounding pace (Akhtar, 2011e), the shape and form of family units and modal child-rearing practices are also changing. These, in turn, might affect the personality attributes (including the capacity for intimacy) upheld as desirable and fitting for survival and progress. *Fifth*, one must not overlook that massive waves of migration are occurring from so-called Third World countries to the Western hemisphere. This provides a great opportunity for people of both regions to develop heteroethnic and homoethnic friendships. Elsewhere, I have elaborated on the differences and similarities of such bonds (Akhtar, 2011e, pp. 81–102). Suffice here to say that in general, homoethnic friendships soothe and provide more intimate contact but can slow down individuation, whereas heteroethnic friendships propel acculturation and enrich culture-specific ego skills but preclude deeper intimacy. *Finally*, it should be remembered that the intimacy–privacy divide is not an 'all or none' phenomenon. It is not that Westerners need and value more privacy and Easterners need and value more intimacy. Both groups need and value both experiences. Their ways of obtaining these experiences might differ and the dramatis personae enlisted for important relationships might vary. More importantly, different layers of psychic structure might be used to achieve these goals. In this context, the astute observation of Roland (1988), a New York-based psychoanalyst with considerable clinical and social experience with Indian and Japanese clients and their respective homelands, is highly pertinent.

> As a counter to permeable outer ego boundaries in the intense familial intimacy relationships where there is little if any privacy, Indians establish another inner ego boundary to protect and enhance a highly private self with its rich feelings and fantasies – thus creating inner psychological space. This kind of ego boundary is as yet unformulated in psychoanalysis in the West – mainly because Western individualism, with its emphasis on strong outer ego boundaries and individual autonomy, precludes the necessity of developing such an inner boundary and private self as central psychological structures.
>
> (p. 227)

Endopsychic considerations such as these are useful reminders of the dialectical ties between anthropology and psychoanalysis (Paul, 2005) while also preparing the ground for us to re-enter the clinical realm. Before doing so, however, I will make a brief foray into some sub-optimally understood aspects of human intimacy.

Three unexplored realms of intimacy

Three areas, not widely recognized in the existing literature on intimacy now draw my attention. Rendered as questions, these are (i) are there variable degrees of intimacy with one's different self-representations, (ii) can intimacy exist between man and animal, and (iii) is there a sort of intimacy between a religious mendicant and his or her god? Allow me to make brief comments on each of these issues.

Intimacy with parts of oneself

A healthy and 'well-formed' self does not imply a monolithic homogeneity. In fact, a rigid and caricatured consistency is often a defence against internal divisions and chaos. A normal, well-integrated, and smoothly functioning self is comprised of many subsets of self-representations (Eisnitz, 1980). Some of these are close to action, others to contemplation. Some are nearer to masculinity, others to femininity. Some express one life agenda, others a differing one. What distinguishes a cohesive self with multiple self-representations from a disordered identity is the former's overall synthesis, comfortable transition between various aspects, and an optimal mixture of reality principle and ego-ideal-dictated life direction in the manifestation or non-manifestation of this or that self-representation.

One might therefore maintain varying distances with different parts of one's self. Note here that Freud's topographic (1900) and structural (1923) models of mind both permit a consideration of this sort and Bouvet (1958), who first wrote about 'optimal distance', was actually talking about "the gap that separates the way in which a subject expresses his instinctual drives from how he would express them if the process of 'handling' or 'managing' (in French: *amenagement*) these expression did not intervene" (p. 211, italics in the original). Besides such formal and dynamic separations, there are content-based divisions within the self. Bach's (1977) concept of 'mirror-complementarity of the self' whereby one consciously experienced and expressed behavioural extreme is almost always associated with its opposite (e.g. greed versus generosity) refers to this very fact. So does Feldman's (2007) paper on the technique of addressing (or, not addressing) repudiated parts of the self during the analytic work.

Thus one's avowed self might maintain a close discourse with one self-representation and deny expression to another. I, for one, have avoided 'intimacy' with two aspects of myself: one pertains to gambling and the other to spirituality. Staying far from the former, I have not frequented casinos (after one mesmerizing trip to Atlantic City) and have never visited Las Vegas. Staying less distant from the latter, I have found promptings to renounce a well-chiselled selfhood alluring as well as frightening. I have flirted with desires to learn more about Buddhism and Sufism, to visit sacred places of the world, and to retreat into non-worldly solitude[9] but found such inner callings a bit scary. A gradual compromise on my part has been to read and write about human attributes such as forgiveness (Akhtar, 2002), goodness (Akhtar, 2009c, 2009d), gratitude (Akhtar, 2013b), generosity (Akhtar, 2013c), patience (Akhtar, 2015a), dignity (Akhtar, 2015b), and humility (Akhtar, 2018). My lack of 'intimacy' with my gambler self has been good for me. My hesitation to fully encounter my 'spiritual self' (Roland, 2011) has produced ambivalent results. My own struggles notwithstanding, the question remains whether we – all of us – can become 'intimate' with all parts of ourselves? And, if not, does such distance enrich or impoverish one's personality? Are compromises possible? And, do such compromises present themselves only in middle or old age or earlier as well?

Intimacy with animals

In *Totem and Taboo*, Freud (1913) famously declared that:

> Children show no trace of the arrogance which urges adult civilized men to draw a hard-and-fast line between their own nature and that of all other animals. Children have no scruples over allowing them to rank as their full equals. Uninhibited as they are in the avowal of their bodily needs, they no doubt feel themselves more akin to animals than to their elders, who may well be a puzzle to them.
>
> (pp. 126–127)

Four years later, Freud (1917b) returned to this topic with the following statement:

> Man is not a being different from animals or superior to them; he himself is of animal descent, being more closely related to some species and more distantly to others. The acquisitions he has subsequently made have not succeeded in effacing the evidences, both in his psychic structure and mental dispositions, of his parity to them.
>
> (p. 141)

Freud's developmental theorizing emphasized the animal substrate of the inner world of human beings while also noting that animals frequently serve as symbolic reservoirs of our projections. Indeed, three out of his 'famous' four cases, namely those of Little Hans (1909a), the Rat Man (1909b), and Wolf Man (1918), involved human fantasies and preoccupations with animals.

This line of exploration in Freud's work was not advanced by later psychoanalysts, with the notable exception of Searles (1960) and, to a lesser extent, by Sperling (1952, 1971) and Shengold (1971). A major impetus was given to such conceptualization by two volumes that Volkan and I edited: *Mental Zoo* (Akhtar and Volkan, 2005a) and *Cultural Zoo* (Akhtar and Volkan, 2005b). We brought together a number of contemporary analysts who advanced Freud's preliminary notions about the role of domesticated or wild animals in the psychic development of a child, in his or her adaptation to the external world, and in the complex and rich tapestry of human culture including mythology, art, music, literature, and cinema.

Now, taking a step towards deeper layers of man–animal relationship, I raise the question whether genuine intimacy can be a part of this bond. Putting aside the sexually perverse use of animals (Krafft-Ebing, 1892; Kinsey et al., 1948a, 1948b; Greenacre, 1951; Shengold, 1967; Stolorow and Grand, 1973; Traub-Werner, 1986) and cruelty towards them (Akhtar and Brown, 2005) where the relationship is exploitative, unempathic, and one-sided, the answer to the question about genuine intimacy between man and animal seems to be affirmative. Experience with my pet dogs – Jackie and Majnun – my children's experiences with cats and horses, my observation of friends and patients who have owned pets, and my reading of novels involving man–animal relationship (e.g. Ackerley, 1956; Parkhurst, 2004) and newer psychoanalytic contributions (Bolognini, 2008; Platt, 2017) support such an assertion on my part.

All the components of intimacy – caring, trusting, sharing of experiences, discarding shame, and facilitating the joyous expansion of the partner's self – can be found in man–animal relationship. The communication and exchange of such feelings occurs less on a verbal and more on a non-verbal, sensual, and intuitive level. Writing specifically about the man–dog relationship, Bolognini (2008) declares that if the owner retains a "sufficiently liberated spirit" (p. 98) and can resist projecting his or her self-representations upon the animal partner, a "operative unity" (p. 99) and "shared directionality" (p. 105) between them can emerge; this can enrich both partners' emotional lives. I agree with this and add that we not only give all sort of nicknames to our animals, we also come up with nicknames we believe our pets have assigned to us. Such reciprocity is further enhanced by mutual play and respectful regard for each other's moods and state-related needs. Khan's (1983d) observation that the presence of a dog in the house[10] can facilitate the master's 'lying fallow' is one shining example of the holding functions of man–animal relationships. Another illustration is contributed by the deeply affectionate mutuality between blind people and their seeing-eye dogs. The use of domesticated animals in nursing homes for the elderly is yet another example of the benefits of man–animal intimacy. More recently, the trust in horses' natural benevolence has been utilized to help crack the shell of impaired mentalization in autistic children (Murphy, 2011; Cahill, 2015), and to create confessional narratives that preclude recidivism for female prisoners nearing release from prison (Rellahan, 2017).

Intimacy with God

The dissolution of the self – or, at least, its partial dismantling – during the state of 'oceanic feeling' was attributed to transcendence by Rolland (letter to Freud, 5 December 1927; cited in Freud, 1930, p. 65) and to regression by Freud (1930). The sense that one is merged with the universe-at-large and all time and space is co-extensive with the ego was seen by the former as an arrival at a higher level of consciousness (where the self renounces its own boundaries) and was regarded by the latter as a return to an early infantile state (where the self is in a state of fusion with its surround, including, of course, the mother). With few exceptions (Rizzuto, 1979, 2001; Meissner, 1984, 2001), subsequent psychoanalysts followed Freud's line of thinking. They adapted his sceptical view of religious belief (Freud, 1927a) and helped create a heuristic atmosphere where psychoanalysis became a conjoint twin of atheism.

In light of this, most analysts might feel uneasy at my suggestion that intimacy can exist between man and God.[11] They might assert that since God is an imaginary creation of man and its existence merely intrapsychic, the question of intimacy with it should not even arise. To this objection, I respond by saying that if differing levels of intimacy can exist with different *self*-representations (as described above) then why not with different *object*-representations as well? Freud's (1927a) argumentative dismissal of God and the fervent advocacy of atheism by some contemporary thinkers (Hitchens, 2007; Dawkins, 2008; Thomson and Aukofer, 2011) cannot – indeed do not – rob people of the need to believe in a divine power and to carry on internal discourse with it. This 'divine internal object' (personal communication,

Father Lee Makowski, 21 January 2001) or 'God representation' (Rizzuto, 2001) can acquire anthropomorphic attributes and content-specificity *or* it can be metaphorical and remain ensconced in the 'intermediate area of experience' (Winnicott, 1953). Projected outward, the former leads to idolatry and submission. Kept inside, the latter enhances gratitude and humility (Akhtar, 2018). My declaration that "God is a majestic poem" (Akhtar, 2008, p. 5) is reflective of this latter stance. Needless to add that one can be informed by a poem and one can add further meanings and richness to it.

Seen this way, we are less surprised (than we would be if we got stuck in the futile debate whether God exists or does not exist) to find that alongside his vociferous claims to be an atheist. Freud paid repeated homage to God.

> Letters throughout Freud's life are replete with words and phrases such as "I passed my examinations with God's help"; "if God so wills"; "the good Lord"; "taking the Lord to task"; "into the keeping of the Lord"; "until after the Resurrection"; "science seems to demand the existence of God"; "God's judgement"; "God's will"; "God's grace"; "God above"; "if someday we meet above"; "in the next world"; "my secret prayer". In a letter to Oscar Pfister, Freud writes that Pfister was "a true servant of God" and was "in the fortunate position to lead others to God".
>
> (Nicholi, 2002, p. 51)

Clearly, Freud revolted against the externalized, stern, father-like God who demanded blind worship while fearlessly expressing humility towards the sublime object of wonder, awe, and gratitude. Fascinatingly, in one of his last writings, Freud (1939) declared that believing in a universal God, typical of monotheistic religions, results in certain "sacrifice of intimacy" (p. 128). To explain by caricature, one can say that the father of twelve children is less likely to be 'intimate' with each of his children than the father of one or two. This opens up the possibility that polytheistic religions which let their followers choose the deity to worship (e.g. male, female, child, animal, half-animal-half man, and so on) might facilitate a greater intimacy between man and God. Hinduism, especially, offers "a transference pantheon" (Rao, 2005, p. 271) and with it, the possibility

> to create, through the plasticity afforded by polytheism, a God in one's very own image. This is exemplified by the common practice of *Ishta Devata* or a personal God of one's liking, a God that a family or family member adopts as personally significant beyond all the other Gods. The idea of choosing the form of God to worship or cherish is unique, but not unlike the practice of seeking the blessings of a Christian patron saint … In India, Gods are transference Gods par excellence, one might go further and say that they are also gods of transference, meaning that in a fundamental way Hindu Gods extends themselves in turn as

transformable beings and transference objects. They do so through the *Avatar* mechanism, usually translated as incarnation of descent (From a more exalted state), a cherished power of Hindu deities that allows for multiple lives, births, appearance, and attributes to suit temporal eras, social customs, and personal wishes.

(pp. 291–292, italics in the original)

Such flexibility stands in sharp contrast to the paternal and paternalistic God of the three Abrahamic faiths. At the same time, softer forms of all these religions (e.g. Kabbalah of Judaism, various mystical sects of Christianity, Sufism of Islam) do permit a more playful and personal dialogue with God. This, in Ostow's (1995) terms, constitutes 'ultimate intimacy'.

Technical implications

Any consideration of the therapeutic implications of intimacy needs to begin by delineating the place such experience occupies in a given psychoanalytic therapy of human development. Two opposite conceptualizations exist. In the classical model (Freud, 1905b, 1915b), seeking release of instinctual tension is the main psychic motivator and the 'object' (that which will facilitate tension reduction) is secondary to the instinct's 'aim' (the particular tension which needs to be discharged). In the later emergent object relations model, "libido is fundamentally object seeking" (Fairbairn, 1963, p. 224), attachment needs are supraordinate to instinctual gratification (Bowlby, 1958), and the child has an 'intimacy need' from the very beginning of his life (Sullivan, 1953). The classical perspective reluctantly permits the value of object specificity, but more on the level of experientially evolved wishes than on the level of hard-wired developmental needs. The object relations perspective emphasizes that fulfilment of intimacy need specifically involving the mother is essential to normal growth and development of the child. The two perspectives yield different therapeutic stances.

The classical perspective discourages intimacy with the patient. It advocates anonymity and abstinence on the therapist's part. Freud's use of the 'surgeon' and 'mirror' metaphors (1912, pp. 115, 118) underscored the dispassionate and personally 'uninvolved' stance that he deemed optimal for the therapist to assume. While he acknowledged the "healing power of love" (1907, p. 22) and even said that "our cures are cures of love" (Freud, cited in Nunberg and Federn, 1962, p. 101), officially, he recommended that the doctor "should be opaque to this patients" (1912, p. 118) and must avoid giving personal information or even a glimpse of his feelings to the patient. Admonitions of this sort encouraged subsequent analysts to adopt a remote and distant stance from the patient's subjective emotionality. A tragic limit was reached when Hartmann (1960) declared that "analytic therapy is a kind of technology" (p. 21). Thus was born a 'non-relational' or what I call 'motherless' psychoanalysis.

Disagreements with such pseudo-scientific austerity were evident from the earlier days of psychoanalysis. Ferenczi (1928, 1931) placed emotional contact between the analyst and the patient at the centre of what was therapeutic about psychoanalysis. And, his attitude was reflected in the later writings of his pupil, Balint (1953, 1968). In the United States, it is the organizationally side-lined and academically unsung Sullivan (1953) who championed this cause. He emphasized that the human need for emotional contact with others is innate and the failure to meet this need leads to disorganization in childhood and loneliness in adult life. Sullivan's notion of treatment included the therapist's becoming, by his very warmth and humanity, a useful presence that transcends transferential fantasy and satisfies the need for intimacy. Representing this way of thinking, Ferreira (1964) stated that "in psychotherapy, it is not the explanation but the experience that counts" (p. 193). Developing the proposal further, Levenson (1974) declared that all interpretations are, in the end, acts of countertransference. The analyst "must not use himself as a tool to lever the patient into change" (p. 365). An additional feature to such therapeutic approach is for the analyst to share something subjective of himself with the patient. In Hirsch's (1983) words, "the exposure of the self of the analyst and the self of the patient reflects analytic intimacy" (p. 327). The analyst's resonating with the patient's experience and helping him find more nuances of it within himself is what is therapeutic about psychoanalysis. This is what I term the 'fatherless' version of psychoanalytic technique.

This classical–relational divide has had many incarnations, beginning with Freud–Ferenczi disagreements through the Klein–Balint schism, down to the current tension between the 'modern ego psychology' and relational, intersubjective approaches to technique. The names keep changing and lineages are highlighted or denied[12] but issues remain the same. The technical impacts of this divergence are too extensive to cover here and we need to keep a tight focus on the issue of intimacy.

In the classical technique, the demand for free association 'forces' the patient to reveal his fantasies and secrets while the analyst remains 'opaque'. This does not seem to qualify as intimacy especially if the mutuality and bilaterality are held as its central ingredients. How can the patient be intimate if the analyst is reserved? In the relational technique, the subjective experience of the patient is regarded as always valid and a shared responsiveness and openness in the clinical dyad is recommended. The therapist is discouraged from ascribing greater significance to his understanding of the patient's experience. Kohut (1977) and Schwaber (2007) both support such 'anti-interpretation posture', though from differing theoretical bases. Nosek (2009) is even more vocal in this regard.

If we are prepared to forgo the violence of knowledge, if we are not incited by the urgency of ontology and the power of positivism, we encounter the territory of hospitality; this means receiving the foreigner as such, allowing him his own existence. This gesture, configured as goodness, does not ennoble or exalt me; its character comes from the infinite to be received, unravelling my possibilities ... For us psychoanalysts, this is a radical hierarchical reflection; psychoanalysis is no longer a talking cure but a listening cure.

(p. 145)

Levenson (1974) seeks a compromise position by saying that "after the experience of the patient and therapist has been validated, a content interpretation has the value of supplying the patient with a coherent myth, an armature on which to hang the story" (p. 365). Giving a little more credit to the usefulness of interpretation, I have noted how the analyst needs to oscillate with the ebb-and-flow of his patient's material, making validating comments at one moment, and deciphering interventions at another (Akhtar, 2002).

The temptation here is to regard the intimacy born out of intersubjective attunement and interpretation derived from 'objective listening' (Akhtar, 2013a) as separate entities. The fact, however, is that an interpretative element is always embedded in the most affirmative of analyst's remarks. The following three vignettes exemplify this assertion.[13]

Clinical vignette: 10

Andrea Hooberman, a fifty-five-year-old divorced and childless schoolteacher, was in the clutches of deep anguish when she sought my help. A botched surgical operation had recently left her with a dysfunction that made it impossible for her to enjoy sex. She had also become fecally incontinent. Multiple consultations with physicians and surgeons confirmed that the damage was irreversible. While she had sued the original surgeon and was expecting a huge monetary settlement, this hardly consoled her.

In her work with me, Andrea would often break down and weep bitterly. Once, pulling herself out of such emotional flooding, she looked at me intently and asked: "So, what are *you* thinking?" Without a moment's delay, I responded: "Actually, I was having two thoughts. One, I want to find you a great surgeon who can fix your problem. And, two, I am thinking how can I kill you painlessly to relieve you of this unbearable suffering". Andrea looked at me, nodded, and mumbled: "Thank you."

Clinical vignette: 11

Lisa Fischetti, a twenty-one-year-old college student, was in treatment with me for a long-term sense of inferiority, inability to say 'no', and doubt about her self-worth. She came across as charming, intelligent, and witty, but felt that she had little to offer and would be of no interest to anyone worthwhile. The two things she acknowledged to be good in her life were her academic performance and the fact that she had developed a good friendship with her roommate. And then one day, a disaster happened: this friend of hers was run over by a drunk driver and died on the spot. Lisa was devastated.

In the session immediately following this accident, Lisa cried and cried: her body curled up in pain, her face wet with tears, her sobs and wails filling up the psychic space between us. I remained mostly silent till almost the end of the session when I said: "You know, being an analyst, I am not permitted to do certain things. Had I not been bound by such ethics, I would have gotten up from my chair and given you a long and tight hug." Lisa looked up, met my eyes, and nodded with understanding and gratitude.

Clinical vignette: 12[14]

Katherine O'Malley had lost her mother to lung cancer at the age of four-and-a-half. Although her father was very loving, her stepmother's duty-bound, anti-instinctual, and humourless attitude left Katherine with a life-long wound of maternal loss. She achieved great success in her profession, married, and raised two kids but always felt that something was missing from her life; a gnawing anguish persisted. This became worse when her teenage daughter got into drugs. Katherine now entered analysis and was surprised to discover the pervasive, even if subtle, effects of the childhood maternal loss upon her psychosocial functioning. Grieving that had been 'deferred' (Freud, 1918) now began in earnest and occupied centre stage for the first two years of her analysis.

In the fourth year, when such mourning seemed to have subsided, a disturbing external event re-kindled the grief. Katherine was overwhelmed and began crying profusely during one session. Barely able to stop heaving and sobbing, she said, "I thought it was over but surely, it is not". I felt moved to respond and said, "You know, two lines from a poem in my mother-tongue came to mind in response to what you just said. I know you will not understand them but let me recite them first and then I will translate them for you". After this, I recited, "*Kitne toofaN uthhaye aankhoN ne // Naao yaadoN ki doobti; hi nahiN*".[15] I then paused and said, "It means that how many, just how many storms my eyes have borne but this goddamn boat of memory never sinks". Feeling understood and well 'held', Katherine nodded and became calmer.

As would be readily evident, these vignettes have many elements in common. In all three instances, the patient was in the throes of powerful emotions and I was correspondingly moved. In all three instances, I made a certain kind of self-disclosure (in the first, of a fantasy I was having; in the second, of an act I would have performed were it not a clinical situation; and in the third, of my need to speak in my mother tongue that was not comprehensible to the patient). In all three instances, there was a marked authenticity and a spontaneity to my intervention. In all three instances, the patient's response to my intervention was feeling deeply understood.

Together these features make such interventions appear akin to what Bion (1970) has called 'acts of faith'; these refer to interventions that arise from a sudden intuition which, for one shining moment, has left all prior experience and knowledge behind. This is true if we focus on my speaking alone. However, if we pay attention to the relational matrix of these vignettes, then Stern et al.'s (1998) 'moments of meeting' seem a more apt designation. A 'moment of meeting' is "a newly created dyadic state ... [and] the point at which the intersubjective context gets altered" (p. 913). Stern et al. emphasize that interpretations can lead to a 'moment of meeting' and a 'moment of meeting' can lead to an interpretation.[16] I agree and add that comments made during such moments carry both affirmative-validating and interpretative-unmasking elements in them.

Thus in the first vignette, my comment not only resonated with the help-lessness of the patient, it also unmasked the temptation towards omnipotence under such circumstances. Similarly, in the second vignette, my comment demonstrated that I was aware of how upset that patient was while simulta-neously deciphering the ordinary human desire for being comforted during grief. Finally, in the third vignette, the choice of the poetic piece was in attunement with the patient's suffering while the use of my mother tongue conveyed that I myself was less 'empty' and could offer her maternal nourishment. To go back to a comment I made in the developmental section of this chapter, both 'maternal intimacy' and 'paternal intimacy' were at work in unison. This, to my mind, erases the sharp distinction between offering intimacy and making an interpretation, thus bridging a schism that has long existed in our theory of technique.

Concluding remarks

In this chapter, I have surveyed the psychoanalytic literature on the concept of intimacy. From this review, I have culled seven components of intimacy, including trust, sharing of private experiences and feelings, relaxation of boundaries, overcoming of personal shame, empathy, tenderness, and transcendence of gender boundaries. I have discussed the developmental prerequisites for the capacity for such intimacy, emphasizing the role played by early maternal attunement to the child's needs and emotions and by the mother's ability to bear some distance from the child and encourage indivi-duation. I have noted that the refinement of the capacity for intimacy occurs in latency and adolescence and true intimacy is achieved by the merger of affection and sexuality at the onset of young adulthood. Following this, I have delineated four psychopathological derailments of this capacity: (i) failed intimacy, (ii) florid intimacy, (iii) fluctuating intimacy and, (iv) false intimacy. Then I have delved into the sociocultural realm as it pertains to the form, extent, and purview of intimacy. And, finally, I have elucidated the place of intimacy in the analytic situation, providing a few clinical illustrations that highlight the analyst's participation in such moments of deep contact.

Before concluding this discourse, I must add that in healthy individuals the capacity for intimacy is not compulsively deployed. It is under voluntary control; one can chose to be intimate with one person and not with another. One can also regulate the velocity of such development. Moreover, the capacity of intimacy does not preclude the ability to relate with others in a non-intimate manner. Even with one's lover, the degree of intimacy undergoes ebb and flow. In this vein and coming back full circle to where I started from, I conclude this contribution with another of my father's *shers* (couplets) which notes that the beloved who has become truly certain of the lover's devotion can become free, at times, to be lovingly indifferent towards him. The actual words of my father (J.N. Akhtar, 1964, p. 32) are:

Aitmaad-e-mohabbat to dekhe koi
Un meiN ik khaas begaana-pun aagaya.

Notes

1 Such literal translation of these couplets has resulted in a regrettable loss of their prosodic beauty. I therefore feel sorry for all three parties involved here – the poet, myself as an amateur translator, and the reader – for this loss.
2 A related question in today's world is whether intimacy – romantic or friendly – can be developed and sustained via electronic communication systems such as Skype, FaceTime, and instant chat applications. The knee-jerk reaction of scepticism regarding such relationships is rapidly becoming old-fashioned. People are carrying on all sorts of meaningful dialogues with each other on such social media: business-related, familial, romantic, erotic, bullying, and sexually perverse. Some of these contacts do qualify as 'intimate'. Psychoanalytically biased idealization of personal contact falls upon its face when we learn of well-meaning and distinguished colleagues conducting analytic treatments across nations and continents. To refute that they are involved in an intimate discourse is to take an ultra-conservative position that is becoming less and less defensible in the contemporary world.
3 Kafka's (1989) concept of the 'primary paradox of individuation' also touches upon this matter. According to him, healthy mother–child symbiosis permits the child to grow and step away from its mother. In such a setting, "love and mutual acceptance of separateness become subjectively equivalent" (p. 33).
4 A striking example of friendly intimacy was recently related by one of my supervisees. She was invited by a close friend of hers to be present in the labour

room as the latter delivered her first child. The friend's husband was also present there but since neither the friend nor her husband had medical backgrounds, the invitation to a physician friend provided healthy rationalization to what, at its depth, might have carried complex emotional motives. On the other hand, this gesture might have simple been a testimonial to friendly intimacy (Ariela Green, personal communication, 21 December 2017).

5 My proposal contains an echo of Herzog's (1984) homeostatic and disruptive attunements, i.e. maternal provision of validity and harmony, and paternal nudge towards self-expansion.

6 I have elsewhere (Akhtar, 2018) elucidated the concept of humility in considerable detail.

7 Freud and Jung, who reported talked incessantly for thirteen continuous hours upon meeting other for the first time (Gay, 1988) unfortunately did not do so well in the long run.

8 Like the proverbial 'return of the repressed', childhood keeps making ferocious claims upon the daily lives of adult Americans. The sight of people carrying water bottles with eyes fixed on their iPhone screens 'confirms' the continued oral-visual cathexis of the maternal breast. Vestimentary distinction between children and adults is blurred. Blockbuster movies centre upon superheroes, magical settings, and animation – all staples of children's imagination. And, television commercials are replete with animal (actually, animated) spokesmen pushing this or that merchandise. Together, such cultural phenomena reflect a desperate clinging to childhood among people who have not had their fill when they really were children.

9 Much to the disbelief of friends to whom I have told this, I was utterly fascinated by (and wanted to follow the lead of) Carmelite mendicants who take a vow of silence and spend their lives in cloistered prayer. More recently, my seeing the photographs of the fourth-century Sumela monastery in Turkey had a similarly alluring effect upon me.

10 While Khan does not specify it, my sense is that it needs a big dog to facilitate the owner's lying fallow. Most small dogs are too frisky and playful to provide such a holding function.

11 The fact is that a large number of books exist that are titled *Intimacy with God* (e.g. Heald, 2000; Keating, 2009; Jakes, 2013; Oberto, 2017).

12 For various 'political' reasons, the current relational analysts do not declare that their conceptual and theoretical ancestry goes back to Sullivan.

13 The names given to patients in these vignettes are fictitious.

14 This case has also been included elsewhere (Akhtar, 2015c) in a different context.

15 The line comes from a poem by the contemporary Urdu poet of India, Akhlaq Mohammad Khan Shahryar (1936–2012).

16 Yerushalmi (2013) has noted that theoretical developments encouraging analysts to create such moments increase the risk of countertransference enactments.

Part III

Titrating and transcending

Chapter 5

Humility

Very little has been written on humility in the field of psychoanalysis. PEP-Web (the electronic compendium of analytic literature of over one hundred years) lists ten papers with the word 'humility' in their titles but most of them focus upon the exhortation for psychoanalysts to exercise modesty and temper their enthusiasm for this or that theoretical persuasion. Only one paper (Weber, 2006) has something to say about the concept of humility itself. In addition to this paper, I have been able to locate a chapter on humility in Paul Marcus' (2013a) book, *In Search of the Spiritual: Gabriel Marcel, Psychoanalysis, and the Sacred* as well as a few passing remarks here and there in the psycho-analytic literature.

This lack of attention to humility is puzzling since (i) the clinical enterprise of psychoanalysis is based upon devoted care and non-selfish concern with the Other, (ii) psychoanalytic developmental theory upholds renunciation of omni-potence and working through the smug certainty of the 'paranoid position' in favour of the self-effacing modesty of the 'depressive position' (Klein, 1940), (iii) contemporary analysts frequently implore their colleagues for 'a measure of humility' (Richards, 2003) and to set aside the allure of theoretical 'purity', (iv) a vast majority of papers on psychoanalytic technique advocate the attitude of humility, and (v) almost all published obituaries of psychoanalysts extol the deceased's humility. All this suggests that 'humility' would be a topic of great interest to psychoanalysts. One expects them to eagerly explore its origins, aims, objects, and relational implications. That this is not true comes as a jolting surprise.

Descriptive characteristics

The English word 'humility' is derived from the Old French *umelite* and the Latin, *humilitas*. The former evokes the qualities of modesty and sweetness. The latter is a noun related to the adjective *humilis*, which can be translated as 'humble' but also as 'well-grounded', or 'from the earth'; the word *humus* in Latin means 'earth'. The dictionary definition of 'humility' characterizes it as "the state or quality of being humble ... freedom from pride and arrogance ...

a modest estimate of one's worth ... [and, also] an act of submission and courtesy" (Mish, 1987, p. 565). Although the word 'humility' appears frequently in a religious context, it is also used outside such context to denote an attitude of modesty and self-restraint from vanity.

Humility seems to enhance self-growth and deepen interpersonal relatedness. The 'lay' press is replete with short, simple, and quickly assembled books on the virtues of humility. Most of them come from Christian evangelists. However, there are three books (Whitfield et al., 2006; Worthington, 2007; Williams, 2016) that keep matters in the secular realm and offer some meaningful insights about humility. Whitfield et al. (2006) make the dialectical bond between humility and gratitude explicit, note that "humility allows for different interpretations of the same event" (p. 31),[1] and observe that humility anchors the self in its finitude. According to them, renunciation of pride and its relentless demands upon the mind opens up psychic space for recognizing the benefits one is drawing from the goodness of others. They also note that humility permits a re-framing of one's interpretative stance; "not attached to being 'right' or 'wrong', we become more inclusive of others and do not compete with their reality" (p. 31). And finally, Whitfield et al. (2006) underscore that humility facilitates (and is facilitated by) the acceptance of the time-limited nature of our existence. It grounds us in reality. Such salutary portrayal, however, leads them to subsume all sorts of desirable qualities under this rubric. They state that: "There are at least twelve key characteristics of humility. These include (1) openness, (2) an attitude of 'don't know', (3) curiosity, (4) innocence, (5) a child-like nature, (6) a spontaneity, (7) spirituality, (8) tolerance, (9) patience, (10) integrity, (11) detachment and (12) letting go" (p. 15). This seems to be an overextension of the concept of humility and detracts from the other, good ideas contained in the Whitfield et al.'s book.

Worthington's (2007) book emphasizes that humility unshackles the ego from self-serving drives and makes it interested in others' pursuits. In this respect, humility resembles altruism. But whereas altruism can exist without 'lowering' oneself, humility cannot. According to Worthington, humility rests upon our discovery and acceptance of "Something bigger than we are. The bigger – God, humanity, the environment, or the cosmos – differs across people, communities, and cultures. But the constant in the question is this: something is bigger than we are. And, we know it" (p. 43). Another feature of humility is that it is noticed more by others than by oneself. Indeed, self-evaluation of humility is always suspect since a truly humble person does not claim to have this "quiet virtue" (p. 17). Worthington goes on to say that maintaining humility over the lifespan and in varying circumstances is no easy task. However, active avoidance of pride, acceptance of one's limits, keeping one's mortality in mind, and cultivation of non-selfish interests can enhance the capacity for humility.

The third 'popular' book on humility is by Pat Williams (2016), the senior vice-president of the NBA's well-known team, Orlando Magic. Williams declares humility to be "a modest and realistic view of one's importance"

(p. 36) and, citing an anonymous source, adds that "humility does not mean thinking less of yourself. It just means thinking of yourself less" (p. 36). Williams goes on to emphasize that those who possess humility treat all others as equals and thus earn trust, respect, and loyalty. His book, even though a bit preachy, contains convincing illustrations of humility from the lives of not only great people like Washington, Lincoln, Gandhi, and Mandela but also from the lives of ordinary individuals. Williams' message is loud and clear: humility begets respect and that, in turn, can bring actual success. More importantly, he states that "humility is a choice" (p. 40) and follows this up by suggesting ways to enhance this personality trait: (i) taking time for self-reflection, (ii) inviting a few friends to be brutally honest with one, and (iii) readily acknowledging one's faults and failures. Williams' cognitive-behavioral approach needs to be 'softened' by the addition of insights that psychoanalysis has to offer on this matter.

Psychoanalytic literature

Freud's views

Freud used the word 'humility' a mere nine times in his entire writing (Guttman et al., 1980, p. 262). He valued this character trait and referred to Frau Emmy von N. as "a true lady" (Freud, 1895b, p. 104) since she possessed, among other qualities, a great "humility of mind" (p. 103). His other references to humility occur in the context of romantic love, man's awe of nature's majesty, and religion. While declaring that "traits of humility, of the limitation of narcissism, and of self-injury occur in *every case* of being in love" (1921, p. 113, emphasis added), Freud regarded the attitude of "humility and the sublime overvaluation of the sexual object characteristic of the male lover" (1920, p. 154). This was true even when the case he was discussing was that of a woman. Thus, in describing a girl's profound erotic attachment to an older woman, he referred to her "humility [as manifesting] the characteristic type of masculine love" (1920, p. 160). Such phallocentric bias in theorizing was also evident in his tracing the female hysterics' "humility towards their lovers" (1897, p. 244) to their dimly recalling the encounter with "the height from which the father looks down upon a child" (1897, p. 244) but never attributing a male lover's humility to a parallel ontogenetic encounter with the mother's height.[2]

A second context in which Freud remarked upon the experience of humility was in man's awe of the mysteries of nature. Talking of the great Leonardo Da Vinci, Freud (1910a) stated the following:

> A man who has begun to have an inkling of the grandeur of the universe with all its complexities and its laws readily forgets his own insignificant self. Left in admiration and filled with true humility, he all too easily forgets that he himself is a part of those active forces and that in

accordance with the scale of his personal strength the way is open for him to try to alter a small portion of the destined coursed of the world – a world in which the small is still no less wonderful and significant than the great.

(pp. 75–76)

In contrast to such 'true humility', Freud traced the "religious sense of humility" (1923, p. 37) to the individual and collective ego of man realizing that it has fallen far short of its wished-for ideal state. Curiously, the word 'humility' does not appear even once in Freud's (1927a) *The Future of an Illusion*, which posits man's struggle to bear his smallness vis-à-vis nature and mortality to be a major contribution to the origin of religious ideas. While interesting and even somewhat instructive, Freud's observations on 'romantic', 'true', and 'religious' humility were largely made in passing and did not delve into the exact nature of this emotional attitude.

Subsequent contributions

Although a few later psychoanalysts (e.g. Clark, 1932; Menninger, 1943; Feldman, 1953; Marcovitz, 1970a; Kirman, 1998) did mention humility in other contexts, only two (Weber, 2006; Marcus, 2013a) wrote papers specifically devoted to this topic. Weber acknowledged that "humility is a loaded word for Americans and escapees from our familiar organized religions" (p. 219) but went on to explore its dynamics in detail. She emphasized that humility necessitates that one renounce "both the arrogance of the superior ego and the wallowing victimization of the sense of inferiority" (p. 221). Unlike the polarities of narcissism and masochism, which draw all one's energy back into oneself, humility spreads the psychic energy broadly and connects one to others. It defeats egotism and prepares ground for respect and awe. Weber declared that human beings are connected to each other not because of instinctual needs or via the repetition of early attachments but owing to the fact that humility drives them to seek out the external world. She recommended that we "surrender humbly" (p. 219) to this inner command and declared that

> we are connected to life because life itself is perfect. Each of us, each moment we experience, is momentarily perfect, even when it is perfectly awful. We can know that perfection through our own experience, in fact only through our own experience. Our duty and our joy are to know it as well as we can, to be open to every vast and mysterious moment.
>
> (pp. 218–219)

Representative of the emerging consilience between psychoanalysis and Buddhism (Coltart, 1985; Epstein, 1995; Rubin, 2005; Hoffer, 2015), Weber anchored her proposal in the psychoanalyst Ghent's (1990) dictum that in each individual there exists "a longing for something in the environment to make possible the surrender, in the sense of yielding, of the false self" (p. 109). Weber's faith in the self-evident and absolute truth of each moment is akin to Bion's (1965) concept of 'O' though she herself does not make this connection.

Weber's 'psychoanalytic spirituality' finds a counterpart in Marcus' (2013a) paper on humility even though his views have little to do with Buddhism. Marcus' perspective arises from the contributions of Gabriel Marcel (1889–1973), a French philosopher, playwright, music critic, and leading Christian existentialist, which focused upon the modern individual's struggle in a technologically dehumanizing society. Drawing upon them, Marcus (2013a) notes that "humility always moves against the prison-house of the self-centric, against inordinate narcissism, selfishness, and other such neuroses" (p. 90). For Marcus, a well-cultivated sense of humility in daily life is "the basis of wholesome personal growth and development, enhanced communality, and a modicum of personal happiness" (p. 92). Humility is not an isolated character trait; it pervades one's entire being.

Marcus acknowledges Marcel's insistent linking of humility to faith in a supreme being – God – but struggles himself to retain a secular view of the attitude. He cites philosophers, scientists, and poets ranging from Socrates to T.S. Eliot and from Gandhi to Einstein in support of his proposal that, even without invoking God, humility involves the acknowledgement that one's self is not the centre of this universe. Thus, humility revolves around a process of radically "un-selving" (Smith, 2005, p. 104) oneself. This profoundly affects the relationship one has to oneself and to others.

Marcus highlights the 'self-relation' in humility as (i) mindfulness of one's relatively insignificant place in the larger scheme of things, (ii) awareness of the time-limited nature of one's existence, (iii) lack of preoccupation with oneself, (iv) realistic self-awareness that is devoid of both inferiority and arrogance, (v) capacity to admit to errors, (vi) openness to new ideas, and (vii) freedom from boredom. In relation to others, a humble person shows respect, hospitality, and non-exploitativeness.

> The humble person can relate to others with greater honesty and openness since he is not afraid to show his imperfections to them. He also sees the best in others and knows that he needs other people to live a satisfying, productive, and decent life, as does everyone. He graciously wants to pass on his "glory", his hard-earned insights on how to live a "good life" to others. He is more than willing to give someone a helping hand and, overall, he tends to a service mentality (serving others is almost always to some extent humbling, the humble spirit is always associated with kindness and compassion).
>
> (p. 106)

Weber's (2006) and Marcus' (2013a) contributions pretty much exhaust what psychoanalysis has to offer regarding the topic of humility. The existence of a few other passing remarks by others will become evident later in this chapter.

Synthesis and critique

Pooling together the various features attributed to 'humility', one finds that the attitude is comprised of (i) *a self-view* of being 'nothing special' without masochistic disavowal of one's assets, (ii) *an emotional state* of gratitude and tenderness, (iii) *a cognitive attitude* of openness to learning and considering one's state of knowledge as non-exhaustive, (iv) *a behavioural style* of interacting with others with attention, respect, and politeness, and (v) *an experiential capacity* for surrender and awe. Passed through the filter of classical metapsychology (Freud, 1915c, 1915d; Rapaport, 1960), the constituents of humility can be re-configured in the following way.

- *Topographic perspective*: the attitude of humility exists mostly on an unconscious basis, though its behavioural aspects might be preconscious or conscious.
- *Genetic perspective*: humility is an outgrowth of a combination of the infantile awe of parents, oedipal phase acceptance of generational differences, and latency phase wonder about the world-at-large. Later, adult life developments also contribute to it.
- *Economic perspective*: humility reflects a psychic state where the instinctual qualities (e.g. pressure, relief upon discharge, cyclical nature) of libido and aggression are renounced and neutralized energy flows peacefully towards the outer world.
- *Dynamic perspective*: humility arises from the ego's capacity to achieve a balance between self-deflation and self-inflation, and to maintain ongoing concern for others. There is also a peaceful tolerance of the gap between the ego and the ego-ideal.
- *Adaptive perspective*: humility results in a relational pattern that is disarming, trust-earning, and therefore interpersonally beneficial.

Humility is regarded as a component of dignity by Marcovitz (1970a); the latter is an elusive concept that has only recently come under psychoanalytic scrutiny (see Chapter Six of this book). Humility also has a close relationship with awe. And this has dual implications. The *first issue* pertains to the ontogenetic origin of the capacity for humility. The intermingling of humility with awe reflects a re-activation of the non-verbal subjective experience of the supine infantile eye. After all, the human infant spends its first year or so in a supine posture, looking upwards towards the much taller parents. Looking up thus becomes associated with safety and protection (and God comes to reside up in the heavens). Freud (1897) did hint at this root of humility but, in his characteristic phallocentrism, restricted it to the female gender only. The psychoanalyst who has elaborated on this notion more meaningfully is Ostow (2000). He declares that:

> Since awe seems to be a response to major discrepancies of scale, it would seem reasonable to attribute its origin to the earliest experiences of the infant who must be impressed by, and responds to, the large sizes, loud sounds, and bright lights that he first encounters at the hands of his parents and the world in which they live. It is inconceivable that there is no affective response to the enormous scale of these perceptions, though it would seem impossible to retrieve them ... I do not know that the awe we experience as adults reproduces literally the affect of this early experience; it may be that the activation of the non-declarative residues of the early experience now yields an affective experience different from that which it originally elicited, but I would suspect that it resembles it in some way.
>
> (pp. 206–207)

To such early infantile experiences, later encounter with oedipal realities[3] and with the latency age requirement to respect school-based hierarchies give further colouration. Awe of parents spreads to that of teachers, principals, and national heroes, strengthening the capacity for humility. All in all, the cadence of humility arises from a safe, bearable, and well-protected sense of smallness that exists in relation to the bigness of others.

The *second issue* raised by the correlation of awe with humility is the essentially hybrid nature of this concept. Like identity (Erikson, 1950) or forgiveness (Akhtar, 2000), the experience of humility is partly intrapsychic and partly interpersonal. And, the latter dimension is not restricted to the human realm; it extends to the non-human environment. This stretches our conventional psychoanalytic theory to its limits.[4] No wonder that psychoanalysts, being uneasy with hybrid concepts of this sort, have tended to avoid the topic all together. The close association between humility and religion has also played a role in their disinterest. With the advent of modern 'anthropological psychoanalysis' (Akhtar, 2013d), however, the possibility of thinking about such concepts has expanded.

Sociocultural realm

Two areas especially demand attention when it comes to the sociocultural dimension of humility. The first pertains to religion and the second to the East–West difference.

Humility across religions

As far as the religious variable is concerned, it is almost reflexive to associate humility with Christianity. The glut of 'popular' books on this topic written by evangelist Christians lends credence to such an impression. And, it is true that the New Testament of the Bible contains passages that are so often quoted as to become a part of daily speech. Take a look at the following.

- "Blessed are the meek for they shall inherit the earth" (Matthew 5: 5).
- "He who exalts himself will be humbled and he who humbles himself will be exalted" (Matthew 23: 12).
- "Do nothing out of selfish ambition or vain conceit. Rather, in humility, value others above yourselves" (Philippians 2: 3).

Moreover, all Christian saints, especially St Augustine and St Thomas Aquinas, uphold humility as a fundamental virtue. Saint Bernard went on to declare Jesus Christ to be the ultimate definition of humility. More recently, C.S. Lewis (1942) declared pride to be an 'anti-God' state and humility to be the true moral stance. All this, and more, has led to a compact of essentialism between humility and Christianity. The fact, however, is that all religions of the world extol the attitude and encourage their followers to adopt it.

Within the other two Abrahamic faiths, Judaism and Islam, there are numerous such 'reminders'. The Old Testament regards humility as a sign of Godly strength and purpose and states that "Moses was a man exceeding meek above all men than dwelt upon earth" (Numbers 12: 3). It underscores the relationship between humility, wisdom, and inner peace and explicitly declares that "God opposes the proud but gives grace to the humble" (Proverbs 3: 34). The influential writings of Jewish philosophers Martin Buber (1878–1965) and Emmanuel Levinas (1906–1995) have consistently emphasized the moral significance of humility. And, Rabbi Lord Jonathan Sacks, perhaps the most respected Jewish theologian of our times, has written that:

> Humility – true humility – is one of the most expansive and life-enhancing of all virtues. It does not mean under-valuing yourself. It means valuing other people. It signals a certain openness to life's grandeur and the willingness to be surprised, uplifted, by goodness wherever one finds it ... Humility, then, is more than just a virtue: it is a form of perception, a language in which the "I" is silent so that I can hear the "thou", the unspoken call beneath human speech, the Divine Whisper within all that moves, the voice of others that calls me to redeem its loneliness with the touch of love. Humility is what opens us to the world.
>
> (Chabad.org, pp. 1–2)

The youngest of Abrahamic religions, Islam, too, celebrates the virtue of humility. The following three quotations from the Quran should suffice to illustrate this, though more examples can readily be given.

- "The servants of the Most Merciful are those who walk upon the earth in humility, and when the ignorant address them, they say words of peace" (Surah-al-Furqan 25: 63).
- "Remember your Lord in yourselves with humility and in private without announcing it in the mornings and evenings, and do not be among the heedless" (Surah-al-A'raq 7: 205).
- "Lower to your parents the wing of humility and of mercy and say: My Lord have mercy upon them as they brought me up when I was small" (Surah-al-Isra 17: 24).

Besides these passages from Quran, there are multiple sayings of Mohammad that uphold humility and its propitious impact upon human bonds.

- "Verily, Allah has revealed to me that you must be humble towards one another, so that no one wrongs another or boasts to another" (Sunnah, reported by Iyad ibn Haman).
- "There is no human being except that the wisdom of his mind is in the hands of an angel. When he shows humility, the angel is ordered to increase his wisdom. When he shows arrogance, the angel is ordered to decrease his wisdom" (Sunnah, reported by Ibn-Albas).

Eastern religions such as Hinduism, Buddhism, Jainism, Sikhism, and Taoism similarly champion the silent force of humility. Sanskrit, the language of Hindu scriptures, contains many words that convey the essence of humility: *viniti* (kindness), *samniti* (respect of others), *amanitvam* (pridelessness), and *namrata* (modest behaviour). And, the great *Bhagwad Gita* (circa second century BCE) explains humility to mean the lack of desire to be honoured by others. Outside of religious texts, though emanating from them, Gandhi (1940) emphasized three aspects of humility: (i) it is an internal state and does not refer merely to good manners, (ii) it cannot be cultivated; it is foundational, and (iii) it does not make itself evident to consciousness; a humble person is not aware of his humility. And between the ancient religious texts and the mid-twentieth-century proposals of Gandhi lies a huge corpus of Hindu philosophy and spiritual exegesis that elucidates humility. The three important derivatives of Hinduism, namely Buddhism, Jainism, and Sikhism, all consider humility to be a virtue and decry conceit and overconfidence. The Far Eastern religion, Taoism, defines humility by an extended Chinese phrase instead of a single word: "*Bugan wei tianxia xian*", which means "daring not to be at the world's front" (cited in Chen, 1989, p. 209). To be in front is to court death while to stay behind is to allow oneself time to fully ripen and bear the fruit of wisdom. All in all, it can be said that both the religions derived from the Abrahamic faith (Judaism, Christianity, and Islam) and from Eastern belief systems (Hinduism, Buddhism, Jainism, Sikhism, and Taoism) uphold humility as a virtue.

Humility across cultures

If all aspects of human life were regulated by religion, the foregoing state-ment would imply a uniform prevalence of the character trait of humility across the globe. But since modal personality patterns, to the extent such generalizations are possible, emerge from a large variety of factors which go far and beyond religious belief (economy, history, folklore, child-rearing practices, ecology, nationalistic agendas, and so on), it seems reasonable to ask whether the prevalence of humility as a character trait is uniform or variable across cultures? No hard data is available to answer this question. However, there are some studies of leadership styles that do shed light on this matter. The prominent Dutch social psychologist, Geert Hofstede (2001), for instance, has found that some countries (e.g. Russia) have high 'power distance' scores (93 on a 1–100 scale), whereas others (e.g. the United States) have far lower scores (40 on a 1–100 scale). This means that organizational leaders in Russia prize hierarchy, inequality, and a top-down decision-making approach whereas those in the United States value collaboration, informality, and team-driven decision-making. Paradoxically, 'subordinates' in Russia display submissiveness and humility whereas 'sub-ordinates' in the United States are encouraged to be independent and contribute to problem-solving.

Commenting upon the parallel difference in the world of pedagogy, I have elsewhere observed that:

> In Western countries, especially the United States, the apprentice (be it a young mechanic or a medical student) is expected to ask questions and learn by active engagement with his teachers. Too quick agreement with what the teacher says is viewed with suspicion. The relationship between the teacher and apprentice is based upon mutual respect and cordiality; it strives to stay away from authoritarianism. In the East, typically, the situation is reverse (Roland, 1988; Moore, 2009). The teacher is authoritarian. His word is not to be questioned. The apprentice is to learn by submission and emulation, not by questioning and challenging the teacher. The relationship between the two is sombre and leaves little doubt about the teachers' authority over the student. If such differences are not taken into account, a Western apprentice (say in yoga, martial arts, or Tibetan Buddhism) in the East can come across as disrespectful to his Eastern mentors. And, an Eastern apprentice in the West can appear inhibited and neurotically tongue-tied. Clearly, misunderstand-ing of this sort can create problems at the workplace. Also to be kept in mind is the fact that over time, these differences in the apprenticeship patterns affect what kind of teacher the respective apprentices become. The assertive and questioning apprentice of the West, over the course of time, turns into a teacher who is modest and willing to be challenged.

The humble and submissive apprentice of the East, in contrast, becomes a more forceful teacher expecting his word to be taken on surface, and without questions asked.

(Akhtar, 2011e, p. 44)

Yet another perspective on the difference vis-à-vis humility between East and West comes from Roland's (1988, 1996) anthropological studies of India and Japan. Roland proposes that unlike highly individualized Westerners (especially North Americans), Indians and Japanese have a powerful familial and spiritual dimension to their selves. Their 'we-self' enhances concern for others and identification with the reputation and honour of their families. Moreover, there is a spiritual flavour to the individuals' existence: this is expressed in India via rituals and meditation and in Japan via aesthetics and communion with nature. Roland asserts that the individualized self typical of Americans is less prominent among Indians and Japanese whose narcissistic cathexis is submerged in the twin rivers of connection and compression. Greater space of humility thus becomes available to them.

Finally, there is the information forthcoming from culturally sensitive studies of self-enhancement patterns. Heine et al. (1999) went so far as to suggest the need for self-enhancement is not universal; it manifests only in some cultures and is most marked in the United States. Their claim was vociferously disputed by a number of subsequent studies (for a comprehensive listing of these, see Lee et al., 2014) which asserted that the difference resided not in the extent of the desire for self-enhancement but in the way people in different cultures went about enhancing their selves. Many such studies found that humility functions as a useful tool for maintaining harmony in collectivist cultures and hence is an important regular of self-esteem (Kim and Cohen, 2010; Lee et al., 2014). A cross-cultural study of Chinese and American subjects (Cai et al., 2011) found that the former reported increased self-respect when instructed to be as modest as possible while the latter did not. The result suggests that being humble is instrumental for self-enhancement in Eastern cultures but not in Euro-American cultures.

Pooling together all the sociocultural observations mentioned above yields a broad-based notion that the trait of humility might be more marked in non-Western cultures. For the clinician who must draw conclusions from deeper contact with a single individual, this information can serve as a gentle reminder to scan his or her non-Western patients' material with a culturally sensitive lens. And, this brings us back to considering the pertinence of humility in the clinical realm.

Psychopathology

Like any other positive personality attribute, humility is subject to distortion and morbidity. Elsewhere, I (Akhtar, 2013e) have delineated the psychopathological syndromes involving generosity, gratitude, and forgiveness. Here, I focus upon the maladaptive variants of humility, including (i) excessive humility, (ii) deficient humility, (iii) false humility, and (iv) compartmentalized humility. Brief comments on each follow.

Excessive humility

There are individuals who are simply too 'humble' and are forever ready to help others. They cannot accept compliments. They underestimate their strengths and often verbally indulge in self-depreciation. Between the polarities of pride and self-abnegation, they seem to have tilted too far in the latter direction. Herein lies an important theoretical and clinical point. Klein's (1940) 'paranoid' and 'depressive' positions are respectively characterized by omnipotence, self-congratulatory certainty, and externalization of all 'badness' *and* by modesty, gratitude, and tolerance of ambivalence. This has given rise to the common misunderstanding that the 'paranoid' position is always unhealthy and the 'depressive' position is always healthy. What is overlooked in this dichotomous vision is that, at times, the opposite is true. Skills of political oratory, trial law, and editorial scrutiny of a manuscript, for instance, benefit by a 'paranoid' position. And, the self-flagellation of the melancholic gives evidence to the 'depressive position' gone awry. Excessive humility wipes out the psychic traces of healthy narcissism and thus represents a morbid extreme of the 'depressive position'. However, 'excessive humility' is not 'false' (see 'false humility' below). It does not mask grandiosity or caricature inferiority. It is merely a guilty intensification of humility that resides in the individual. Excessive humility is a collusive concoction of a ferocious superego and a slavish ego.

Deficient humility

This symptom constitutes the 'negative twin' of pathological narcissism. Experiencing and expressing humility requires lowering oneself in the given matrix of object relations; the self is accorded less value than the object. Taking such a 'risk' is difficult for a pathological narcissist. Continually warding-off this inferiority-laden and morose self-representation (Kernberg, 1984; Akhtar, 1989), such an individual cannot bring himself to say 'sorry' or 'thank you', both of which acknowledge the higher status of his object. Full of self-concern, the narcissist is empty of remorse and gratitude. He lacks humility. And, so does the antisocial individual who holds the world accountable for his humiliating and deprived childhood.

False humility

Not all that looks like humility is humility. Many mental mechanisms can lead to the appearance of humility while matters at the psychic core are quite different. In fact, the spectrum of such 'false humility' is broad. On its benign end resides the air of 'affected humility' (Feldman, 1953) that one sometimes encounters in poets and artists. On the malignant end, is the anti-social individuals' crafty façade of humility for extracting favors from others. Superego-driven reaction formation against anal-phase megalomania can give one's character a flavour of undue reticence which is mistaken for humility (Menninger, 1943). In the 'shy narcissist' (Akhtar, 2000), the competing pressures of exhibitionism and modesty can also result in false humility.

False humility needs to be distinguished from what Green (1986) has termed 'moral narcissism'. The falsely humble person wears his self-effacement on his sleeve and desires admiration from onlookers. In contrast, the moral narcissist seeks to destroy his instinctual needs and free himself from all libidinal ties to others. Both of them can appear self-depriving but the former is propelled by object hunger and the latter by an attack against that very hunger.

An entirely different pathway for the evolution of false humility is via the defence called 'denial by exaggeration' (Fenichel, 1945). Here, a person correctly estimates his status in a given relationship as low but plays up this inferiority for moralistic and sadomasochistic purposes Long before the description of this mechanism though, Clark (1932) had noted that "many children are known to disguise their underlying neuroses by a mock humility" (p. 48).

Compartmentalized humility

In certain individuals, the sector of personality that is suffused with genuine politeness and humility shows a 'mirror complimentarity' (Bach, 1977) with another sector of personality that is brimming with self-centeredness and vanity. Dramatic examples of this in the lives of renowned individuals (e.g. politicians and socially conscious movie personalities) draw great public attention but 'compartmentalized humility' can as easily be found in less illustrious citizens. Regardless of their social stature, those with compartmentalized humility can be seen performing humble acts of religious devotion and public service on the one hand and exercising ruthless control over their subordinates and children on the other. The important point to remember here is that their subjective experience of both extremes is authentic and devoid of fakery. Thus, Gandhi could clean latrines and stay overnight in the poor abodes of India's 'untouchables', but could also be "extremely dictatorial when dealing with his closest relatives or followers" (Kapoor, 2017, p. 117); when enraged, he could easily slap his wife. His humility, even though marked and genuine, was certainly compartmentalized.

Technical implications

As we begin to consider the role of humility in clinical work, we are immediate struck by a peculiar contradiction in our profession's attitude towards this matter. On the one hand, there exist numerous – in fact, too numerous to mention here – reminders in the literature on psychoanalytic technique that one ought to sustain an attitude of humility. On the other hand, none of these remarks explains what humility is and how exactly having this attitude might affect clinical technique. Dissatisfied with such unhelpful complacency and having given the matter serious thought, I have concluded that humility plays – or should play – an important role in the way we: (i) select the patients with whom we work, (ii) conduct ourselves vis-à-vis matters of daily life with our patients, (iii) listen to our patients, (iv) speak with our patients, and (v) decide about the longevity of our professional careers as psychoanalysts.

Humility in selecting patients

Before saying anything at all about this matter, it should be acknowledged that not all clinicians have the luxury of selecting who they work with. Young professionals who are just opening a private practice might therefore wince at my idea of 'selecting' patients and even consider it a bit arrogant. I acknowledge that, with gaining some experience and after getting more or less established, one does acquire greater choice in what sort of individual one would take into treatment. However, upon closer scrutiny, the matter turns out to be less simple than this.

The widespread, even though unspoken, assumption that any psychoanalyst can help any patient is open to question. No one says this publicly but when analysts refer a patient to someone, they often select the colleague who will be 'best' for that particular person.[5] In this choice is embedded the unmentalized belief that other analysts might not do so well by this patient and it will not be too far-fetched to assume that a few others might not be at all suitable for this particular referral. And this should not be surprising. After all, psychoanalyst have their own 'pathos' and 'ethos' just as does the patient and a reasonable 'fit' between such interpersonal concavities and convexities is best for a decent therapeutic alliance to emerge. Of course, such 'fit' must not become a nidus for 'shared ethnic scotoma' (Shapiro and Pinsker, 1973), 'nostalgia collusions' (Akhtar, 2006), and countertransference-based 'deaf spots' (Akhtar, 2013a).

Let me put it bluntly. All of us do better work with certain kinds of patients than others. Whether the determining factor is diagnosis, age, race, religion, gender, social class, sociopolitical leanings, or something more elusive remains variable. Some psychoanalysts seem to work better with severely traumatized patients, others do not. Some can retain the same quality of empathy and efficiency with patients of diverse cultural backgrounds, others cannot. A few have the knack of working with sociopathic individuals while most others get uneasy and avoid taking such patients into their practices. Some can work with older individuals. Others are better with children and adolescents.

Besides such patient-related variables, there are state and trait variables in psychoanalysts themselves that can and should affect patient selection. Here are a few questions to ponder upon:

- Should an analyst who is undergoing a bitter and contentious divorce take a new analytic patient, especially one with serious marital difficulties?
- Is it appropriate for an analyst over eighty years of age, no matter how physically healthy he or she is, to start a fresh analysis?
- Can a stridently atheistic psychoanalyst treat a deeply religious patient in a meaningful manner?

The point I am trying to make is simply this: we psychoanalysts accept our characterological and situational limitations and exercise utmost humility in taking on patients. We delude ourselves if we hold on to the idea that we can treat anyone who shows up at our doors. The fact is that most of us cannot do so and will do great service to those seeking our counsel by sending them to others who might be better situated to help. A related consideration here is also of differential therapeutics. Being a psychoanalyst should not make one overlook that other treatment modalities (e.g. couple's therapy, family therapy, medication, ECT) might, at times, be better for the individual sitting in our offices. Psychoanalysis is not the treatment for all emotional suffering and psychoanalysts are not the only useful mental health professionals.

Humility in our daily conduct with patients

Elsewhere, I have commented upon the need for the analyst to behave in accordance with 'good manners' (Akhtar, 2009d). I also entered some caveats to his doing so. Here, I wish to extend that discussion to the analyst conducting himself with humility. To be sure, judicious accommodations of the therapeutic frame to the patients' cultural idiom (Akhtar, 1999b, 2011e), adjustment of fee during periods of patients' financial difficulties, respecting the patient's academic- or work-related absences, and other sundry 'silent sacrifices' (David Sachs, personal communication, 15 April 2001) give evidence to the analyst's humility. However, there is something deeper at stake here.

It is by regarding the patient to be a full human being, capable of moral and, yes, therapeutic, reciprocity and by discarding the view of the patient as infantile and unwanted, that the analyst shows true humility. Viewing both the patient and himself as 'works in progress' and capable of further growth is yet another constituent of the analyst's humility. In elaborating upon such matters, Frank (2004) reminds us that the analyst, having been the beneficiary of a training analysis, carries within himself the "obligation of the cured" (p. 55) and this imparts tenderness and humility to his stance. Griffith (2010) evokes the writings of the Jewish philosopher, Emmanuel Levinas (1906–

1995), who proposed that ethical relatedness to the Other is the foundational stone of the psychic self and requires the acceptance of difference. Erasing self–other distinction leads to totalization and sets the stage for domination and control. Commitment to dialogue, in contrast, endorses a relation to the Other while accepting the autonomy of both parties. No partner in a dialogue has all the answers and each can enrich the process between them.

While applicable to all clinical situations, this stance becomes even more important when a cultural chasm exists between the therapist and the patient. Here, a position of 'cultural humility' (Tervalon and Murray-Garcia, 1998) is badly needed. It encourages the therapist to be open-minded, accept his ignorance of the patient's ethos, and learn from the patient. For instance, the therapist with cultural humility asks a culturally diverse patient how his or her name is pronounced, rather than making it up himself. It should be noted that the stance of 'cultural humility' has the prerequisite of 'cultural neutrality' (Akhtar, 1999b, pp. 113–116). Cultural neutrality means that the therapist does not assume any particular culture to be inherently superior than another. Holding such a belief is in essence "anti-humanity and in the widest sense, anti-sanity" (Kareem, 1992, p. 21). It is only by sustaining cultural neutrality that the therapist can achieve a state of cultural humility.

Humility in the act and attitude of listening

Listening is in itself an act of humility. One can discern in it the remote echoes of an infant taking in the maternal breast and a near-archetypal identification with receptivity of the maternal vagina to the father's penis. Listening involves creating internal space for someone else. It is essentially an act of surrender and its servile dimension (if the expression can be used without any derogatory implications) becomes more marked when listening is done with "evenly suspended attention" (Freud, 1912, p. 111). One does not exert personal choice and listens with equal consideration to all that is offered.

Resolute avoidance of listening in only one way (i.e. objective, subjective, empathic, and intersubjective; for elaboration on these models, see Akhtar, 2013b) and from only one theoretical perspective (e.g. Freudian, Kleinian, Winnicottian) is also evidence of an analyst's humility. To listen in only one way and from only a theoretical perspective narrows the analyst's receptive capacities and pushes him towards arrogance. He 'knows' what the patient means. In an admittedly exaggerated fashion, I have portrayed the impact of such heuristic arrogance upon the analyst's listening.

An "ego psychologist" sees only drive-defense sort of compromises in the patient's material. A "Kernbergian" sees idealization as a defense against regression and a "Kohutian" sees it as a resumption of a thwarted developmental need. A "Mahlerian" regards patients' fluctuating levels of intimacy as representing merger-abandonment anxieties while a "relationist" sees a craftily enacted scenario of mutual teasing and seduction in the same oscillation. A "Kleinian" views patients' hatred of the analyst's silence as an envious attack on a withholding breast while a "Winnicottian" views that very outrage as manifestation of hope (that the analyst can "survive" the patient's assault) and therefore of love!

(Akhtar, 2013a, p. 107)

Such listening lacks humility. It declares that one theoretical perspective of psychoanalysis is inherently superior to others and is the preferred model for all sorts of clinical material and all varieties of patients. In contrast is the listening attitude of the analyst who is forever mindful of the 'principle of multiple determination' (Waelder, 1936) and of the 'four psychologies of psychoanalysis' (Pine, 1988), with their own respective claims upon the hermeneutics of the clinical exchange. The psychoanalyst who can oscillate between various levels of attunement (Killingmo, 1989), maintain allegiance to the existence of multiple determinants of all psychic material, and be comfortable with diverse theoretical models shows humility. Greater 'analytic humility' might also be inherent in the current two-person, intersubjective perspective on listening provided it is not carried to an extreme.[6]

Humility in the manner of intervening

It is rare that a working analyst feels suddenly, sharply, and absolutely clear about what is going on between him and his patient, which aspect of it needs to be interpreted, and in what manner and to what extent. Such moments of uncanny clarity do occur (Bion, 1967, 1970; Brottman, 2011) but are infrequent and sporadic. Most of the time, the work of analysis involves patient listening, careful 'collection' of data (within a single session or spanning over many sessions), clarification, development of 'conjectures' (Brenner, 1976) and then making interpretations or reconstructions. Throughout such work, an attitude of tentativeness is maintained. This attitude is mostly private and allows the analyst (on a preconscious or unconscious basis) to mull over the material, cross-check competing hypotheses, sort out countertransference, and 'choose' the most suitable form and extent of the intervention to be made. At other times, the tentativeness might be shared with the patient. For instance, the analyst might say something like this: "You know, what you are saying seems like the very complaint that you have voiced, at other times, about your sister, and actually about me as well. What do you think? Does this make sense?" At another occasion, the analyst might 'invite' the patient to consider his 'still-not-so-clear-about-it' sort of interpretation. Thus, the analyst might say: "Allow me, please, to put a thought in front of you and see what you make of it. I am not sure about this but, behind this reserve of yours, I sense a deep anxiety about loving. Do you have any further thoughts about this?"

Ehrenberg's (1995) recommendation of "inviting the patient to engage collaboratively" (p. 215) in the therapeutic exchange reflects this very spirit. At the same time, I am aware that some colleagues regard such manner of talking 'too didactic' and 'Freudian pussy-footing' (as a senior Kleinian analyst once referred to it). I, for one, believe that maintaining such humility precludes the sort of certainty that we analysts can rarely possess. It also demonstrates to the patient an open and receptive attitude towards not only our interventions but towards his or her own therapeutic strivings.

A related measure pertains to the analyst's occasionally demystifying the basis for his interventions. The German analyst, Helmut Thomä, has written most cogently on this topic. He suggests that the analyst not only explain, at the outset, why free association is required but, from time to time during the treatment, share with the patient his reasons for making a particular intervention. Thomä states that "it is nothing special for me to offer a patient insight into my psychoanalysis thinking" (cited in Thomä and Kachele, 1994, p. 86). In fact, he feels that decisive and salutary shifts in the relationship between transference and therapeutic alliance can occur as a result of such disclosure.

Yet another manifestation of humility in the analyst's manner of speaking is his persistent regard for the principles of 'over-determination' (Freud, 1895b) and 'multiple function' (Waelder, 1936). The analyst makes interventions that are inclusive of psychic and external reality of multiple vectors in psychic reality, and of his and the patient's take on the material under consideration. Moreover, the analyst remains open to correction by the patient, to seek consultation from colleagues when in difficulty, and to apologize to the patient (Goldberg, 1987) if he makes a 'hurtful' mistake in his behaviour or interventions.

Humility in deciding upon the longevity of our professional careers

A footnote I appended to my elucidation of greed (2014a), including analytic greed, read as follows:

> An analytic colleague and a good friend, Ira Brenner, told me that early on in his career, he marveled at senior analysts who kept working well in their eighties, and sometimes even in their nineties. With greater maturity, he has tempered this idealization and thinks that a combination of love of psychoanalysis, anxiety about aging, and greed for prestige and money drives such professional longevity (personal communication, November 6, 2013). This latter dynamic became especially apparent to me during a recent visit to a North American psychoanalytic institute where younger training analysts confided their dismay at their seniors' (who were far along in their eighties) grabbing all the attractive and well-paying applicants for training analyses.
>
> (p. 65)

This sad state of affairs came even closer to my own experience when an eighty-two-year-old colleague asked me to support his starting a new training analysis since his institute had raised objections to it. And, incredible though it might sound, more recently in a North American psychoanalytic institute, a ninety-two-year-old training analyst expressed his desire to take on a fresh candidate into treatment.

Clearly, such practices betray an alarming degree of arrogance. The denial of aging, increased potential for infirmity, and the proximity with one's own death[7] in such cases is truly disturbing. Even under the rationale and rationalization of continuing good health, continuing to take on new analytic patients beyond a certain age carries not only a kernel of arrogance but also of compromised ethics; after all, one is knowingly exposing the new patient to the potential of a devastating loss.

Fortunately a trend is now evolving where matters of aging and death are deemed topics for serious consideration. Many training institutes are setting age limits after which analysts may not take on new cases in analysis. But this is externally imposed. What about the analyst's own humility in limiting his or her professional career? The now-deceased San Francisco-based analyst, Alan Skolnikoff (1933–2016) has been the only colleague to have told me, when he was seventy-one years old, that he had decided to stop taking new analytic cases upon turning seventy-three and to restrict his practice to teaching, supervision, and finishing ongoing cases. This, to my mind, was an expression of great humility. Skolnikoff died at the age of eighty-three but it is to be noted that he was considering ending his career as an analytic clinician some twelve years before his death. Instead of quibbling over this or that number of years as the upper limit for continuing to practice as an analyst, we – all of us – need to exercise a modicum of humility in making such decisions and not go on and on despite failing bodies and minds.

Concluding remarks

In this chapter, I have delineated the phenomenological terrain, ontogenetic roots, sociocultural dimensions, psychopathological variants, and technical implications of the concept of humility. I have noted that humility comprises modesty, self-effacement, regard for a higher power be it religious or secular, openness to fresh input, and a capacity for awe. Humility arises from infantile respect for parents' psychophysical stature, is strengthened by phallic-oedipal surrender to them, and is deepened by the latency age wonder at the mysteries of the world-at-large. Humility is upheld by all religions as a virtue. However, the purported East–West difference in the trait is less clear. What *is* clear is that humility exists in both normal and pathological (e.g. excessive, deficient, false, and compartmentalized) forms. The conduct of psychotherapy and psychoanalysis is affected by the analyst's humility in multiple ways outlined in the immediately preceding section of this chapter.

Two issues still remain to be addressed. One pertains to gender and the other to the unfolding of the human lifespan. Let us take up the first issue. Are men more humble than women? Or, vice versa? And, if a difference does exist, what might be its explanation? Averse to generalizations, psychoanalytic literature has no answers to these questions. Turning to general psychology research, we find two interesting studies. The first, asking 213 American, 229 British, and 114 Japanese students to assess their own IQ levels and those of their parents and siblings (Furnham et al., 2001) revealed that, regardless of the country of origin, male students consistently noted their own, their fathers', and their brothers' IQs higher than those of their mothers and their sisters. This suggested a lack of humility in them as compared to their female counterparts who demonstrated no such bias in their assessments. A second study involving 202 Swedish students (Kajonius and Dåderman, 2014) found that the 'honesty-humility' trait was strongly correlated with liberal values and was endorsed at a higher level by women (M=12.8, SD=3.4) than men (M=12.0, SD=3.7). Meagre as research is in this area, it does suggest that on a 'gross' level, at least, men are less humble than women.[8]

The second unaddressed realm pertains to lifespan. It involves the question whether humility is a trait that is discernible early on or, like Erikson's (1950) 'generativity', makes its appearance only with mature adulthood? Little information is available to answer this question with certainty. However, it seems reasonable to assume that while the ingredients of humility (e.g. wonder, awe, gratitude) originate in childhood, its fully consolidated experience does not emerge until mid to late adulthood. It is only after experiencing a sustained sense of commonality with fellow human beings, the puncture of omnipotence in the process of child-rearing, and repeated encounter with limits and failures, that humility sets in. Aging and infirmity also affect one's value system and mobilize a re-assessment of one's place in this world; this enhances the capacity for humility. The acknowledgement and acceptance of one's approaching mortality acts as an even stronger stimulus for realizing the small space that one ultimately has occupied in this world. If one can bear this realization, one becomes truly humble. If not, one regresses into defensive omnipotence and conceit.

Talking of infirmity and old age and their relationship to the arrogance–humility dialectic brings to mind the following joke told to me by my friend, the noted historian, Norman Itzkowitz (personal communication, 21 April 2003).

A highly-respected teacher of Torah, Rabbi Goldstein, had turned ninety-three and was now quite frail. One day, while instructing three students who sat in great awe of him, the Rabbi fell asleep. Not daring to disturb him, the students spoke to each other in hushed whispers. One said: "I respect Rabbi Goldstein for his immense knowledge of the Torah". The second student said: "I agree with you but respect him more for how he imparts that knowledge to others". The third expressed his agreement with both of them and added that he respects the Rabbi even more for his living a life that is true to the Scriptures. At this time, Rabbi Goldstein opened one of his eyes, looked with bemused dismay at his three protégés, and said: "And, not a word about my humility?"

Notes

1 This aspect of humility is of great significance to the clinical enterprise of psychoanalysis, as will be highlighted in a later section of this chapter.
2 Another striking example of such bias in Freud's (1924a) thinking is his coining the term 'feminine masochism' based upon clinical work with two *male* patients who wished to be beaten.
3 In a frequently cited paper, Greenacre (1956) traced the human capacity for awe to the child's feelings about the larger bodies of parents and especially to his or her seeing the father's erect penis.
4 Most psychoanalysts view man's relationship to the known human environment as a displaced and symbolic derivative of his ties to the primary human objects. Only a few (Searles, 1960; Bollas, 1992, 2009; Akhtar, 2003) allow for the possibility that there might be a 'direct' relationship between man and 'things'.
5 The highly respected British psychoanalyst, Nina Coltart (1927–1997), was known for her skill of finding the analyst who would be best suited for the needs of a given patient. This talent earned her the affectionate moniker of 'The Matchmaker'!
6 Kirman (1998) has provided a thorough review of the literature on this matter.
7 Upon hearing the subtitle of one of my edited books, *Fear, Denial, and Acceptance of Death*, a prominent analyst said, "Well, I don't accept death". It took me some effort to resist shooting back, "But death accepts you; in fact, it is going to get you".
8 It is worth nothing that colloquial references to arrogance often invoke that most-prized part of the male anatomy: the penis. Thus, an arrogant person is called 'cocky', 'dick-head', 'prick', and so on.

Chapter 6

Dignity

Dignity is an elusive concept. Upon encountering the term, we feel an intuitive familiarity with its nosological contours. But when asked to put our 'understanding' into words, we fumble, wander in and out of various conceptual alleys, and return with lexical baskets that are empty. Solace comes from finding out that the concept has been mired in controversy, ambiguity, and imprecision since its appearance centuries ago. Taken up largely by philosophers, the notion of dignity has led to considerable debate and division. Some, like Frederick Nietzsche and Arthur Schopenhauer, reject it outright, considering it a redundant and pompous façade for man's sagging self-esteem. Others like Immanuel Kant, Francis Bacon, and Thomas Aquinas, champion the concept and offer painstakingly detailed discourse on it. More recent opponents of the validity and usefulness of the notion of dignity include Ruth Macklin (2003) and James Griffin (2002). And, more recent proponents of the concept include George Kateb (2011) and Michael Rosen (2012). The interesting fact though is that even the proponents do not seem to agree on what is it that they are talking about and to what realm the concept they are advancing applies. Four areas of discord exist. Formulated as questions, these include:

- Is dignity a specifically human trait or is it inherent in all that exists in this world including animals, plants, and even inanimate objects?
- Is dignity confined to the morally upright, the socially powerful, and the aesthetically refined, or is it an asset of all human beings since they carry an inviolable transcendental kernel within themselves?
- Does the concept of dignity have religious overtones or is it a secular concept, even though existing on an 'anagogic' (Silberer, 1914) level?[1]
- Can an attitude of religious humility be consonant with dignity or is surrender to God contrary to human dignity?

Clearly the field is rife with descriptive and conceptual conundrum. It might serve us well, therefore, to briefly go over the various definitions of dignity that exist in philosophical and, to a lesser extent, in psychoanalytic literature.

Familiarity with them seems necessary for addressing the sociocultural and technical implications of this concept.

Various definitions

The dictionary definition of 'dignity' comprises of such phrases as "the quality or state of being worthy, honored, or esteemed ... high-rank, office, or position ... a legal title of nobility or honor ... [and] formal reserve of manner or language" (Mish, 1987, p. 354). This amalgam of respect, status, and restraint is uplifting but leaves the concept somewhat ambiguous. Matters become more murky when we approach the philosophical definitions of dignity. In citing them, I borrow heavily from Rosen's (2012) meticulous and thorough survey of this literature.

- Cicero (106–43 BC) considered that it is the capacity for self-reflection and thoughtfulness that separates human beings from other species and gives them dignity.
- St Thomas Aquinas (1225–1274) gave an explicit definition of the concept, stating that "dignity signifies something's goodness on account of itself" (cited in Rosen, 2012, pp. 16–17). In his view, dignity is not restricted to human beings and all things created by God possess their own dignity.[2]
- Francis Bacon (1561–1626) emphasized that dignity is not associated with social status and that it is by painful and laborious effort that man achieves the elevated and respectable quality of dignity.
- Immanuel Kant (1724–1804) wrote extensively on dignity. He seemed to present many, occasionally divergent, views on the subject. One view is implicit in this passage: "In the Kingdom of ends everything has either a *price* or a *dignity*. What has a price can be replaced by something else as its *equivalent*; what, on the other hand, is raised above all price and therefore admits of no equivalent has a dignity" (cited in Rosen, 2012, pp. 20–21, italics in the original). This view permits, I assert, the extension of the concept of dignity to a breath-taking piece of art, a soulful poem, or even a single line from a poem (for instance, "what is sadder than a train stopped in rain?" by Pablo Neruda or "there is a door that I have closed till the end of this world" by Jorge Luis Borges), or a lilting movement in music. Kant's other, more restrictive view, curiously, is enunciated later in the same paragraph: "Morality, and humanity insofar as it is capable of morality, is that which alone has dignity" (cited in Rosen, 2012, p. 21). A third view could be derived from Kant's declaration that "autonomy is the ground of the dignity of human nature" (cited in Rosen, 2012, p. 21). This view would make dignity akin to a sense of agency, be it physical, intellectual, or moral. However, Rosen (2012) reminds us that Kant's use of the word 'autonomy' was different from its

contemporary meaning of self-determination; it referred to a willing commitment to the path of morality. What thus appears to be Kant's third view gets rapidly subsumed in his second view, though not without a remnant trace of ambiguity. What remains certain is that Kant's view of dignity does not depend upon God; in fact, he regarded religious submission to be antithetical to human dignity.

- Friedrich Schiller (1788–1805) regarded dignity as an aesthetic quality. For him, dignity was evident through 'tranquility in suffering'. Moreover, unlike Kant who thought genuinely moral behaviour emanated from strenuous thinking and making difficult choices, Schiller underscored the 'grace' with which a person acts morally without any kind of internal struggle. Schiller declared that "Just as grace is the expression of a beautiful soul, so dignity is the expression of a sublime disposition" (cited in Rosen, 2012, p. 35).
- Reinhold Niebuhr (1892–1971) emphasized the elements of thought and free will in his view of dignity. He held that the dignity of man consists of his capacity to rise above the laws of nature and, at times, even those of logic and reason in order to help others and for the betterment of society-at-large.

Moving on from the philosophical terrain to the realm of psychoanalysis immediately makes one aware of the paucity of literature on this subject. The word 'dignity' does not appear in the indices to the complete works of Sigmund Freud and Melanie Klein. Nor is it mentioned in the painstakingly detailed glossaries of Bion's (Lopez-Corvo, 2003) and Winnicott's (Abram, 2007) writings. None of the major psychoanalytic dictionaries (Eidelberg, 1968; Moore and Fine, 1968, 1990; Laplanche and Pontalis, 1973; Akhtar, 2009b; Auchincloss and Samberg, 2012) contain a definition of dignity. And, the PEP Web[3] yields only seven papers (De Rosis, 1973; Abelson, 1978; Abelson and Margolis, 1978; Margolis, 1978; Shabad, 2000, 2011; Zachary, 2002) which contain 'dignity' in their title. And, frankly, not all of these have something significant to offer. Nonetheless, these meagre morsels demand to be savoured.

De Rosis (1973) equates dignity with a kind of psychic wholeness by which the individual can maintain his or her nascent being and yet remain able to be influenced by others. The freedom to be oneself exists alongside ongoing engagement with others. To constantly retain these two modes of being is the essence of dignity. This results in living deeply and fully "within the scope of interplay" (p. 18) between the private self and the object world. And, it is only then one can have a sense of value as a unique individual as well as a responsible partner in the wider circle of humanity.

Abelson (1978) views dignity as emerging from accepting responsibility for one's actions and from insisting upon one's rights as a person including the right to one's psychic privacy. In a provocative assertion, Abelson finds seeking psychotherapy (or, for that matter, psychoanalysis) incompatible with personal dignity. Indeed, in his view, expecting someone else to help with one's psychological trepidation entails a denial of responsible for one's affect and action, hence a loss of personal dignity. Abelson's stance touches upon, but does not fully embody, the poignancy of Francis Bacon, who stated that "by indignities, men come to dignities" (cited in Rosen, 2012, p. 15). Abelson is criticized by Margolis (1978; see also Abelson and Margolis, 1978) who points out that no forfeiture of dignity is warranted if psychic pain needing remediation is clearly generated by others' actions. Moreover, while it is acceptable that a person be morally responsible for his actions, this does not mean

> that one ceases to be a person when events and actions involving one as a putative person are, *at times*, causally accounted for in terms of forces over which he lacked sufficient control or knowledge or which involved inconsistencies with his sincerely avowed reasons and intentions.
>
> (Margolis, 1978, p. 222, italics in the original)

Two other psychoanalysts have commented upon the concept of dignity. Shabad (2000) equates dignity with self-respect and finds some instances of spite and opposition as the ways to regain dignity.[4] Though Shabad does not cite him, the view he is advancing echoes Winnicott's (1960a) concept of 'antisocial tendency' whereby outrageousness becomes a vehicle for the unconscious hope for psychic repair by the environment. Zachary (2002), in discussing the psychic shifts that occur in the wake of menopause, uses the term 'dignity' to convey resilience and growth in the face of developmental crises.

In addition to the foregoing papers derived from the PEP Web, there are the pioneering contributions of Marcovitz (1970a, 1970b) and the quite recent work of Marcus (2013b). Since Marcovitz's contribution is truly pioneering in this realm and not widely known, I will devote considerable space to it. Delivered as a plenary address to the Southeastern Pennsylvania Mental Health Association on 4 November 1966, and published four years later (1970a), this paper is a tour de force. Noting that dignity is both an intrapsychic and social phenomenon, Marcovitz made the following powerful declaration:

> I believe that the development and maintenance of the dignity of the individual human being, both his own sense of worth and its reflection in the attitudes of others toward him, is a necessity to give meaning to existence, to make life worth living. It is simultaneously a prerequisite, a constituent and a sign of mental health. Its failure to develop, or its diminution, as well as the efforts to gain or to regain it, are most important aspects of various forms of mental illness as well as of other problems of personality or behavior that are unhealthy or destructive.
>
> (p. 120)

Marcovitz, rather courageously, emphasized that the feeling of having some superiority over others is often necessary in order to have a sense of dignity. Even the oppressed and the conquered can thus retain dignity by harbouring contempt for their tormentors. However, there also exist healthier avenues to sustain one's dignity under adverse circumstances: these include humour, art, music, and religion.

Among the fundamental components of dignity, Marcovitz listed (i) self-respect, (ii) self-assertion, (iii) a sense of power and agency, (iv) a sense of justice, and, significantly, (v) an amalgam of pride and humility. He added that

> There is another important ingredient to dignity – the feeling of being part of something important, something worth living for, fighting for, sacrificing for. The struggle to produce the kind of changes one aspires to will itself contribute to the dignity of all those involved in it.
>
> (p. 120)

Marcovitz also spoke of how large sections of society that live in states of poverty and deprivation are encumbered on a daily basis with indignities of life. He outlined (1970b) pathological (e.g. narcissistic hedonism, drug-induced oblivion, violence) and healthy (e.g. creativity, education, sports) measures to combat such threats to self-esteem. Finally, Marcovitz addressed the impact of gender upon the experience of dignity. He stated that:

> Although it is true that men envy women and in rare cases men want to become women, men are rarely ashamed of being men – they are usually ashamed of not being man enough, and use all sorts of means to enhance the dignity which depends on their picture of masculinity. With women the problem is different – it is not only that they envy men, but that they are ashamed of being women. Both of these shames, that of men and that of women, originate in the anatomy and in the weakness of childhood. Then social and cultural differences tend to increase or to diminish these primary feelings of shame. In the culture of poverty the woman's position in enhanced so that it is easier for her to get over her shame and to have dignity, because she is the prime wage earner and the head of the family; whereas the man's feeling of inadequacy tends to be fostered and he is forced into various symbolic or substitute or exaggerated forms of masculinity. In the middle classes the women have a more difficult time getting over their primary shame and in accepting their femininity with dignity. They tend to have more complicated forms of the problems of attaining a feeling of worthiness.
>
> (p. 126)

To be sure, these comments are dated and both social and psychoanalytic perspectives have moved ahead. But, Marcovitz deserves credit for at least confronting the gender-based dimension of dignity head on. He is an exception since all the philosophical and psychoanalytic writings on dignity skirt the fact that many cultures and many religious traditions have accorded women less dignity than men. And, in certain parts of the world, this remains true to this day.

Jumping from the earliest to the most contemporary contribution to the concept of dignity, we find the views of Marcus (2013b). He equates dignity with a proper sense of self-worth and self-respect, and declares that

> A person with a dignified being is one who exhibits behavior that is "worthy of himself" and does what needs to be done to shield himself from emotional wounding and other forms of harm. Dignity is also the state of being worthy of respect, esteem, or honour. To treat others with dignity involves, among other things, not psychologically or physically harming others.
>
> (p. 136)

A psychoanalytic exponent of the twentieth-century French philosopher Gabriel Marcel (1889–1973), Marcus notes the centrality of the traits of integrity, fraternity, and freedom in the former's concept of "inalienable dignity" (Marcel, cited in Marcus, 2013b, p. 137) of human beings. Marcel was passionate about the human striving towards a life of beauty, truth, and love, as well as towards the protection (and restoration) of the sacred from the intrusions of technology and totalitarianism. He emphasized that dignity is not associated with social class, but with compassion, empathy with the suffering of others, and courage to resist tyranny. Such courage, in turn, does not reflect a mere affirmation of the self but emanates from a deeply-awakened sense of morality. All in all, Marcel's concept of dignity subsumes integrity, autonomy, compassion, self-respect, courage, and a firm conviction it the sacred nature of life. With the thoughts of a Catholic philosopher presented to us by a Jewish psychoanalyst, we find ourselves at a propitious confluence of the two strands (philosophical and psychoanalytic) with which we began our consideration of how to define the notion of dignity. Time now to put the pieces of this puzzle together.

An attempt at synthesis

By bringing together the foregoing philosophical and psychoanalytic observations together in a harmonious gestalt, we end up with three types of dignity. While subtle overlaps between them exist, these categories actually refer to different phenomena, exist on different levels of abstraction, possess different evocative potentials, produce different praxis, and have different degrees of proximity with psychoanalytic metapsychology. A close look at the three categories I am proposing here would confirm my assertions of their distinct nature.

Metaphysical dignity

This refers to the view that all that exists in this universe is sacred and inherently worthy of respect. All human beings have dignity but dignity is not limited to human beings. Animals, plants, and inanimate objects also have dignity; their intrinsic coherence, purpose, and role in the mysterious operations of nature confer such honour upon them. The imperious lion, the majestic elephant, the sombre pyramids, the mesmerizing Taj Mahal, and yes, even an old oak tree, a beautifully carved grandfather clock, and an intricately woven Persian rug possess dignity. Searles' (1960) lamentably unread treatise on non-human environment and Bion's (1965) concept of 'O' undergird what I have termed 'metaphysical dignity' here. The former offers a detailed analysis of how our ecological surround and the physical objects as well as the big and little animals that populate it silently contribute to our psychic development and functioning. The latter posits the omnipresence of absolute truth which is inherent in the universe and can be readily found by an unthinking mind (yes, you read it right; Bion declares that truth and even thought itself pre-exists the human mind which can only elaborate upon it, not create it). The advantage of the concept of 'metaphysical dignity' is that it yields a sense of tenderness and consideration for all things; a Buddhist calm flows from the heart to the entire universe.[5] The disadvantages of the concept is that it is too broad, can be taken to absurd extremes (e.g. conferring dignity on a mosquito, a broken shoelace, a sewage pump),[6] and poses the risk of putting unrelated phenomena (e.g. respect for plants and for human freedom) on equal footing.

Existential dignity

This refers to the view that only the human species possess dignity. The argument states that since only human beings are capable of forging discontinuities with nature and also evolving and subscribing to an inner sense of morality, they exist on a higher plane than other species. This sentiment is evident in the Holy Quran's declaration that "We have bestowed dignity on the children of Adam and conferred upon them special favors above the greater part of our Creation" (17: 70). Each single human being is bestowed with dignity simply by belonging to a distinguished species and also partly because being human implies the capacity for transcendence within the hearts and souls of each individual. The psychoanalytic concept akin to existential dignity is that of 'belief-in-species' (Erikson, 1975). This concept proposes that an individual must possess and safeguard the understanding that all human beings belong to the same species, *Homo sapiens*, and therefore share the same characteristics; the tendency to divide a human being into more or less human, to the extent of considering some people infra-human or non-human, is 'pseudo-speciation' which assaults the basic commonality and dignity of human beings. The advantage of the concept of 'existential dignity' is that it propels equal respect for all human beings; the notion of fundamental human rights, equality of all human beings, and justice for all arise from this very substrate. The disadvantage of the concept is two-fold. First, by restricting dignity to only human beings, it can unleash wanton and remorseless exploitation of animals, things, and nature at large (Kateb, 2011). Second, by imparting dignity to every single human being, it risks obliterating the important moral difference between the oppressed and the oppressor and the cruel perpetrator and the innocent victim. Think about it. Does the ruthless Nazi officer with a bayonet share the same sort of dignity as his hapless captive?

Characterological dignity

This refers to a constellation of personality traits that are largely derived from the epigenetic unfolding of human psychic development and therefore might not exist in all individuals to comparable extent. These traits include integrity, restraint, authenticity, empathy, self-esteem, and courage. Seen this way, dignity is not a given but a developmentally 'earned' attribute. An implication of such thinking is that while an infant might have 'metaphysical' and 'existential' forms of dignity, it lacks 'characterological' dignity. Even when a separate and coherent sense of self first emerges (Mahler et al., 1975), the child can be seen to have a sort of 'proto-dignity' at best. Much ego growth and mastery of many developmental tasks before full 'characterological' dignity appears on the horizon.

The individual with such dignity can stick to moral pathways, tolerate states of fear, immerse himself in the subjective experiences of others, maintain appropriate caution and reserve, express himself with elegance, and remain true to his own core beliefs. Marcovitz (1970a, 1970b) stands heads and shoulders above the psychoanalytic contributors to such delineation of dignity. However, since characterological dignity denotes a composite of self-respect, confidence, integrity, inner morality, authenticity, and courage, all those who have addressed these topics implicitly contribute to the understanding of this type of dignity. It is not possible to list all such contributions but mention must be made of Freud's (1923, 1924b) and Jacobson's (1964) writings on superego, Benedek's (1938) concept of 'confident expectation', Rangell's (1954) delineation of poise, Erikson's concepts of 'integrity' (1950) and 'care' (1982), Winnicott's (1960a) proposal of true self, and the recent psychoanalytic papers on courage by Levine (2006), O'Neil (2009), and Akhtar (2013c). The advantage of the concept of 'characterological dignity' is that being a personality trait, it can be psychoanalytically studied and, with improved child-rearing, can be cultivated more and more often. The disadvantage of this concept is that it facilitates a certain kind of psychic elitism; some people are seen as having dignity (or, at least, more dignity) while others as lacking it. Such division creates the potential (however un-intentionally) of prejudice and discrimination against the latter group and, worse, deliberate jettisoning of disliked individuals and minorities into the less-dignified category.

Further synthesis of these three perspectives becomes feasible if we lump the first two categories (metaphysical and existential) together and designate the resulting concept as 'dignity in the broad sense' of the word and call the remaining category (characterological) as 'dignity in the narrow sense' of the word. Precedent for such classification does exist in psychoanalysis in the forms of 'reality principle in broad sense' and 'reality principle in narrow sense' (Hartmann, 1956, 1964) and 'self-psychology in broad sense' and 'self-psychology in narrow sense' (Kohut, 1977). Yet another way of thinking about these three groupings (metaphysical, existential, and characterological) is to consider them 'perspectives' rather than categories per se. At the same time, it cannot be overlooked that no matter how neat is the nosological packaging of the concept of dignity, some slippage inevitably occurs.

Before closing this section on the nosology of dignity, it is worthwhile to consider what might be its exact opposite. While experiences of shame, ego-infirmity, cowardice, helplessness, and feelings of inferiority can be seen as contributing to it, the designation 'indignity' seems preferable as the antonym in this regard. The advantage of such thinking is that it keeps the matter open and invites further investigation into the compromises and deficiencies in the area of dignity.

Technical implications

The foregoing elucidation of human dignity has enormous sociopolitical implications. The concept forms the backbone of the theory of human rights. In civilized societies, such rights include those pertaining to freedom of speech, freedom of religion, freedom of association, freedom of movement, entitlement to one's privacy, and access to due process of law. Inherent in human rights is a commitment to the equality of all human beings. Each human being has the same and equal rights. The state cannot abridge or deny the rights of any individual and cannot treat any person as a second-class citizen or practice discrimination against any group by law. Such under-standing of dignity of each human being and of the human species in general plays a vital role in the United Nation's Universal Declaration of Human Rights of 1948, Geneva Convention of 1949, and the Constitution of the United States. With various hues and nuances, each of these documents insists upon the dignity of human beings, even in dire circumstances such as imprisonment, judicial retribution, and war.

Such profound matters and debates surrounding them (Rosen, 2012; Kateb, 2011), however, are not daily concerns of the practising psychoanalyst. Nonetheless, dealing with the most private and sensitive core of human psychic life and the 'boundary crossings' (Gabbard and Lester, 1995) inherent in such enterprise necessitates that the analyst be mindful of dignity-related issues in the clinical situation. In my way of thinking, there are four ways in which concerns about dignity crop up in the course of our work.

Safeguarding the dignity of the analytic space

The expression 'analytic space' has both literal and metaphorical dimensions. On the literal level, it refers to the waiting room and the consulting room. The former mostly constitutes a space for private, introspective reverie (Wolman, 2007) but can be used for all sorts of different psychic purposes by patients (Abbasi, 2014; Kieffer, 2014). The latter, i.e. the consulting room, is where the 'real' work of analysis takes place. Elsewhere, I have written in detail about the diverse manners in which the analyst's office (and the physical objects contained in it) impact upon the clinical process (Akhtar, 2009a, pp. 113–133). I have elaborated upon the dimensions of location, comfort, authenticity, and constancy of the analyst's office and the analyst's need to safeguard its holding functions. Here, however, I want to emphasize that a certain 'metaphysical dignity' characterizes the consulting room and imparts to it a sacred quality. The wall next to the couch becomes a containing limit, the *objets d'art* acquire the status of 'mnemic objects' (Bollas, 1992) that evoke and contain affects and memories, the furniture and the lamps offer themselves as objects of 'non-human transferences' (Akhtar, 2009a). The inanimate is a silent ally of the analytic process. Hence, it must be treated with dignity and its sacredness protected from intrusions of the profane.[7] To put it bluntly, accoutrements of instinctual gratification (e.g. condoms, pornographic material, bottles of alcohol) must not be stored in the nooks and crannies of the analyst's office nor should activities of direct instinctual gratification (e.g. sexual intercourse, physical violence) take place inside the analytic office, even outside of the clinical hours and even if involving individuals other than patients. The principle of abstinence applies not only to the analyst's attitude during clinical work but also to his or her respect for the analytic office. If an analyst smokes pot, masturbates, or has sex with someone in the office, memory traces of such acts continue to haunt the space and pervert its sacrosanct nature. Two lines from my father, the renowned Urdu poet, Jan Nisar Akhtar (1914–1976) come to mind in this context:

> Aayeene ke aage na badalna kapde
> Aayeene meiN aks reh be jaate haiN sakhi.[8]

Needing to protect the dignity of the analytic space, however, goes beyond its literal level. On a metaphorical level, analytic space refers to the dialectically created, psychic realm of discourse between the unconscious of the patient and the unconscious of the analyst (Freud, 1912; Bolognini, 2011;

Akhtar, 2013a). This space is not static. It shrinks and expands. It deepens and becomes shallow. It might seem ephemeral but it is always there and must be treated with dignity. It accommodates what is present and positive but realizes that "engaging the negative is also a dignifying action" (Gerrard Fromm, personal communication, January 2014). Quick, clever, and deep interpretations might impress the patient but often foreclose the analytic space and preclude the emergence of the 'waiting beast' (Coltart, 2000) from within the depths of the patient's psyche. Treating the analytic space with dignity warrants patience, respect for the essential Otherness of the patient, and keeping tight reins upon the analyst's 'compulsion to interpret' (Epstein, 1979).

Protecting the dignity of the analytic process

Two points must be made clear at the outset here. One, that the analyst must possess, display, and behave with the sort of 'characterological dignity' outlined above. Two, that the analyst is, by the very nature of his role, open to be moulded, constructed, destructed, formed, deformed, and even defiled (to a certain extent) by his patient's transferences. Both these points are well-accepted. The rub comes when the patient's projective intrusions (and, at times, real-life actions) begin to collapse the analytic space and violate the core dignity of the analytic process. Undoubtedly the patient, in a state of frustration and rage, can call his Jewish analyst a 'kike', his African-American analyst a 'nigger', his Hindu analyst a 'monkey-worshipping asshole', and his Muslim analyst a 'fucking Arab terrorist'. But when such attacks are cold, calculating, and chronic, and when the patient's speech becomes a predominant vehicle of instinctual discharge, matters take a different turn. Pertinent in this context is the following observation of Ella Sharpe (1940):

> The discharge of feeling tension, when this is no longer relieved by physical discharge, can take place through speech. The activity of speaking is substituted for the physical activity now restricted at other openings of the body, while words themselves become the very substitutes for the bodily substances.
>
> (p. 157)

This applies to the sharp and narrow-minded interrogation by the malignantly paranoid, blood-curdling screams of the severely borderline, and the lascivious 'dirty talk' of the defiant pervert. The latter, though on surface referring to matters erotic, is also at its base hostile. And, insofar as such verbalizations (perhaps better called vocalizations) turn speaking into acting, they constitute attacks on the dignity of the analytic process. The existence of hostility in such talking is approached by Aulagnier (2001) from a novel perspective.

If one considers the auditory function, what one notes is the absence in this register of any system of closure comparable to the closing of eyelids or lips, or to the tactile retreat that muscular movement allows. The auditory cavity cannot remove itself from the irruption of sound waves; it is an open orifice in which, in a state of waking, the outside continuously penetrates … [consequently] the voice-object may so easily become the embodiment of the persecutory object.

(p. 60)

The point to remember here is that such behaviours on the part of the patient are attacks against the analyst's dignity as an analyst (not so much as his or her dignity as a human being, though that too might be involved to a certain extent). It is therefore that such behaviours must be curtailed. Ferenczi (1919, 1921), Kolansky and Eisner (1974), Amati-Mehler and Argentieri (1989), and more recently, I (Akhtar, 2013a) have dealt in detail with technical measures (including refusal to listen to certain kinds of material) indicated under such circumstances. Here, it would suffice to say that it is the analyst's responsibility to protect his dignity as an analyst, his dignity as a person, and, above all, the dignity of his clinical work.

Maintaining contact with the patient's dignity

Besides transference, countertransference, and therapeutic alliance, the analytic pair is also involved in a real relationship. Constituents of it are manifest in their loyalty to the frame (e.g. punctuality, regularity, payment of fees) and the spirit (e.g. respect for complexity, quest for knowledge, and a fundamental attitude of decency and affection towards each other) of their work. Noted by a number of authors (A. Freud, 1954; Stone, 1961; Greenson, 1967), such 'real relationship' demands that the analyst must not ignore the patient's 'existential dignity' at any point. The occasions where the analyst's diligence in this regard is tested vary. An admittedly incomplete list consists of the following:

- The patient is in advanced state of pregnancy and, at the end of one session, needs assistance to get up from the couch.
- The patient has severe post-nasal drip and cannot lie down on the couch, and wants to sit up.
- The patient is a doctoral student and has been regular in attendance and payment. She learns that, for the purposes of her dissertation, she has to spend six weeks in another country. Since this is not to occur for another four to five months, she expects that a long notice like this would mean that she does not have to pay for the sessions missed.
- The patient belongs to a religion other than that of his analyst and cannot keep two appointments due to certain observances. He thinks he should not be charged for those sessions.

- The patient reports that he eats his snot on a regular basis.
- The patient notices that the analyst is quite sick. The analyst has been quiet about this but the patient has learned from the grapevine that the analyst has a terminal illness. Then one day as the session ends, the patient notices that the analyst's face is quite ashen, he is very weak, and having difficulty getting up from his chair. He asks the analyst what is the matter.

All these situations might have individualized responses to them that would be appropriate. No one attitude can be legislated as being correct. But these situations do have something in common. They test the resilience of the analytic technique and provide opportunities for treating our patients with the dignity they deserve. In accepting their basic rights as human beings, and their entitlement to empathy, respect, and honesty, we preserve their dignity. Simply put, we assist the pregnant woman in getting up from the couch, let the patient with post-nasal drip sit up, not charge the doctoral student and the religious Other for the missed sessions, listen with equanimity to the one who eats snot, and let the patient know the truth about our not being well. If, however, we exert psychoanalytic autocracy, hide behind 'proper' technique, and remain stonily silent or turn interpretive in these circumstances, we end up offending them to their very core. We must not forget that respect for the patient as an autonomous and worthy individual is central to our clinical work. The views of the French philosopher, Emanuel Levinas (1906–1995) turn out to be the most reliable guides for appropriate conduct in the sort of situations mentioned above. Levinas (1961, 1981) states that ethical related-ness to the other requires recognition of and respect for difference. Erasing self–other distinction leads to totalization and sets the stage for domination and control. Commitment to dialogue, in contrast, endorses a relation between self and Other while accepting the 'strangeness' and autonomy of both parties. No partner in a dialogue has all the answers and each can enrich the process between them. Needless to add that the judicious accommoda-tions to frame and offering well-titrated 'gratifications' that might emanate from such an attitude do not oppose the interpretive work of psychoanalysis.[9] In fact, they strengthen the possibility of such work to continue.

Empathizing with the indignities faced by the patient

Many of our patients suffer from indignities, either those which were afflicted upon them during childhood or those which are their lot as adults. In an impressive confluence of ideas, the psychoanalyst Leonard Shengold and the political theorist George Kateb address the devastating impact of being robbed of one's dignity upon the human mind. Shengold (1989) designates the result of assaults upon human dignity as 'soul murder'. Deliberately inflicted by an individual upon the (usually dependent and weaker) other, such trauma consists of (i) attack upon the capacity for rational thought, (ii) erasure of the victim's identity and, (iii) brain-washing that leads to confusion in the victim's mind about what actually took place and that what did take place was highly pathological. Kateb (2011) makes similar observations within the socio-political context and I take the liberty of quoting him at some length.

> Beyond oppression, there are systems of suffering that are so extreme as to efface the personhood of individuals and leave only biological entities that do anything to survive, at whatever cost to those around them and to their own dignity. Degraded human beings therefore lose their identity as human beings and as particular persons, at least for a significant stretch of time. They have been forced to lose almost all uniquely human and personal characteristics. Thus through no fault of their own, they no longer manifest the reason for which incomparable dignity is assigned to human beings. The assault on dignity has achieved its aim when the ever possibility of the idea of human dignity is forced out of the mind of the victim by extreme suffering.
>
> (p. 20)

Kateb emphasizes that since such existential loss often fails to register on the victim, it is the responsibility of the observer to highlight the evil treatment. Now, this is as true in the setting of one nation, one tribe, one ethnic group (usually the majority) abusing the other nation, tribe, or ethnic group as it is in the less magisterial but no less sinister setting of one individual being abused by another. Here the validating role of the psychoanalyst gains para-mount importance. Take a look at the following situations:

- The patient reports that during his childhood, his enraged father would ask him to lie still on the floor while he took a few steps back, came rapidly towards him, and kicked him with full force in his head.
- The patient reports that after his mother's death when he was five years old, his maternal grandfather sodomized him, saying that this should make him feel close to his deceased mother; the grandfather declared himself to be the substitute for the boy's mother.
- The patient says that his wife routinely calls him 'scumbag', worse than an animal, psychotic, antisocial, and so ugly that she feels like vomiting each time she looks at his face.
- The patient, an international medical graduate from the Far East, reports sitting in a departmental meeting where senior faculty members were unrelentingly mocking the name of one Dr Ha who had applied for a job there.
- The patient is eight-three years old and often loses control of his bowels, soiling his underwear. He cannot see or hear as sharply as before and feels ashamed about his shuffling gait and stooped posture.[10]

To a greater or lesser degree, all the situations cited above call for validation from the analyst that the patient's dignity is or was being endangered. Of course, deciphering the meanings of each event to each particular individual will be necessary and would form the cornerstone of the psychoanalytic approach. However, such work must be preceded by 'affirmative interventions' (Killingmo, 1989) that are intended not at unmasking what lies under the surface but at establishing plausibility that the patient's anguish is valid and meaningful. The confirmation that the patient's dignity is threatened paradoxically restores the valued asset.

Concluding remarks

In this chapter, I have surveyed the wide-ranging literature on the topic of dignity. I have reviewed its definitions in philosophical and psychoanalytic writings and attempted to synthesize them by outlining three categories of dignity which can be seen as phenomenological clusters, points of views, as well as levels of abstraction. These are (i) metaphysical dignity, which extends the concept of dignity beyond the human species to all that exists in this world, (ii) existential dignity, which applies to human beings alone, and (iii) characterological dignity, which applies to some human beings more than to others. I have detailed some pros and cons of each category and acknowledged the limitations of my classification. Finally, I have elucidated the sociopolitical and therapeutic implications of the dignity concept, though my emphasis has remained upon the latter.

I now wish to conclude by briefly taking up three matters that exist on the remote but challenging periphery of the topic at hand. The first pertains to whether someone's dignity can be trampled upon without their conscious or unconscious surrender to such assault. The second pertains to dignity's link with goodness. The third pertains to the role of dignity in certain kinds of suicide. As far as the first issue is concerned, it seems that during infancy and childhood when one is weak and dependent, and in concentration camps and terrorizing totalitarian regimes, human dignity can be crushed even without the individual's participation in such abuse. However, in adult life situations and in relatively calm social circumstances, one has to almost willingly surrender one's dignity in order for the tormentor to be really successful. The fact is that an adult retains choice and this is especially true when people can undertake collective revolt against oppression and occupation. While true of many populations of today's world, the following poem by Chogyam Trungpa (1998, p. 5) captures this sentiment in the context of the Tibetan occupation by Chinese forces.

The red flag flies above Potala,
The people of Tibet are drowned in an ocean of blood;
A vampire army fills the mountains and plains,
But self-existing dignity never wanes.

The second matter pertains to the connection between dignity and goodness. The components of dignity (integrity, morality, authenticity, poise, self-respect, and courage) have a remarkable overlap with what I have elsewhere (Akhtar, 2009c) delineated as the components of human goodness (restraint, epistemic enthusiasm, gratitude, concern, empathy, authenticity, generativity, and faith). Dignity and goodness thus appear closely related. And we witness their confluence in the lives of Gandhi, Martin Luther King, and Nelson Mandela, to name but a few shining stars of humanity. But do all 'good people' have dignity? Or, is there some additional element that imparts the aura of personal dignity to an individual? More fortitude? More charm? A certain kind of noble reserve? Physical grace? Frankly, we do not know. Further complexity is added when we consider whether 'bad people' can exude dignity. Forgive my audacity but might we consider Don Corleone, the Mafia boss from Mario Puzo's (1969) novel, *The Godfather* (and its celluloid incarnation in the person of Marlon Brando), as possessing dignity? He was restrained. He was authentic and courageous. He had a certain sort of integrity and, in his own way, was even 'moral'. So would we be correct in assuming that he, and other high-level gangsters and criminals like him, have dignity? We cringe at that thought but a moralizing countertransference is hardly a sufficient response to this question. It is not easy to spot the boundary between the charisma and power resulting from pathological narcissism and the transcendental calm emanating from morally anchored concern for others, deep empathy, and genuine fortitude. Keeping these two phenomenological postures blurred is the hallmark of messianic cult-leaders in whom pseudo-humility cloaks omnipotence and charm masquerades as kindness. Clearly more thought is needed about the presence or absence of dignity under such circumstances.

Finally, there is the link between dignity and certain kinds of suicide. Sociopolitical and ethical debates regarding the practice of euthanasia and the self-righteous crusades of Jack Kevorkian (1928–2011) notwithstanding, the question whether killing oneself can, at times, be the only way left to preserve one's dignity is important. Within psychoanalysis, two passages help us think about this matter. One is by Klein (1935) and the other by Winnicott (1960a). Talking of the suicidal individual, Klein states:

> In committing suicide, his purpose may be to make a clean breach in his relation to the outside world because he desires to rid some real object – or the "good" object which the whole world represents and which the ego is identified with – of himself, or of that part of his ego which is identified with his bad objects and his id.
>
> (p. 276)

This is 'morally clean' or altruistic suicide. Self-destruction is undertaken because it appears undignified to go on burdening others with one's needs and demands. Many suicides in the context of incurable terminal illness fall in this category.

Another pathway that links personal dignity and suicide is to be found in the following passage from Winnicott (1960a):

> The False Self has as its main concern a search for conditions which will make it possible for the true self to come into its own. If conditions cannot be found then there must be organized a new deference against exploitation of the True Self, and if there be doubt, then the clinical result is suicide. Suicide in this context is the destruction of the total self in avoidance of the annihilation of the True Self. When suicide is the only defence left against betrayal of the True Self, then it becomes the lot of the False Self to organize the suicide. This, of course, involves its own destruction, but at the same time eliminates the need for its continued existence, since its function is the protection of the True Self from insult.
>
> (p. 143)

In simpler words, this amounts to saying that if one has no hope whatsoever left to lead a life of authentic self-expression (an important component of dignity), then it makes sense to end one's life. One might agree or disagree about the applicability of such dynamics to some acts of political martyr-dom but at its operation in certain personal situations appears convincing. In fact, an admixture of the altruistic motive outlined by Klein (1935) and the self-preservatory motive outlined by Winnicott (1960a) often underlies the suicides of great men who, due to old age, illness, and infirmity, find themselves unable to lead a life of dignity. While examples can be given from many realms of human enterprise, it might be humbler to cite only those from within our own field. Prominent psychoanalysts who thus choose to leave this world at their own command include Victor Tausk, Paul Federn, Bruno Bettleheim, Nina Coltart, Thomas Szasz, and, long before all of them, Sigmund Freud himself. Suffering from cancer, living in chronic pain, tolerating repeated surgeries, sustaining himself on injectable opiates, becoming unable to talk, turning foul-smelling due to infection towards his final days, and feeling rejected by his beloved dog, Jofi, Freud asked his physician, Max Schur, to give him a lethal injection of morphine (Gay, 1988). He had led a rich and highly accomplished life and his time to exit this world had come. He could have lived a few more days, perhaps even a few more weeks or months. But rather than cling to mere biological survi-val, he elected to exercise power over his destiny, including how and when his life would end. Being the *mensch*[11] that he was, Freud rejected lingering with indignity and chose a death of dignity.

Notes

1 Silberer originated the term 'anagogic interpretation' for a mode of decoding symbolism that brings out its universal 'transcendent' and ethical dimension. Unlike the customary psychoanalytic tendency to decipher symbols along personal and sexual lines, *anagogic* (Greek for 'to bear upwards') interpretations elevate the concrete into the spiritual.

2 Generally speaking, the three Middle Eastern religions (Judaism, Christianity, Islam) have a hierarchy whereby God, angels, prophets, and man – all, and in that order – exist above animals. Eastern religions (e.g. Hinduism, Buddhism, Jainism) do not subscribe to such a view. Their God resides everywhere and can exist within human beings as well as within animals. As a result, they ascribe greater dignity to animals.

3 The PEP Archive (1871–2008) contains the complete text of forty-six premier journals in psychoanalysis, seventy classic psychoanalytic books, and the full text and editorial notes of the twenty-four volumes of the *Standard Edition* as well as the eighteen-volume German *Gesammelte Werke*. PEP Archive spans over 137 publication years and contains the full text of articles whose source ranges from 1871 through 2008. There are approximately 75,000 articles and 8,728 figures that originally resided in 1,449 volumes with a total of over 650,000 printed pages.

4 Although Shabad uses the expression 'spite' throughout his paper, righteous opposition to assaults upon one's dignity need not be termed as such. Rosa Parks' (1913–2005) refusal to yield her seat to someone only because of their being White did not have a spiteful quality. It was a gesture of robust self-assertion to maintain her dignity.

5 For details on how contact with one's own dignity opens one's heart and eyes to the dignity of all creation, see the October 2008 Special Issue of *Soku Gakkai International Quarterly: A Buddhist Forum for Peace, Culture, and Education.*

6 A Buddhist friend of mine responded to this statement by saying that why should these things not have dignity? The mosquito and the sewage pump are doing what they are required to do. And, the broken shoelace is like a great poet who has had a stroke. Simply because he is no longer able to write poetry, do we withdraw our respect for him?

7 The word 'profane' is derived from the Latin *profamus*, itself comprised of 'pro' (before) and 'famus' (temple). In other words, 'profane' means something that has to be left outside of the temple.

8 An admittedly inelegant translation is "Don't change clothes in front of the mirror; images of your nudity would linger in it long afterwards".

9 The word 'gratification' has been unduly maligned in psychoanalytic discourse. One reason for this is the lack of distinction in many analyst's minds between the satisfying prohibited and id wishes versus meeting developmentally unrealistic appropriate ego needs (see Akhtar, 1999a, for a detailed discussion of the need–wish distinction).

10 See Lax (2008) for what she calls the 'indignities' of getting really old.

11 A Yiddish expression, *mensch*, denotes an honest, courageous, reliable, and strong man.

References

Abbasi, S. (2014). *The Rupture of Serenity: External Intrusions and Psychoanalytic Technique*. London: Karnac Books.

Abelson, R. (1978). Psychotherapy and personal dignity. *Psychoanalysis and Contemporary Thought*: 203–216.

Abelson, R., and Margolis, J. (1978). A further exchange on psychotherapy, personal dignity, and persons. *Psychoanalysis and Contemporary Thought* 1: 227–235.

Abend, S. (1982). Serious illness in the analyst: countertransference considerations. *Journal of the American Psychoanalytic Association* 30: 365–379.

Abraham, K. (1907). The experience of sexual traumas as a form of sexual activity. In: *Selected Papers on Psychoanalysis*, pp. 47–63. New York: Bruner/Mazel.

Abraham, K. (1913). Restrictions and transformation of scophophilia in psychoneurotics. In: *Selected Papers on Psychoanalysis*, pp. 169–234. New York: Bruner/Mazel.

Abraham, K. (1924). The influence of oral eroticism on character formation. In: *Selected Papers of Karl Abraham, M.D.*, pp. 393–406. New York: Brunner/Mazel.

Abraham, K. (1925). The history of an impostor in the light of psychoanalytical knowledge. In: *Clinical Papers and Essays on Psychoanalysis*, pp. 291–305. New York: Brunner/Mazel, 1955.

Abram, J. (2007). *The Language of Winnicott: A Dictionary of Winnicott's Use of Words* (2nd edn). London: Karnac.

Ackerley, J. (1956). *My Dog, Tulip*. New York: New York Review Book Classics, 2011.

Aisenstein, M., and Moss, D. (2014). Desire and its discontents. In: *On Sexualities*, ed. A. Lemma, pp. 63–80. London: Karnac Books.

Akhtar, J.N. (1964). *Nazr-e-Butaan*. New Delhi: Star Publications.

Akhtar, J.N. (1975). *Pichhale Pehar*. New Delhi: Maktaba Jamia.

Akhtar, S. (1984). The syndrome of identity diffusion. *American Journal of Psychiatry* 141: 1381–1385.

Akhtar, S. (1985). The other woman: phenomenological, psychodynamic, and therapeutic considerations. In: *Contemporary Marriage*, ed. D. Goldberg, pp. 215–240. Homeswood, IL: Dow Jones–Irwin.

Akhtar, S. (1989). Narcissistic personality disorder. *Psychiatric Clinics of North America* 12: 505–529.

Akhtar, S. (1990). Concept of interpersonal distance in borderline personality disorder (Letter to Editor). *American Journal of Psychiatry* 147: 2.

Akhtar, S. (1992a). *Broken Structures: Severe Personality Disorders and Their Treatment*. Northvale, NJ: Jason Aronson.

Akhtar, S. (1992b). Tethers, orbits, and invisible fences: clinical, developmental, sociocultural, and technical aspects of optimal distance. In: *When the Body Speaks: Psychological Meanings in Kinetic Clues*, ed. S. Kramer and S. Akhtar, pp. 21–57. Northvale, NJ: Jason Aronson.

Akhtar, S. (1994). Needs, disruptions, and the return of ego instincts: some explicit and implicit aspects of self psychology. In: *Mahler and Kohut: Perspectives on Development, Psychopathology, and Technique*, ed. S. Kramer and S. Akhter, pp. 99–116. Northvale, NJ: Jason Aronson.

Akhtar, S. (1996). "Someday … " and "if only … " fantasies: pathological optimism and inordinate nostalgia as related forms of idealization. *Journal of American Psychoanalytic Association* 44: 723–753.

Akhtar, S. (1999a). The distinction between needs and wishes: implications for psychoanalytic theory and technique. *Journal of the American Psychoanalytic Association* 47: 113–151.

Akhtar, S. (1999b). *Immigration and Identity: Trauma, Treatment, and Transformation*. Northvale, NJ: Jason Aronson.

Akhtar, S. (2000). The shy narcissist. In: *Changing Ideas in a Changing World: Essays in Honor of Arnold Cooper*, ed. J. Sandler, R. Michels, and P. Fonagy, pp. 111–119. London: Karnac Books.

Akhtar, S. (2001). From mental pain through manic defense to mourning. In: *Three Faces of Mourning – Melancholia, Manic Defense and Moving On*, ed. S. Akhtar, pp. 95–115. Northvale, NJ: Jason Aronson.

Akhtar, S. (2002). Forgiveness: origins, dynamics, psychopathology, and clinical relevance. *Psychoanalytic Quarterly* 71: 175–212.

Akhtar, S. (2003). Things: developmental, psychopathological, and technical aspects of inanimate objects. *Canadian Journal of Psychoanalysis* 11: 1–44.

Akhtar, S. (2005). *Objects of Our Desire*. New York: Harmony Press.

Akhtar, S. (2006). Technical challenges faced by the immigration analyst. *Psychoanalytic Quarterly* 75: 21–43.

Akhtar, S. (2007). From unmentalized xenophobia to messianic sadism: some reflections on the phenomenology of prejudice. In: *The Future of Prejudice: Psychoanalysis and the Prevention of Prejudice*, ed. H. Parens, A. Mahfouz, S.W. Twemlow, and D.E. Scharff, pp. 7–19. Lanham, MD: Jason Aronson.

Akhtar, S. (2008). Introduction. In: *On Freud's "The Future of an Illusion"*, ed. M.K. O'Neil and S. Akhtar, pp. 1–8. London: Karnac Books.

Akhtar, S. (2009a). *The Damaged Core: Origins, Dynamics, Manifestations, and Treatment*. Lanham, MD: Jason Aronson.

Akhtar, S. (2009b). *Comprehensive Dictionary of Psychoanalysis*. London: Karnac Books.

Akhtar, S. (2009c). Psychoanalysis and human goodness: theory. In: *Good Feelings: Psychoanalytic Reflections on Positive Emotions and Attitudes*, ed. S. Akhtar, pp. xxv–xxxv. London: Karnac.

Akhtar, S. (2009d). Psychoanalysis and human goodness: technique. In: *Good Feelings: Psychoanalytic Reflections on Positive Emotions and Attitudes*, ed. S. Akhtar, pp. 453–467. London: Karnac.

Akhtar, S. (2011a). ed. *The Electrified Mind: Development, Psychopathology, and Treatment in the Era of Cell Phones and the Internet.* Lanham, MD: Jason Aronson.

Akhtar, S. (2011b). Orphans. In: *Matters of Life and Death: Psychoanalytic Perspectives,* pp. 147–180. London: Karnac Books.

Akhtar, S. (2011c). Mortality. In: *Matters of Life and Death: Psychoanalytic Perspectives,* pp. 87–122. London: Karnac Books.

Akhtar, S. (2011d). Graves. In: *Matters of Life and Death: Psychoanalytic Perspectives,* pp. 123–146. London: Karnac Books.

Akhtar, S. (2011e). *Immigration and Acculturation: Mourning, Adaptation, and the Next Generation.* Lanham, MD: Jason Aronson.

Akhtar, S., ed. (2011f). *Unusual Interventions: Alterations of the Frame, Method, and Relationship in Psychotherapy and Psychoanalysis.* London: Karnac Books.

Akhtar, S. (2013a). *Psychoanalytic Listening: Methods, Limits, and Innovations.* London: Karnac Books.

Akhtar, S. (2013b). Gratitude. In: *Good Stuff: Courage, Generosity, Resilience, Gratitude, Forgiveness, and Sacrifice,* pp. 53–73. Lanham, MD: Jason Aronson.

Akhtar, S. (2013c). Generosity. In: *Good Stuff: Courage, Generosity, Resilience, Gratitude, Forgiveness, and Sacrifice,* pp. 75–102. Lanham, MD: Jason Aronson.

Akhtar, S. (2013d). Psychoanalysis and culture: Freud, Erikson, and beyond. In: *Psychoanalysis in Asia: China, India, Japan, South Korea, and Taiwan,* ed. A. Gerlach, M.T. Hooke, and S. Varvin, pp. 19–42. London: Karnac Books.

Akhtar, S. (2013e). *Good Stuff: Courage, Generosity, Resilience, Gratitude, Forgiveness, and Sacrifice.* Lanham, MD: Jason Aronson.

Akhtar, S. (2014a). *After Landing.* Charlottesville, VA: Pitchstone Publishing.

Akhtar, S. (2014b). Meanings, manifestations, and management of greed. In: *Sources of Suffering: Fear, Greed, Guilt, Deception, Betrayal, and Revenge,* ed. S. Akhtar, pp. 131–158. London: Karnac Books.

Akhtar, S. (2015a). Patience. *Psychoanalytic Review* 102: 93–122.

Akhtar, S. (2015b). Some psychoanalytic reflections on the concept of dignity. *American Journal of Psychoanalysis* 75: 244–266.

Akhtar, S. (2015c). Where is India in my psychoanalytic work? *Psychoanalytic Review* 102: 873–911.

Akhtar, S. (2016). Mistrust, suspiciousness, and paranoia during adulthood. In: *Mistrust: Developmental, Cultural, and Clinical Realms,* ed. S. Akhtar, pp. 41–60. London: Karnac.

Akhtar, S. (2017). Bereavement: the spectrum of emotional reactions. In: *Bereavement: Personal Experiences and Clinical Reflections,* ed. S. Akhtar and G. Kanwal, pp. 3–17. London: Karnac Books.

Akhtar, S. (2018). Humility. *American Journal of Psychoanalysis* 78: 1–27.

Akhtar, S., and Billinkoff, Z. (2011). Developmental tasks of early marriage: "Barefoot in the Park" (1967), "Raising Arizona" (1987), "The Quiet Man" (1952). *American Journal of Psychoanalysis* 71: 110–120.

Akhtar, S., and Brown, J. (2005). Animals in psychiatric symptomatology. In: *The Mental Zoo: Animals in the Human Mind and Its Pathology,* ed. S. Akhtar and V. Volkan, pp. 3–38. Madison, CT: International Universities Press.

Akhtar, S., and Kumar, M. (2008). Destiny and nationalism: Mohammad Ali Jinnah. In: *The Crescent and the Couch: Cross-Currents Between Islam and Psychoanalysis,* ed. S. Akhtar, pp. 79–102. Lanham, MD: Jason Aronson.

Akhtar, S., and O'Neil, M.K., eds (2012). *On Freud's "The Unconscious"*. London: Karnac Books.

Akhtar, S., and Volkan, V. (2005a). *Mental Zoo: Animals in the Human Mind and its Pathology*. Madison, CT: International Universities Press.

Akhtar, S., and Volkan, V. (2005b). *Cultural Zoo: Animals in the Human Mind and its Sublimations*. Madison, CT: International Universities Press.

Alfonso, C.A. (2002). Frontline: writing psychoanalytic case reports – safeguarding privacy while preserving integrity. *Journal of the American Academy of Psychoanalysis* 30: 165–171.

Alperin, R. (2001). Barriers to intimacy: an object relations perspective. *Psychoanalytic Psychology* 18: 137–156.

Altman, L. (1977). Some vicissitudes of love. *Journal of the American Psychoanalytic Association* 25: 35–52.

Amati-Mehler, J., and Argentieri, S. (1989). Hope and hopelessness: a technical problem? *International Journal of Psychoanalysis* 70: 295–304.

Angel, A. (1934). Eingie Bemerkungen uber den optimismus. *International Zeitschr. Of Psychoanalysis* 20: 191–199.

Anthony, E.J. (1987). Risk, vulnerability, and resilience: an overview. In: *The Invulnerable Child*, ed. E.J. Anthony and B.J. Cohler, pp. 3–47. New York: Guilford Press.

Anzieu, D. (1990). Formal signifiers and the ego skin. In: *Psychic Envelopes*, ed. D. Anzieu, pp. 1–26. London: Karnac Books.

Arango, A. (1989). *Dirty Words: Psychoanalytic Insights*. Northvale, NJ: Jason Aronson.

Arlow, J. (1961). Silence and the theory of technique. *Journal of the American Psychoanalytic Association*: 44–55.

Armstrong, L. (2009). *Patience: Harvesting the Spirits' Fruit*. Minneapolis, MN: Faithprobe Publications.

Auchincloss, E.L., and Samberg, E., eds. (2012). *Psychoanalytic Terms and Concepts*. New Haven, CT: Yale University Press.

Aulagnier, P. (2001). *The Violence of Interpretation; From Pictogram to Statement*. London: Brunner-Routledge.

Bach, S. (1977). On narcissistic state of consciousness. *International Journal of sychoanalysis* 58: 209–233.

Balint, M. (1953). *Primary Love and Psychoanalytic Technique*. London: Tavistock.

Balint, M. (1958). *The Basic Fault*. New York: Bruner/Mazel.

Balint, M. (1968). *The Basic Fault: Therapeutic Aspects of Regression*. London: Tavistock.

Balsam, R. (2015). Eyes, ears, lips, fingertips, secrets: Dora, psychoanalysis, and the body. *Psychoanalytic Review* 102: 33–58.

Barale, F., and Minazzi, V. (2008). Off the beaten track: Freud, sound and music: statement of a problem and some historico-critical notes. *International Journal of Psychoanalysis* 89: 937–957.

Bauer, M., and Chytilova, J. (2013). Women, children, and patience: experimental evidence from India villages. *Review of Developmental Economics* 17: 662–675.

Benedek, T. (1938). Adaptation to reality in early infancy. *Psychoanalysis Quarterly* 7: 200–214.

Bergler, E. (1939). On the psychoanalysis of the ability to wait and of impatience. *Psychoanalytic Review* 26: 11–32.

Bergman, A. (1980). Ours, yours, mine. In: *Rapprochements: The Critical Subphase of Separation-Individuation*, ed. R. Lax, S. Bach, and J.A. Burland, pp. 199–216. New York: Jason Aronson.

Bergman, A. (1999). *Ours, Yours, Mine. Mutuality and the Emergence of the Separate Self.* Northvale, NJ: Jason Aronson.

Bick, E. (1968). The experience of the skin in early object relations. *International Journal Psychoanalysis* 49: 484–486.

Bion, W.R. (1957). On arrogance. In: *Second Thoughts: Selected Papers on Psychoanalysis*, pp. 86–92. New York: Basic Books.

Bion, W.R. (1962a). A theory of thinking. *International Journal of Psychoanalysis* 43: 306–310.

Bion, W.R. (1962b). *Learning from Experience.* London: Karnac Books, 1984.

Bion, W.R. (1963). *Elements of Psychoanalysis.* London: Karnac Books, 1984.

Bion, W.R. (1965). *Transformations.* London: Karnac Books, 1984.

Bion, W.R. (1967). Notes on memory and desire. *The Psychoanalytic Forum* 2: 272–273.

Bion, W.R. (1970). *Attention and Interpretation.* London: Karnac Books, 1984.

Binstock, W. (1973). On the two forms of intimacy. *Journal of the American Psychoanalytic Association* 21: 93–107.

Blos, P. (1967). The second individuation process of adolescence. *Psychoanalytic Study of the Child* 22: 162–186.

Boesky, D. (1989). The questions and curiosity of the psychoanalyst. *Journal of the American Psychoanalytic Association* 37: 579–603.

Bollas, C. (1979). The transformational object. *International Journal of Psychoanalysis* 60: 97–107.

Bollas, C. (1992). *Being a Character: Psychoanalysis and Self-Experience.* New York: Hill & Wang.

Bollas, C. (1999). *The Mystery of Things.* London: Routledge.

Bollas, C. (2009). *The Evocative Object World.* London: Routledge.

Bolognini, S. (2008). *Secret Passages: The Theory and Technique of Interpsychic Relations.* Transl. G. Atkinson. London: Karnac Books.

Bolognini, S. (2011). Secret passages towards the unconscious: styles and techniques of exploration. *Italian Psychoanalytic Annual* 5: 75–87.

Boris, H.N. (1976). On hope: its nature and psychotherapy. *International Review of Psycho-Analysis* 3: 139–150.

Bouvet, M. (1958). Technical variations and the concept of distance. *International Journal of Psychoanalysis* 39: 211–221.

Bowlby, J. (1958). The nature of the child's tie to his mother. *International Journal of Psychoanalysis* 39: 350–373.

Bowlby, J. (1969). *Attachment and Loss, Vol I: Attachment.* New York: Basic Books.

Bowlby, J. (1973). *Attachment and Loss, Volume 2.* New York: Basic Books.

Bowlby, J. (1980). *Attachment and Loss, Volume III: Loss – Sadness and Depression.* New York: Basic Books.

Brenner, C. (1976). *Psychoanalytic Technique and Psychic Conflict.* New York: International Universities Press.

Brenner, C. (2000). Brief communication: evenly hovering attention. *Psychoanalytic Quarterly* 69: 545–549.

Brody, E.B. (1978). Intimacy and the fantasy of becoming both sexes. *Journal of the American Academy of Psychoanalysis* 6: 521–531.

Brottman, M. (2011). *Phantoms of the Clinic: From Thought-Transference to Projective Identification*. London: Karnac Books.

Burch, N. (2004). Closeness and intimacy. *British Journal of Psychotherapy* 20: 361–371.

Burnham, D.L., Gladstone, A.E., and Gibson, R.W. (1969). *Schizophrenia and the Need-Fear Dilemma*. New York: International Universities Press.

Cahill, L. (2015). Healing horses: how therapeutic riding lessons can help children with special needs. *The Irish Field*, 6 March 2015. Accessed on 28 December 2017.

Cai, H., Sedikides, C., Gaertner, L., Wang, C., Carvallos, M., Xu, Y., O'Mara, E., and Jackson, L. (2011). Tactical self-enhancement in China: is modesty at the service of self-enhancement in East Asian cultures? *Social Psychological and Personality Science* 2: 59–64.

Carpelan, H. (1981). On the importance of the setting in the psychoanalytic situation. *Scandinavian Psychoanalytic Review* 4: 151–161.

Cath, S. (1989). Readiness for grandfatherhood and the shifting tide. In: *Fathers and Their Families*, ed. S. Cath, A. Gruwitt, and L. Gunsberg, pp. 99–118. Hillsdale, NJ: Analytic Press.

Cecchin, G. (1987). Hypothesizing, circularity, and neutrality re-visited: an invitation to curiosity. *Family Process* 26: 405–413.

Celenza, A. (2015). *Erotic Revelations: Clinical Applications and Perverse Scenarios*. London: Routledge.

Chasseguet-Smirgel, J. (1984). *Creativity and Perversion*. New York: W.W. Norton.

Chen, E.M. (1989). *The Te Tao Ching: A New Translation with Commentary*. New York: Paragon House.

Cheshire, N.M. (1996). The empire of the ear: Freud's problem with music. *International Journal of Psychoanalysis* 77: 1127–1168.

Clark, L.P. (1932). Can child analysis prevent neuroses and psychoses in later life? *Psychoanalytic Review* 19: 46–55.

Clarke, R.A. (2004). *Against All Enemies: Inside America's War on Terrorism*. New York: Free Press.

Cliff, M.A. (1986). Writing about psychiatric patients: guidelines for disguising case material. *Bulletin of the Menninger Clinic* 50: 511–524.

Coltart, N. (1985). The practice of psychoanalysis and Buddhism. In: *Slouching Towards Bethlehem…and Further Psychoanalytic Explorations*, pp. 164–175. New York: Other Press.

Coltart, N. (2000). *Slouching Towards Bethlehem*. New York: Other Press.

Cooper, S. (2008). Privacy, reverie, and the analyst's ethical imagination. *Psychoanalytic Quarterly* 77: 1045–1073.

Covington, C. (2003). A question of confidence: privacy under pressure. *British Journal of Psychotherapy* 20: 131–133.

Dalai Lama (1997). *Healing Anger: The Power of Patience from a Buddhist Perspective*. Ithaca, NY: Snow Lion Publications.

Dawkins, R. (2008). *The God Delusion*. Boston: Mariner Books.

De Rosis, L.E. (1973). Self-esteem, dignity, or the sense of being. *American Journal of Psychoanalysis* 33: 16–27.

de Waal, F. (2016). *Are We Smart Enough to Know How Smart Animals Are?* New York: W.W. Norton.

Denford, S. (1981). Going away. *International Review of Psychoanalysis* 59: 325–332.

Deutsch, H. (1933). The psychology of manic-depressive states with particular reference to chronic hypomania. In: *Neuroses and Character Types*, pp. 203–217. New York: International Universities Press, 1965.

Devereux, G. (1966). Mumbling: the relationship between a resistance and frustrated auditory curiosity in childhood. *Journal of the American Psychoanalytic Association* 14: 478–484.

Dewald, P. (1982). Serious illness in the analyst: transference, countertransference, and reality aspects. *Journal of the American Psychoanalytic Association* 30: 347–363.

Easwaran, E. (2012). *Patience: A Little Book of Inner Strength*. Tomales, CA: Nilgiri Press.

Ehrenberg, D. (1995). Self-disclosure: therapeutic tool or indulgence? *Contemporary Psychoanalysis* 31: 213–228.

Ehrlich, H.S. (1998). On loneliness, narcissism, and intimacy. *American Journal of Psychoanalysis* 58: 135–162.

Eidelberg, L., ed. (1968). *The Encyclopedia of Psychoanalysis*. New York: The Free Press.

Eisnitz, A. (1980). The organization of the self-representation and its influence on pathology. *Psychoanalytic Quarterly* 49: 361–392.

Emde, R. (1980). Toward a psychoanalytic theory of effect. In: *The Course of Life: Psychoanalytic Contributions Towards Understanding Personality Development. Vol. I: Infancy and Childhood*, ed. S.I. Greenspan and G.H. Pollock, pp. 63–112. Rockville, MD: National Institute of Mental Health Publications.

Emde, R. (1981). Changing models of infancy and the nature of early development: remodeling the foundation. *Journal of the American Psychoanalytic Association* 29: 179–219.

Emde, R. (1991). Positive emotions for psychoanalytic theory: surprises from infancy research and new directions. *Journal of the American Psychoanalytic Association* 39: 5–44.

Epstein, L. (1979). Countertransference with borderline patients. In: *Countertransference*, ed. L. Epstein and A.H. Feiner, pp. 375–406. New York: Jason Aronson.

Epstein, M. (1995). Thoughts without a thinker – Buddhism and psychoanalysis. *Psychoanalytic Review* 92: 291–406.

Erikson, E.H. (1950). *Childhood and Society*. New York: W.W. Norton, 1963.

Erikson, E.H. (1968). *Identity, Youth, and Crisis*. New York: W.W. Norton.

Erikson, E.H. (1975). *Life History and the Historical Moment*. New York: W.W. Norton.

Erikson, E.H. (1982). *The Life Cycle Completed: A Review*. New York: W.W. Norton.

Fairbairn, W. (1940). Schizoid factors in the personality. In: *An Object Relations Theory of Personality*, pp. 3–27. New York: Basic Books, 1952.

Fairbairn, W. (1952). *An Object Relations Theory of Psychoanalysis*. New York: Basic Books.

Fairbairn, W. (1963). Synopsis of an object-relations theory of the personality. *International Journal of Psychoanalysis* 44: 224–225.

Feldman, A.B. (1953). The confessions of William Shakespeare. *American Imago* 10: 113–166.

Feldman, M. (2007). Addressing parts of the self. *International Journal of Psychoanalysis* 88: 371–386.

Fenichel, O. (1945). *The Psychoanalytic Theory of Neurosis*. New York: W.W. Norton.

Ferenczi, S. (1909). Introjection and transference. In: *First Contributions to Psychoanalysis*. Transl. E. Jones, pp. 35–93. New York: Bruner/Mazel, 1980.

Ferenczi, S. (1913). A little Chanticleer. In: *First Contributions to Psychoanalysis*. Transl. E. Jones, pp. 240–252. New York: Bruner/Mazel, 1980.

Ferenczi, S. (1915). Talkativeness. In: *Further Contributions to the Theory and Technique of Psychoanalysis*, p. 252. London: Hogarth Press, 1948.

Ferenczi, S. (1919). On the technique of psychoanalysis. In: *Further Contributions to the Theory and Technique of Psychoanalysis*. Transl. J. Suttie, pp. 177–189. London: Karnac Books, 1980.

Ferenczi, S. (1921). The further development of the active therapy in psychoanalysis. In: *Further Contributions to the Theory and Technique of Psychoanalysis*, pp. 198–217. London: Hogarth Press, 1955.

Ferenczi, S. (1928). The elasticity of psychoanalytical technique. In: *Final Contributions to the Problems and Methods of Psychoanalysis*, pp. 87–101. New York: Basic Books, 1955.

Ferenczi, S. (1929). The unwelcome child and his death instinct. *International Journal of Psychoanalysis* 10: 125–129.

Ferenczi, S. (1931). Child-analysis in the analysis of adults. *International Journal of Psychoanalysis* 12: 468–482.

Ferreira, A. (1964). The intimacy need in psychotherapy. *American Journal of Psychoanalysis* 24: 190–194.

Firestein, S. (1990). Death of the analyst: termination, interruption, what? In: *Illness and the Analyst: Implications for the Treatment Relationship*, ed. A.J. Schwartz and A.S. Silver, pp. 333–340. Washington, DC: American Psychiatric Press.

Fivush, R. (2010). Speaking silence: the social construction of silence in autobiographical and cultural narratives. *Memory* 18: 88–98.

Fonagy, P., and Target, M. (1998). Mentalization and the changing aims of child psychoanalysis. *Psychoanalytic Dialogues* 8: 87–114.

Francis, L.P., and Francis, J.G. (2017). *Privacy: What Everyone Needs to Know*. Oxford: Oxford University Press.

Frank, A. (1969). The unrememberable and the unforgettable: passive primal repression. *The Psychoanalytic Study of the Child* 24: 48–77.

Frank, A.W. (2004). *The Renewal of Generosity: Illness, Medicine, and How to Live*. Chicago: University of Chicago Press.

Frankel, V. (1959). *Man's Search for Meaning*. Boston: Beacon Press, 2006.

Freedman, A. (1990). Death of the psychoanalyst as a form of termination of psychoanalysis. In: *Illness in the Analyst: Implications for the Treatment Relationship*, ed. H.J. Schwartz and A.S. Silver, pp. 299–332. Washington, DC: American Psychiatric Press.

Freud, A. (1954). Psychoanalysis and education. *Psychoanalytic Study of the Child* 9: 9–15.

Freud, S. (1895a). Project for a scientific psychology. *Standard Edition* 1: 295–343.

Freud, S. (1895b). Studies on hysteria (with Joseph Breuer). *Standard Edition* 2: 1–323.

Freud, S. (1897). Extracts from the Fleiss Papers: Letter 57. *Standard Edition* 1: 242–244.

Freud, S. (1900). The interpretation of dreams. *Standard Edition* 4–5: 1–626.

Freud, S. (1905a). On psychotherapy. *Standard Edition* 7: 257–268.

Freud, S. (1905b). Three essays on the theory of sexuality. *Standard Edition* 7: 135–243.

Freud, S. (1907). Delusions and dreams in Jensen's "Gradiva". *Standard Edition* 9: 1–96.

Freud, S. (1908a). On the sexual theories of children. *Standard Edition* 9: 209–226.

Freud, S. (1908b). "Civilized" sexual morality and modern nervous illness. *Standard Edition* 9: 177–204.

Freud, S. (1908c). Creative writers and day-dreaming. *Standard Edition* 9: 141–154.

Freud, S. (1909a). Analysis of a phobia in a five year old boy. *Standard Edition* 10: 5–149.

Freud, S. (1909b). Notes upon a case of obsessional neurosis. *Standard Edition*: 151–244.

Freud, S. (1910a). Leonardo da Vinci and a memory of his childhood. *Standard Edition* 11: 63–138.

Freud, S. (1910b). A special type of object choice made by men. *Standard Edition* 11: 163–175.

Freud, S. (1911). Formulation of the two principles of mental functioning. *Standard Edition* 12: 213–226.

Freud, S. (1912). Recommendations to physicians practising psycho-analysis. *Standard Edition* 12: 109–120.

Freud, S. (1913). Totem and taboo. *Standard Edition* 13: 1–161.

Freud, S. (1914a). On narcissism: an introduction. *Standard Edition* 14: 69–102.

Freud, S. (1914b). Remembering, repeating, and working through. *Standard Edition* 12: 145–156.

Freud, S. (1915a). Observations on transference love. *Standard Edition* 12: 157–171.

Freud, S. (1915b). Instincts and their vicissitudes. *Standard Edition* 14: 117–140.

Freud, S. (1915c). Repression. *Standard Edition* 14: 141–158.

Freud, S. (1915d). The unconscious. *Standard Edition* 14: 159–216.

Freud, S. (1915e). A case of paranoia running counter to the psychoanalytic theory of the disease. *Standard Edition* 14: 261–272.

Freud, S. (1917a). Mourning and melancholia. *Standard Edition* 14: 237–258.

Freud, S. (1917b). A difficulty in the path of psychoanalysis. *Standard Edition* 17: 137–144.

Freud, S. (1918). From the history of an infantile neurosis. *Standard Edition* 17: 1–122.

Freud, S. (1920). The psychogenesis of a case of homosexuality in a woman. *Standard Edition* 18: 145–172.

Freud, S. (1921). Group psychology and the analysis of the ego. *Standard Edition* 18: 65–144.

Freud, S. (1923). The ego and the id. *Standard Edition* 19: 1–66.

Freud, S. (1924a). The economic problem of masochism. *Standard Edition* 19: 157–170.

Freud, S. (1924b). The dissolution of the Oedipus complex. *Standard Edition* 19: 171–188.

Freud, S. (1925). Some psychical consequences of the anatomic distinction between the sexes. *Standard Edition* 19: 241–258.

Freud, S. (1926). Address to the society of B'nai B'rith. *Standard Edition* 20: 273–274.

Freud, S. (1927a). The future of an illusion. *Standard Edition* 21: 5–56.

Freud, S. (1927b). Fetishism. *Standard Edition* 21: 152–157.

Freud, S. (1930). Civilization and its discontents. *Standard Edition* 21: 64–145.

Freud, S. (1933). Why war? (Letter to Albert Einstein). *Standard Edition* 22: 203–215.

Freud, S. (1939). Moses and monotheism. *Standard Edition* 23: 7–137.

Furnham, A., Hosoe, T., and Tang, T. (2001). Male hubris and female humility? A cross- cultural study of ratings of self, parental and sibling multiple intelligence in America, Britain and Japan. *Intelligence* 30: 101–115.

Gabbard, G. (2015). Privacy, the self and psychoanalytic practice in the era of the internet. *Revista di Psicoanalisi* 61: 529–542.

Gabbard, G.O., and Lester, E. (1995). *Boundaries and Boundary Violations in Psycho-analysis*. New York: Basic Books.

Gabbard, G., and Williams, P. (2001). Preserving confidentiality in the writing of case reports. *International Journal of Psychoanalysis* 82: 1067–1068.

Gandhi, M.K. (1940). *An Autobiography: The Story of My Experiments with Truth.* Transl. M. Desai. Boston: Beacon Press, 1957.

Gay, P. (1988). *Freud: A Life for Our Time.* New York: W.W. Norton.

Gediman, H. (1985). Impostor, inauthenticity, and feeling fraudulent. *Journal of American Psychoanalytic Association* 39: 911–936.

Glover, E. (1955). *The Technique of Psychoanalysis.* New York: International Universities Press.

Goffman, E. (1959). *The Presentation of Self in Everyday Life.* New York: Doubleday Anchor.

Goldberg, A. (1987). The place of apology in psychoanalysis and psychotherapy. *International Review of Psychoanalysis* 14: 409–422.

Goldberg, C. (2002a). An exploration of analyst's impeded curiosity. *Contemporary Psychoanalysis* 38: 141–151.

Goldberg, C. (2002b). Escaping the dark side of curiosity. *American Journal of Psychoanalysis* 63: 185–199.

Green, A. (1986). Réponses à des questions inconcevables. *Topique* 37: 11–30.

Greenacre, P. (1951). Respiratory incorporation and the phallic phase. *Psychoanalytic Study of the Child* 6: 180–205.

Greenacre, P. (1953). Certain relationships between fetishism and the faulty development of the body image. *Psychoanalytic Study of the Child* 8: 79–97.

Greenacre, P. (1956). Experience of awe in childhood. *Psychoanalytic Study of the Child* 11: 9–30.

Greenson, R. (1960). Empathy and its vicissitudes. *International Journal of Psychoanalysis* 41: 418–424.

Greenson, R. (1967). *The Technique and Practice of Psychoanalysis.* New York: International Universities Press.

Greenspan, S. (1989). *The Development of the Ego: Implications for Personality Theory, Psychopathology and the Psychotherapeutic Process.* Madison, CT: International Universities Press.

Greenspan, S. (2005). *Infant and Early Childhood Mental Health: A Comprehensive Developmental Approach to Assessment and Intervention.* Washington, DC: American Psychiatric Publishing, Inc.

Griffin, J. (2002). A note on measuring well-being. In: *Summary Measures of Population Health: Concepts, Ethics, Measurement and Applications,* ed. C.J.L. Murray, J. Salomon, and C. Mathers, p. 31. Geneva: World Health Organization.

Griffith, J.L. (2010). *Religion that Heals, Religion that Harms: A Guide for Clinical Practice.* New York: Guilford Press.

Grinberg, R. (1962). On curiosity. *Psychoanalytic Quarterly* 31: 593.

Gross, A. (1951). The secret. *Bulletin of the Menninger Clinic* 15: 37–44.

Grotstein, J. (2007). *An Intense Beam of Darkness: Wilfred Bion's Legacy in Psychoanalysis.* London: Karnac Books.

Gunderson, J. (1985). *Borderline Personality Disorder.* Washington, DC: American Psychiatric Press.

Guntrip, H. (1969). *Schizoid Phenomena, Object Relations and the Self.* New York: International Universities Press.

Guttman, S.A., Jones, R.L., and Parrish, S.M., eds (1980). *The Concordance to the Standard Edition of the Complete Psychological Works of Sigmund Freud*. Boston: G.K. Hall.

Hartmann, H. (1939). *Ego Psychology and the Problem of Adaptation*. Transl. D. Rapaport. New York: International Universities Press, 1958.

Hartmann, H. (1952). The mutual influences of the development of ego and id. *Psychoanalytic Study of the Child* 7: 9–30.

Hartmann, H. (1956). Notes on the reality principle. *Psychoanalytic Study of the Child* 11: 31–53.

Hartmann, H. (1960). *Psychoanalysis and Moral Values*. New York: International Universities Press.

Hartmann, H. (1964). *Essays on Ego Psychology*. New York: International Universities Press.

Harvard's Project Zero program (2010). *Research Project: Visible Thinking*. Cambridge, MA: Harvard University Press.

Heald, C. (2000). *Intimacy with God*. Colorado Springs, CO: NavPress.

Heaney, S. (1995). *A Redress for Poetry*. New York: Farrar, Straus and Giroux.

Heine, S.J., Lehman, D.R., Markus, H.R., and Kitayama, S. (1999). Is there a universal need for positive self-regard? *Psychological Review* 106: 766–779.

Herold, C.M. (1942). Critical analysis of the elements of psychic functions. *Psychoanalytic Quarterly* 11: 59–82.

Herzog, J. (1984). Fathers and young children: fathering daughters and fathering sons. In: *Foundations of Infant Psychiatry, Vol II*, ed. J.D. Kall, E. Galenson, and R. Tyson, pp. 335–343. New York: Basic Books.

Hirsch, I. (1983). Analytic intimacy and the restoration of nurturance. *American Journal of Psychoanalysis* 43: 325–343.

Hitchens, C. (2007). *God is Not Great*. New York: Twelve.

Hoffer, A., ed. (2015). *Freud and the Buddha: The Couch and the Cushion*. London: Karnac Books.

Hoffman, I. (1983). The patient as interpreter of the analyst's experience. *Contemporary Psychoanalysis* 19: 389–422.

Hofstede, G. (2001). *Culture's Consequences: International Differences in Work-Related Values* (2nd edn). London: Sage Publications.

Horner, A. (1986). *Being and Loving*. Northvale, NJ: Jason Aronson.

Hoyt, M. (1978). Secrets in psychotherapy: theoretical and practical considerations. *International Journal of Psychoanalysis* 5: 231–241.

Hoyt, M. (1980). Secrets in psychotherapy. *International Journal of Psychoanalysis* 7: 407–408.

Ingram, D.H. (1986). Remarks on intimacy and the fear of commitment. *American Journal of Psychoanalysis* 46: 76–79.

Irwin, R. (2011). *Memoirs of a Dervish: Sufis, Mystics, and the Sixties*. London: Profile Books.

Isherwood, C. (1980). *My Guru and His Disciple*. New York: Farrar, Straus and Giroux.

Jablow, P. (2016). Review of "Bush", by J.E. Smith. *Philadelphia Inquirer*, p. H-10. October 9, 2016.

Jacobs, T. (1980). Secrets, alliances, and family fictions: some psychoanalytic observations. *Journal of the American Psychoanalytic Association* 28: 21–42.

Jacobson, E. (1964). *The Self and the Object World*. New York: International Universities Press.

Jakes, T.D. (2013). *Intimacy with God*. Ada, MI: Bethany House Publishing.

Kafka, J. (1989). *Multiple Realities in Clinical Practice*. New Haven, CT: Yale University Press.

Kajonius, P.J., and Dåderman, A.M. (2014). Exploring the relationship between honesty-humility, the big five, and liberal values in Swedish students. *Europe's Journal of Psychology* 10: 104–117.

Kantrowitz, J. (2009). Privacy and disclosure in psychoanalysis. *Journal of the American Psychoanalytic Association* 57: 787–806.

Kaplan, H. (1990). Sex, intimacy, and the aging process. *Journal of American Academy of Psychoanalysis and Dynamic Psychiatry* 18: 185–205.

Kapoor, P. (2017). *Gandhi: An Illustrated Biography*. New York: Black Dog and Leventhal Publishers.

Kareem, J. (1992). The Nafsiyat Intercultural Therapy Centre: ideas and experience in intercultural therapy. In: *Intercultural Therapy: Themes, Interpretations, and Practice*, ed. J. Kareem and R. Littlewood, pp. 14–37. London: Blackwell Scientific Publications.

Kateb, G. (2011). *Human Dignity*. Cambridge, MA: Harvard University Press.

Keating, T. (2009). *Intimacy with God*. New York: Crossroad Publishing Company.

Keizer, G. (2012). *Privacy*. New York: Picador.

Kernberg, O.F. (1970). A psychoanalytic classification of character pathology. *Journal of the American Psychoanalytic Association* 18: 800–822.

Kernberg, O.F. (1975). *Borderline Conditions and Pathological Narcissism*. New York: Jason Aronson.

Kernberg, O.F. (1984). *Severe Personality Disorders: Psychotherapeutic Strategies*. New Haven, CT: Yale University Press.

Kernberg, O.F. (1992). *Aggression in Personality Disorders and Perversions*. New Haven, CT: Yale University Press.

Kernberg, O.F. (1995). *Love Relations: Normality and Pathology*. New Haven, CT: Yale University Press.

Khan, M. (1963). The concept of cumulative trauma. In: *The Privacy of the Self*, pp. 42–58. New York: International Universities Press, 1974.

Khan, M. (1972). The finding and becoming of self. In: *The Privacy of the Self*, pp. 294–305. New York: International Universities Press, 1974.

Khan, M. (1979). *Alienation in Perversions*. New York: International Universities Press.

Khan, M. (1983a). From secretiveness to shared living. In: *Hidden Selves: Between Theory and Practice in Psychoanalysis*, pp. 88–96. New York: International Universities Press.

Khan, M. (1983b). Secret as potential space. In: *Hidden Selves: Between Theory and Practice in Psychoanalysis*, pp. 97–107. New York: International Universities Press.

Khan, M. (1983c). Infancy, aloneness, and madness. In: *Hidden Selves: Between Theory and Practice in Psychoanalysis*, pp. 181–182. New York: International Universities Press.

Khan, M. (1983d). On lying fallow. In: *Hidden Selves: Between Theory and Practice in Psychoanalysis*, pp. 183–188. New York: International Universities Press.

Kieffer, C. (2014). *Mutuality, Recognition, and the Self: Psychoanalytic Reflections.* London: Karnac Books.

Killingmo, B. (1989). Conflict and deficit: implications for technique. *International Journal of Psycho-Analysis* 70: 65–79.

Kim, Y.H., and Cohen, D. (2010). Information, perspective, and judgements about the self in "face" and "dignity" cultures. *Personality and Social Psychology Bulletin* 36: 537–550.

Kinsey, A., Pomeroy, W., and Martin, C. (1948a). *Sexual Behavior in the Human Male.* Philadelphia: W.B. Saunders.

Kinsey, A., Pomeroy, W., and Martin, C. (1948b). *Sexual Behavior in the Human Female.* Philadelphia: W.B. Saunders.

Kirman, J.H. (1998). One-person or two-person psychology? *Modern Psychoanalysis* 23: 3–22.

Kleeman, J. (1967). The peek-a-boo game. *Psychoanalytic Study of the Child* 22: 239–273.

Klein, M. (1924). The role of the school in the libidinal development of the child. *International Journal of Psychoanalysis* 5: 312–331.

Klein, M. (1925). A contribution to the psychogenesis of tics. In: *Love, Guilt and Reparation: And Other Works 1921–1945*, pp. 106–127. New York: The Free Press, 1975.

Klein, M. (1930). The importance of symbol formation in the development of ego. *International Journal of Psychoanalysis* 11: 24–39.

Klein, M. (1931). A contribution to the theory of intellectual inhibition. *International Journal of Psychoanalysis* 12: 206–218.

Klein, M. (1935). A contribution to the psychogenesis of manic depressive states. In: *Love, Guilt and Reparation and Other Works – 1921–1945*, pp. 262–289. New York: Free Press, 1975.

Klein, M. (1940). Mourning and its relation to manic depressive states. In: *Love, Guilt and Reparation and Other Works – 1921–1945*, pp. 344–369. New York: Free Press, 1975.

Klumpner, G., and Frank, A. (1991). On methods of reporting clinical material. *Journal of the American Psychoanalytic Association* 39: 537–551.

Kohut, H. (1971). *Analysis of the Self.* New York: International Universities Press.

Kohut, H. (1977). *Restoration of the Self.* New York: International Universities Press.

Kolansky, H., and Eisner, H. (1974). The psychoanalytic concept of preoedipal developmental arrest. Paper presented at the fall meetings of the American Psychoanalytic Association. Cited in: *Inner Torment: Living Between Conflict and Fragmentation*, ed. S. Akhtar, p. 231. Northvale, NJ: Jason Aronson, 1999.

Krafft-Ebing, R. von (1892). *Psychopathia Sexualis.* New York: Arcade Publishing, 1998.

Kramer, S. (1983). Object-coercive doubting: a pathological defensive response to maternal incest. *Journal of the American Psychoanalytic Association* 31S: 325–351.

Kramer, S. (1996). The development of intimacy and its relationship with the ability to have friends. In: *Intimacy and Infidelity: Separation-Individuation Perspectives*, ed. S. Akhtar and S. Kramer, pp. 1–18. Northvale, NJ: Jason Aronson.

Kretschmer, E. (1925). *Physique and Character.* Transl. W.J.H. Sprott. New York: Harcourt Brace.

Kris, A.O. (1977). Either-or dilemmas. *Psychoanalytic Study of the Child* 32: 91–117.

Kris, E. (1952). *Psychoanalytic Explorations in Art.* New York: International Universities Press.

Kulish, N. (2002). Female sexuality: the pleasures of secrets and the secret of pleasure. *Psychoanalytic Study of the Child* 57: 151–176.

Kundera, M. (1991). *Immortality*. New York: Faber & Faber.

Kurtz, S. (1992). *All The Mothers Are One: Hindu India and the Cultural Re-shaping of Psychoanalysis*. New York: Columbia University Press.

Laplanche, J., and Pontalis, J.-B. (1973). *The Language of Psychoanalysis*. Transl. D. Nicholson-Smith. New York: W.W. Norton.

Lasch, C. (1979). *The Culture of Narcissism: American Life in an Age of Diminishing Expectations*. New York: W.W. Norton.

Laufer, M. (1968). The body image, the function of masturbation, and adolescence: problem of the ownership of the body. *Psychoanalytic Study of the Child* 23: 114–137.

Lax, R.F. (2008). Becoming really old: the indignities. *Psychoanalytic Quarterly* 77: 835–857.

Lee, H.I., Leung, A.K., and Kim, Y.H. (2014). Unpacking East-West differences in the extent of self-enhancement from the perspective of face versus dignity culture. *Social and Personality Psychology Compass* 8: 314–327.

Lerner, H.E. (1976). Parental mislabelling of female genitals as a determinant of penis envy and learning inhibitions in women. *Journal of the American Psychoanalytic Association* 24S: 269–283.

Levenson, E.A. (1974). Changing concepts of intimacy in psychoanalytic practice. *Contemporary Psychoanalysis* 10: 359–368.

Levenson, R. (1984). Intimacy, autonomy, and gender: developmental differences and their reflection in adult relationships. *Journal of the American Academy of Psychoanalysis* 12: 529–544.

Levinas, E. (1961). *Totality and Infinity*. Transl. A. Lingis. Pittsburgh, PA: Dusquesne University Press.

Levinas, E. (1981). *Otherwise than Being*. Transl. A. Lingis. Pittsburgh, PA: Dusquesne University Press.

Levine, S. (2006). Catching the wrong leopard: courage and masochism in the psychoanalytic situation. *Psychoanalytic Quarterly* 75: 533–565.

Levine, S., ed. (2016). *Dignity Matters: Psychoanalytic and Psychosocial Perspectives*. London: Karnac Books.

Lewis, C.S. (1942). *The Screwtape Letters*. New York: HarperCollins.

Lichtenberg, J. (1982). Reflections on the first year of life. *Psychoanalytic Inquiry* 1: 695–730.

Lichtenberg, J. (1989). *Psychoanalysis and Motivation*. Hillsdale, NJ: Analytic Press.

Lichtenberg, J. (2005). Sanderian activation waves: a hypothesis of a nonsymbolic influence on moods. *Psychoanalytic Quarterly* 74: 485–505.

Lifton, R.J. (1971). Protean man. *Archives of General Psychiatry* 24: 298–304.

Limentani, A. (1989). *Between Freud and Klein: The Psychoanalytic Quest for Knowledge and Truth*. London: Free Association Books.

Loewenstein, R.M. (1961). The silent patient: introduction. *Journal of the American Psychoanalytic Association* 9: 2–6.

Lokos, A. (2012). *Patience: The Art of Peaceful Living*. New York: Tarcher.

Lopez-Corvo, R. (2003). *The Work of W.R. Bion*. London: Karnac Books.

Low, B. (1935). The psychological compensations of the analyst. *International Journal of Psychoanalysis* 16: 1–8.

Macklin, R. (2003). Dignity is a useless concept. *British Medical Journal* 327: 1419–1420.

Maddow, L. (1997). On the way to a second symbiosis. In: *The Seasons of Life: Separation-Individuation Perspectives*, ed. S. Akhtar and S. Kramer, pp. 157–170. Northvale, NJ: Jason Aronson.

Mahler, M. (1942). Pseudo-imbecility: a magic cap of invisibility. In: *Selected Papers of Margaret S Mahler*, pp. 3–16. New York: Jason Aronson, 1979.

Mahler, M.S., Pine, F., and Bergman, A. (1975). *The Psychological Birth of the Human Infant: Symbiosis and Individuation*. New York: Basic Books.

Maldonado, J.L. (2005). A disturbance of interpreting, of symbolization, and of curiosity in the analyst-analysand relationship: the patient without insight. *International Journal of Psychoanalysis* 86: 413–432.

Marcovitz, E. (1970a). Dignity. In: *Bemoaning the Lost Dream: Collected Papers of Eli Marcovitz, MD*, ed. M.S. Temeles, pp. 120–130. Philadelphia: Philadelphia Association for Psychoanalysis, 1983.

Marcovitz, E. (1970b). Aggression, dignity, and violence. In: *Bemoaning the Lost Dream: Collected Papers of Eli Marcovitz, MD*, ed. M.S. Temeles, pp. 131–149. Philadelphia: Philadelphia Association for Psychoanalysis.

Marcus, P. (2013a). *In Search of the Spiritual: Gabriel Marcel, Psychoanalysis, and the Sacred*. London: Karnac Books.

Marcus, P. (2013b). On the quiet virtue of humility. In: *In Search of the Spiritual: Gabriel Marcel, Psychoanalysis, and the Sacred*, pp. 89–110. London: Karnac Books.

Margolis, G. (1966). Secrecy and identity. *International Review of Psychoanalysis* 47: 517–522.

Margolis, G. (1974). The psychology of keeping secrets. *International Journal of Psychoanalysis* 1: 291–296.

Margolis, J. (1978). Psychotherapy and persons: reply to R. Abelson. *Psychoanalysis and Contemporary Thought* 1: 217–226.

Martin, G. (2008). *Gabriel Garcia Marquez: A Life*. New York: Alfred Knopf.

Max Planck Society. (2007). Personality gene makes songbirds curious. www.mpg.de/English/illustrations/documentation. Accessed on 2 May 2007.

May, R. (1953). *Man's Search for Himself*. New York: W.W. Norton, 2009.

May, R. (1969). *Love and Will*. New York: W.W. Norton, 2007.

Mayes, L. (1991). Exploring internal and external worlds: reflections on being curious. *Psychoanalytic Study of the Child* 46: 3–36.

McDermott, M. (2009). Researchers discover first ever link between intelligence and curiosity. www.PhysOrg.com/news. Accessed on 14 September 2009.

Meares, R. (1994). A pathology of privacy: towards a new theoretical approach to obsessive compulsive disorder. *Contemporary Psychoanalysis* 30: 83–100.

Meissner, W. (1984). *Psychoanalysis and Religious Experience*. New Haven, CT: Yale University Press.

Meissner, W. (2001). So help me God! Do I help God or does God help me? In: *Does God Help? Developmental and Clinical Aspects of Religious Belief*, ed. S. Akhtar and H. Parens, pp. 74–126. Northvale, NJ: Jason Aronson.

Melges, F.T., and Swartz, M.S. (1989). Oscillations of attachment in borderline personality disorder. *American Journal of Psychiatry* 146: 1115–1120.

Meltzer, D. (1986). *Studies in Extended Metapsychology: Clinical Applications of Bion's Ideas*. London: Karnac Books.

Melzak, S. (1992). Secrecy, privacy, survival, repressive regimes, and growing up. *Bulletin of the Anna Freud Centre* 15: 205–224.

Menninger, W.C. (1943). Characterologic and symptomatic expressions related to the anal phase of psychosexual development. *Psychoanalytic Quarterly* 12: 161–193.

Migdow, J.S. (2008). A failure of curiosity. *Psychoanalytic Social Work* 15: 43–52.

Miller, J.F. (2013). *The Triumphant Victim: A Psychoanalytical Perspective on Sadomasochism and Perverse Thinking*. London: Karnac Books.

Mish, F.C., ed. (1987). *Merriam Webster's Collegiate Dictionary* (10th edn). Springfield, MA: Merriam Webster Press.

Modell, A. (1984). *Psychoanalysis in a New Context*. New York: International Universities Press.

Moore, B., and Fine, B., eds. (1968). *A Glossary of Psychoanalytic Terms and Concepts*. New York: American Psychoanalytic Association.

Moore, B., and Fine, B., eds. (1990). *Psychoanalytic Terms and Concepts*. New Haven, CT: Yale University Press.

Moore, M. (2009). *Wa*: harmony and sustenance of the self in Japanese life. In: *Freud and the Far East: Psychoanalytic Perspectives on the People and Culture of China, Japan, and Korea*, ed. S. Akhtar, pp. 79–88. Lanham, MD: Jason Aronson.

Murphy, C. (2011). Unique therapy uses horses to help children. *Farm Ireland*, 6 July 2011. Accessed on 28 December 2017.

Nersessian, E. (1995). Some reflections on curiosity and psychoanalytic technique. *Psychoanalytic Quarterly* 64: 113–135.

Nersessian, E. (2000). The role of curiosity in psychoanalysis: changes in my technique in the past fifteen years. In: *Changing Ideas in a Changing World: Essays in Honor of Arnold Cooper*, pp. 103–109. London: Karnac Books.

Nersessian, E., and Silvan, M. (2007). Neutrality and curiosity: elements of technique. *Psychoanalytic Quarterly* 76: 863–890.

Nicholi, A. (2002). *The Question of God: C.S. Lewis and Sigmund Freud Debate God, Love, Sex, and the Meaning of Life*. New York: Free Press.

Niederland, W. (1968). Clinical observations on the "survivor syndrome". *International Journal of Psychoanalysis* 49: 313–315.

Nin, A. (1966). *In Favor of the Sensitive Man, and Other Essays*. Boston: Mariner Books.

Nosek, L. (2009). Body and infinite: notes for a theory of genitality. *Revista Brasiliera de Psicanalise* 43: 139–151.

Novick, J., and Novick, K.K. (2008). Expanding the domain privacy, secrecy, and confidentiality. *The Annual of Psychoanalysis* 36: 145–160.

Nunberg, H. (1931). The synthetic function of the ego. *International Journal of Psychoanalysis* 12: 123–140.

Nunberg, H. (1961). *Curiosity*. New York: International Universities Press.

Nunberg, H., and Federn, P. (1962). *Minutes of the Vienna Psychoanalytic Society, Vol I: 1906–1908*. New York: International Universities Press.

Oberto, R. (2017). *Intimacy with God*. New York: Opened Heart Publications.

Ogden, T.H. (1996). Reconsidering three aspects of psychoanalytic technique. *International Journal of Psychoanalysis* 77: 883–899.

O'Neil, M.K. (2007). Confidentiality, privacy, and the facilitating role of psychoanalytic organizations. *International Journal of Psychoanalysis* 88: 691–711.

O'Neil, M.K. (2009). Commentary on "courage". In: *Good Feelings: Psychoanalytic Reflections on Positive Emotions and Attitudes*, ed. S. Akhtar, pp. 55–63. London: Karnac Books.

Orbach, S. (2007). Separated attachments and sexual aliveness: how changing attachment patterns can enhance intimacy. *Attachment: New Directions in Psychotherapy and Relational Psychoanalysis* 1: 8–17.

Ostow, M. (1995). *The Ultimate Intimacy: Psychoanalysis and Jewish Mysticism*. London: Karnac.

Ostow, M. (2000). Three archaic contributions to the religious instinct: awe, mysticism, and apocalypse. In: *Does God Help: Developmental and Clinical Aspects of Religious Belief*, ed. S. Akhtar and H. Parens, pp. 197–233. Northvale, NJ: Jason Aronson.

Paris, J. (1985). Boundary and intimacy. *Journal of the American Academy of Psychoanalysis* 13: 505–510.

Parkhurst, C. (2004). *The Dogs of Babel*. Boston: Back Bay Books.

Parsons, M. (2007). Raiding the inarticulate: the internal analytic setting and listening beyond countertransference. *International Journal of Psychoanalysis* 88: 1441–1456.

Paul, R. (2005). Anthropology. In: *Textbook of Psychoanalysis*, ed. E.S. Person, A.M. Cooper, and G.O. Gabbard, pp. 479–490. Washington, DC: American Psychiatric Publishing.

Peeping Tom (1960). Directed and produced by Michael Powell.

Pine, F. (1988). The four psychologies of psychoanalysis and their place in clinical work. *Journal of the American Psychoanalytic Association* 36: 571–596.

Platt, C. (2017). Death of pet. In: *Bereavement: Personal Experiences and Clinical Reflections*, ed. S. Akhtar and G.S. Kanwal, pp. 143–166. London: Karnac.

Poland, W. (2000). The analyst's witnessing and otherness. *Journal of the American Psychoanalytic Association* 48: 17–34.

Poland, W. (2009). Problems of collegial learning in psychoanalysis. *International Journal of Psychoanalysis* 90: 249–262.

Puzo, M. (1969). *The Godfather*. New York: G.P. Putnam's Sons.

Racker, H. (1968). *Transference and Countertransference*. London: Hogarth Press.

Rangell, L. (1954). The psychology of poise – with a special elaboration on the psychic significance of the snout or perioral region. *International Journal of Psychoanalysis* 35: 313–332.

Rangell, L. (1969). Choice conflict and the decision-making function of the ego. *International Journal of Psychoanalysis* 50: 599–602.

Rao, D. (2005). Manifestations of God in India: a transference patheon. In: *Freud Along the Ganges: Psychoanalytic Reflections on the People and Culture of India*, ed. S. Akhtar, pp. 271–308. New York: Other Press.

Rapaport, D. (1960). *The Structure of Psychoanalytic Theory: A Systematic Attempt*. New York: International Universities Press, Inc.

Reed, G. (1997). The analyst's privacy and the patient's curiosity. *Journal of Clinical Psychoanalysis* 6: 517–531.

Reik, T. (1948). *Listening with the Third Ear*. New York: Farrar, Straus and Giroux.

Rellahan, M. (2017). Equine therapy helps Chesco inmates. *Philadelphia Inquirer B-4*, December 26, 2017.

Renik, O. (1994). Publication of clinical facts. *International Journal of Psychoanalysis* 75: 1245–1250.

Renik, O. (1995). The ideal of the anonymous analyst and the problem of self-disclosure. *Psychoanalytic Quarterly* 64: 466–495.

Richards, A. (2003). Psychoanalytic discourse at the turn of our century: a plea for a measure of humility. *Journal of the American Psychoanalytic Association* 51S: 73–89.

Richards, A.K., and Spira, L. (2003). On being lonely: fear of one's own aggression as an impediment to intimacy. *Psychoanalytic Quarterly* 72: 257–374.

Rilke, R.M. (1929). *Letters to a Young Poet*. New York: Vintage Books, 1986.

Ritchhart, R., and Perkins, D. (2005). Learning to think: the challenges of teaching thinking. In: *Cambridge Handbook of Thinking and Reasoning*, ed. K.J. Holyoak and R.G. Morrison, pp. 775–802. New York: Cambridge University Press.

Ritchhart, R., and Perkins, D. (2008). Making thinking visible. *Educational Leadership* 65: 57–61.

Rizzuto, A.M. (1979). *The Birth of the Living God*. Chicago: University of Chicago Press.

Rizzuto, M. (2001). Does God help? What God? Helping whom? The convolutions of divine help. In: *Does God Help? Developmental and Clinical Aspects of Religious Belief*, ed. S. Akhtar and H. Parens, pp. 19–52. Northvale, NJ: Jason Aronson.

Roland, A. (1988). *In Search of Self in India and Japan*. Princeton, NJ: Princeton University Press.

Roland, A. (1996). *Cultural Pluralism and Psychoanalysis: The Asian and North-American Experience*. New York: Routledge.

Roland, A. (2011). *Journeys to Foreign Selves: Asians and Asian Americans in a Global Era*. New Delhi: Oxford University Press.

Ronningstam, E. (2006). Silence: cultural function and psychological transformation in psychoanalysis and psychoanalytic psychotherapy. *International Journal of Psychoanalysis* 87: 1277–1296.

Rosen, M. (2012). *Dignity: Its History and Meaning*. Cambridge, MA: Harvard University Press.

Rotenberg, M. (1977). "Alienating-individualism" and "reciprocal-individualism": A cross-cultural conceptualization. *Journal of Humanistic Psychology* 17: 3–17.

Rubin, J. (2005). Psychoanalytic and Buddhist history and theory. In: *Freud Along the Ganges: Psychoanalytic Reflections on the People and Culture of India*, ed. S. Akhtar, pp. 335–354. New York: Other Press.

Rubin, T. (1989). Editorial: intimacy and cultural pressures. *American Journal of Psychoanalysis* 49: 1–4.

Rudnytsky, P. (2011). *Rescuing Psychoanalysis from Freud and Other Essays in Re-Vision*. London: Karnac Books.

Ryan, M.J. (2013). *The Power of Patience*. New York: Conari Press.

Salmon, A.K. (2010). Engaging children in thinking routines. *Childhood Education* 86: 132–137.

Sandler, J., and Sandler, A.M. (1998). *Internal Objects Re-Visited*. London: Karnac Books.

Sarphatie, H. (1993). On shame and humiliation: some notes on early development and pathology. In: *The Dutch Annual of Psychoanalysis 1993*, ed. H. Groen-Prakken and A. Ladan, pp. 191–204. Amsterdam: Swets and Zietlinger.

Schimel, J. (1987). On failed intimacy. *Journal of the American Academy of Psychoanalysis and Dynamic Psychiatry* 15: 553–557.

Schlesinger, H. (2003). Responding to patients' questions. In: *The Texture of Treatment: On the Matter of Psychoanalytic Technique*, pp. 171–178. Hillsdale, NJ: Analytic Press.

Schopenhauer, A. (1851). *Parerga und Paralipomena, Vol II*. Transl. E.F.J. Payne. Oxford: Clarendon Press, 2000.

Schore, A. (2001). Minds in the making: attachment, the self-organizing brain, and developmentally-oriented psychoanalytic psychotherapy. *British Journal of Psychotherapy* 17: 299–313.

Schwaber, E. (2007). The unending struggle to listen. In: *Listening to Others: Developmental and Clinical Aspects of Empathy and Attunement*, ed. S. Akhtar, pp. 17–39. Lanham, MD: Jason Aronson.

Schwartz, H., and Silver, A., eds. (1990). *Illness in the Analyst: Implications for the Treatment Relationship.* Washington, DC: American Psychiatric Press.

Searles, H.F. (1960). *The Non-Human Environment in Normal Development and in Schizo-phrenia.* New York: International Universities Press.

Searles, H.F. (1979). *Countertransference and Related Subjects: Selected Papers.* New York: International Universities Press.

Shabad, P. (2000). Giving the devil his due: spite and the struggle for individual dignity. *Psychoanalytic Psychology* 17: 690–705.

Shabad, P. (2011). The dignity of creating: the patient's contribution to the "reachable enough" analyst. *Psychoanalytic Dialogues* 21: 619–629.

Shapiro, E., and Pinsker, H. (1973). Shared ethnic scotoma. *American Journal of Psychiatry* 130: 1338–1341.

Sharpe, E. (1930). The technique of psychoanalysis. *International Journal of Psychoanalysis* 11: 361–386.

Sharpe, E. (1940). Psychophysical problems revealed in language: an examination of metaphor. *International Journal of Psychoanalysis* 41: 201–220.

Sharpe, E. (1947). The psychoanalyst. *International Journal of Psychoanalysis* 28: 1–21.

Shengold, L. (1967). The effects of overstimulation: rat people. *International Journal of Psychoanalysis* 48: 403–415.

Shengold, L. (1971). More about rats and rat people. *International Journal of Psychoanalysis* 52: 277–288.

Shengold, L. (1989). *Soul Murder: The Effects of Childhood Abuse and Deprivation.* New Haven, CT: Yale University Press.

Sherman, J.R. (1987). *Patience Pays Off.* New York: Pathway Books.

Silberer, H. (1914). *Problem der Mystik und ihrer Symbolik.* Leipzig: Hugo Heller.

Smith, M.B. (2005). *Toward the Outside: Concepts and Themes in Emmanuel Levinas.* Pittsburgh, PA: Duquesne University Press.

Smolen, A. (2013). A seduced child is a betrayed child. In: *Betrayal: Developmental, Literary, and Clinical Realms*, ed. S. Akhtar, pp. 19–36. London: Karnac Books.

Smolen, A. (2018). The concerns of privacy in the treatment of children and adolescents. In: *Privacy: Developmental, Cultural, and Clinical Realms*, ed. S. Akhtar and A. Abbasi. London: Routledge.

Sperling, M. (1952). Animal phobias in a 2-year old child. *Psychoanalytic Study of the Child* 7: 115–125.

Sperling, M. (1971). Spider phobias and spider fantasies: a clinical contribution to the study of symbol and symptom choice. *Journal of the American Psychoanalytic Association* 19: 472–498.

Stafford, T. (2012). How curiosity can protect the mind from bias. www.BBC.com/future/story/20160907. Accessed on 8 September 2016.

Stekel, W. (1924). *Peculiarities of Behavior: Wandering Mania, Dipsomania, Cleptomania, Pyromania, and Allied Impulsive Acts*, Vols I and II. Transl. J. Van Teslaar. New York: Boni and Liveright.

Stern, D. (1985). *The Interpersonal World of the Infant: A View from Psychoanalysis and Developmental Psychology*. New York: Basic Books.

Stern, D. (1998). Introduction. In: *The Interpersonal World of the Infant: A View from Psychoanalysis and Developmental Psychology* (2nd edn), pp. i–xxv. New York: Basic Books.

Stern, D. (2009). Curiosity: dealing with divergent ideas in the ideal psychoanalytic institute. *Contemporary Psychoanalysis* 45: 292–305.

Stern, D., Sander, L., Nahum, J., Harrison, A., Lyons-Ruth, K., Morgan, A., Bruschweler-Stern, N., and Tronick, E. (1998). Non-interpretative mechanisms in psychoanalytic therapy: the "something more" than interpretation. *International Journal of Psychoanalysis* 79: 903–922.

Stolorow, R.D., and Grand, H.T. (1973). A partial analysis of a perversion involving bugs. *International Journal of Psychoanalysis* 54: 349–360.

Stone, L. (1961). *The Psychoanalytic Situation: An Examination of its Development and Essential Nature. Freud Anniversary Lecture*. New York: International Universities Press, 1977.

Strean, H. (1981). Extra-analytic contacts: theoretical and clinical considerations. *Psychoanalytic Quarterly* 50: 238–259.

Strenger, C. (1989). The classic and the romantic visions in psychoanalysis. *International Journal of Psychoanalysis* 70: 595–610.

Sullivan, H.S. (1953). *The Interpersonal Theory of Psychiatry*. New York: W.W. Norton.

Sullivan, H. (1956). *Clinical Studies in Psychiatry*. New York: W.W. Norton.

Sulzberger, C. (1953). Why it is hard to keep secrets. *Psychoanalysis* 2: 37–43.

Tähkä, V. (1993). *Mind and Its Treatment: A Psychoanalytic Approach*. Madison, CT: International Universities Press.

Tarnower, W. (1966). Extra-analytic contacts between the psychoanalyst and the patient. *Psychoanalytic Quarterly* 35: 399–413.

Tausk, V. (1933). On the origin of the "influencing machine" in schizophrenia. *Psychoanalytic Quarterly* 2: 519–556.

Tervalon, M., and Murray-Garcia, J. (1998). Cultural humility versus cultural competence: a critical distinction in defining physician training outcomes in multicultural education. *Journal of Health Care for the Poor and the Underserved* 9: 117–125.

The Holy Quran, ed. and transl. A.Y. Ali. Lahore: Ashraf Publications, 1968.

Thomä, H., and Kachele, H. (1994). *Psychoanalytic Practice, Volume 2: Clinical Studies*. Northvale, NJ: Jason Aronson.

Thomson, J.A., and Aukofer, C. (2011). *Why We Believe in God(s)?* Charlottesville, VA: Pitchstone Publishing.

Thorne, B. (1991). The quality of tenderness. In: *Person-Centred Counselling*, pp. 73–81. London: Whurr.

Traub-Werner, D. (1986). The place and value of bestophilia in perversions. *Journal of the American Psychoanalytic Association* 34: 975–992.

Trungpa, C. (1998). *Timely Rain: Selected Poetry of Chogyam Trungpa*. Ed. D.I. Rome, transl. A. Ginsberg. Boston: Shambhala Publications.

Tuckett, D. (2000). Reporting clinical events in the Journal: toward the construction of a special case. *International Journal of Psychoanalysis* 81: 1065–1069.

Tyson, P., and Tyson, R. (1999). *Psychoanalytic Theories of Development*. New Haven, CT: Yale University Press.

Viola, M. (1992). From curiosity to the capacity to think: elements of a clinical experience. *Revista Di Psicoanalisi* 38: 352–378.

Vincent, D. (2016). *Privacy: A Short History*. Malden, MA: Polity Press.

Volkan, V.D. (1981). *Linking Objects and Linking Phenomena: A Study of the Forms, Symptoms, Metapsychology, and Therapy of Complicated Mourning*. New York: International Universities Press.

Wacks, R. (2010). *Privacy: A Very Short Introduction*. Oxford: Oxford University Press.

Waelder, R. (1936). The principle of multiple function: observations on multiple determination. *Psychoanalytic Quarterly* 41: 283–290.

Wagner, C. (1997). *It's Taking Too Long: A Book about Patience*. New York: Time Life Medical Books.

Warren, S.D., and Brandeis, L.D. (1890). The right to privacy. *Harvard Law Review* 4: 193–220.

Weatherill, R. (1995). Violence and privacy: what if the container fails? *Free Associations* 5: 150–170.

Weber, S.L. (2006). Doubt, arrogance, and humility. *Contemporary Psychoanalysis* 42: 213–223.

Weiss, J., and Sampson, H. (1986). *The Psychoanalytic Process: Theory, Clinical Observation, and Empirical Research*. New York: Guilford Press.

Westin, A. (1967). *Privacy and Freedom*. New York: Atheneum.

Wheelis, A. (1966). *The Illusionless Man*. New York: Harper & Row.

Wheelis, A. (1973). *How People Change*. New York: Harper & Row.

Wheelis, A. (1975). *On Not Knowing How to Live*. New York: Harper & Row.

Wheelis, A. (1994). *The Way Things Are*. Fort Worth, TX: Baskerville Publishers.

Whitfield, C.L., Whitfield, B.H., Park, R., and Prevatt, J. (2006). *The Power of Humility*. Deerfield Beach, FL: Health Communications, Inc.

Williams, M. (2008). *The Pigeon Wants a Puppy*. Los Angeles: Hyperion Books for Children.

Williams, P. (2016). *Humility: The Secret Ingredient of Success*. Uhrichsville, OH: Shiloh Run Press.

Winnicott, D. (1953). Transitional objects and transitional phenomena. *International Journal of Psycho-Analysis* 34: 89–97.

Winnicott, D. (1954). Metapsychological and clinical aspects of regression within the psychoanalytic set-up. In: *Collected Papers: Through Paediatrics to Psychoanalysis*, pp. 53–63. London: Hogarth Press, 1975.

Winnicott, D. (1956). Primary maternal preoccupation. In: *Collected Papers: Through Paediatrics to Psychoanalysis*, pp. 300–305. New York: Basic Books, 1958.

Winnicott, D.W. (1958). The capacity to be alone. *International Journal of Psycho-analysis* 39: 416–420.

Winnicott, D. (1960a). Ego distortion in terms of true and false self. In: *Maturational Processes and the Facilitating Environment*, pp. 140–152. New York: International Universities Press, 1965.

Winnicott, D. (1960b). The theory of parent-infant relationship. In: *The Maturational Processes and the Facilitating Environment*. New York: International Universities Press, 1965, pp. 37–55.

Winnicott, D. (1962). Ego integration in child development. In: *Maturational Processes and the Facilitating Environment*, pp. 45–53. New York: International Universities Press.

Winnicott, D. (1963). Communicating and not communicating leading to a study of certain opposites. In: *The Maturational Processes and the Facilitating Environment*, pp. 179–192. New York: International Universities Press, 1965.

Winnicott, D. (1966). Ordinary devoted mother. In: *Babies and Their Mothers*, ed. C. Winnicott, R. Shepherd, and M. Davis, pp. 3–4. Reading, MA: Addison-Wiley, 1987.

Winnicott, D. (1971). *Playing and Reality*. London: Tavistock.

Winnicott, D. (1984). *Home is Where We Start From*. New York: W.W. Norton.

Wolman, T. (1990). The death of the analyst in the post-termination phase of analysis: impact and resolution. In: *Illness in the Analyst: Implications for the Treatment Relationship*, ed. H.J. Schwartz and A.S. Silver, pp. 253–266. Washington, DC: American Psychiatric Press.

Wolman, T. (2007). Human space, psychic space, analytic space, geopolitical space. In: *The Geography of Meanings: Psychoanalytic Perspectives on Place, Space, Land, and Dislocation*, ed. M.T.S. Hooke and S. Akhtar, pp. 23–45. London: International Psychoanalytic Association.

Wolstein, B. (1977). Countertransference, counterresistance, counteranxiety: the anxiety of influence and the uniqueness of curiosity. *Contemporary Psychoanalysis* 13: 16–29.

Woodward, B., and Bernstein, C. (1974). *All the President's Men*. New York: Simon & Schuster.

Woodward, R. (2004). *Plan of Attack*. New York: Simon & Schuster.

Worthington, Jr., E.L. (2007). *Humility: The Quiet Virtue*. Philadelphia: Templeton Foundation Press.

Wright, K. (1991). *Visions and Separation: Between Mother and Baby*. Northvale, NJ: Jason Aronson.

Yalom, I. (1980). *Existential Psychotherapy*. New York: Basic Books.

Yerushalmi, H. (2013). On the therapist's yearning for intimacy. *Psychoanalytic Quarterly* 82: 671–687.

Zachary, A. (2002). The menopause: dignity and development at the end of the reproductive cycle. *Psychoanalytic Psychotherapy* 16: 20–36.

Zuckerman, J., and Horlick, L. (2006). The affective experience of the analyst in the extra-analytic moment. *American Journal of Psychoanalysis* 66: 351–371.

Zusman, J.A., Cheniaux, E., and De Freitas, S. (2007). Psychoanalysis and change: between curiosity and faith. *International Journal of Psychoanalysis* 88: 113–125.

Index